Human and International Security in India

With its common colonial experience, an overarching cultural unity despite apparent diversities, and issues of nation-building cutting across national frontiers, South Asia offers a critical site on which to develop a discourse on regional security that centres on the notion of human security. This book analyses the progress that has been achieved since independence in multiple intersecting areas of human security development in India, the largest nation in South Asia, as well as considering the paradigms that might be brought to bear in future consideration and pursuance of these objectives.

Providing original insights, the book analyses the idea of security based on specific human concerns cutting across state frontiers, such as socio-economic development, human rights, gender equity, environmental degradation, terrorism, democracy, and governance. It also discusses the realisation that human security and international security are inextricably interlinked. The book gives an overview of Indian foreign policy, with particular focus on India's relationship with China. It also looks at public health care in India, and issues of microfinance and gender. Democracy and violence in the country is discussed in-depth, as well as Muslim identity and community.

Human and International Security in India will be of particular interest to researchers of contemporary South Asian History, South Asian Politics, Sociology and Development Studies.

Crispin Bates is a Professor of Modern and Contemporary South Asian History in the School of History, Classics and Archaeology at the University of Edinburgh.

Akio Tanabe is a Professor in South Asian Area Studies and Anthropology in the Graduate School of Asian and African Area Studies and Director of the Centre for the Study of Contemporary India at Kyoto University.

Minoru Mio is an Associate Professor at the National Museum of Ethnology, Osaka, Japan (NME), and the Director of the Centre for Contemporary Indian Area Studies at NME.

Routledge New Horizons in South Asian Studies
Series Editors: Crispin Bates, *Edinburgh University*;
Akio Tanabe, *Kyoto University*;
Minoru Mio, *National Museum of Ethnology, Japan*

Democratic Transformation and the Vernacular Public Arena in India
Edited by Taberez Ahmed Neyazi, Akio Tanabe and Shinya Ishizaka

Cities in South Asia
Edited by Crispin Bates and Minoru Mio

Human and International Security in India
Edited by Crispin Bates, Akio Tanabe and Minoru Mio

Human and International Security in India

Edited by Crispin Bates, Akio Tanabe
and Minoru Mio

LONDON AND NEW YORK

First published 2016
by Routledge
2 Park Square, Milton Park, Abingdon, Oxon OX14 4RN

and by Routledge
711 Third Avenue, New York, NY 10017

Routledge is an imprint of the Taylor & Francis Group, an informa business

© 2016 selection and editorial material, Crispin Bates, Akio Tanabe and Minoru Mio; individual chapters, the contributors

The right of Crispin Bates, Akio Tanabe and Minoru Mio to be identified as authors of the editorial material, and of the individual authors as authors of their contributions, has been asserted by them in accordance with sections 77 and 78 of the Copyright, Designs and Patents Act 1988.

All rights reserved. No part of this book may be reprinted or reproduced or utilised in any form or by any electronic, mechanical, or other means, now known or hereafter invented, including photocopying and recording, or in any information storage or retrieval system, without permission in writing from the publishers.

Trademark notice: Product or corporate names may be trademarks or registered trademarks, and are used only for identification and explanation without intent to infringe.

British Library Cataloguing in Publication Data
A catalogue record for this book is available from the British Library

Library of Congress Cataloging-in-Publication Data
Human and international security in India / edited by Crispin Bates, Akio Tanabe, and Minoru Mio.
   pages cm. — (Routledge new horizons in South Asia studies)
  1. Human security—India. 2. Security, International—India.
 I. Bates, Crispin, 1958–
   JC599.I4H569 2015
   355'.033054—dc23
   2015012723

ISBN: 978-1-138-90866-6 (hbk)
ISBN: 978-1-315-69429-0 (ebk)

Typeset in Times New Roman
by Apex CoVantage, LLC

Printed and bound in the United States of America by Publishers Graphics, LLC on sustainably sourced paper.

Contents

List of figures vii
List of tables viii
Acknowledgments ix
Notes on contributors x

Introduction: looking back on human and international security in India since independence 1
CRISPIN BATES

1 **The paradoxes of Indian politics: a dialogue between political science and history** 15
SUBHO BASU AND CRISPIN BATES

2 **India's foreign relations: an overview** 32
JAYANTA KUMAR RAY

3 **The transformation of India's external posture and its relationship with China** 50
TAKENORI HORIMOTO

4 **India's macroeconomic performance in the long run** 65
TAKAHIRO SATO

5 **Public health and human security in India: poised for positive change** 86
SUNIL CHACKO

6 **Being Muslim in India today** 101
MUSHIRUL HASAN

7 **Democracy and violence in India: the example of Bihar** 110
KAZUYA NAKAMIZO

8 Microfinance and gender: the *Magalir Thittam* in Tamil Nadu 128
ANTONYSAMY SAGAYARAJ

9 Rural lives and livelihoods: perceptions of security in a Rajasthan village 146
ANN GRODZINS GOLD

10 As hierarchies wane: explaining intercaste accommodation in rural India 162
JAMES MANOR

11 Epilogue: human and international security in an age of new risks and opportunities 175
AKIO TANABE AND MINORU MIO

Index 185

Figures

4.1	Economic growth rate	69
4.2	Per capita income at constant price (1999–2000)	71
4.3	Poverty ratio (%)	73
4.4	Inflation rate of GDP deflator (%)	74
4.5	Agriculture	76
4.6	Fiscal balance (% of GDP)	78
4.7	Current account balance (% of GDP)	81
4.8	Exchange rate against US dollar	83
4.9	Net capital inflow (% of GDP)	84
8.1	Sharma Nagar layout	140
8.2	High-rise buildings in Street No. 3	141
8.3	SHG meeting held under a tree in front of an original house in Street No. 7	141

Tables

3.1	Global GDP – top ten countries, 2008–13	55
3.2	Global military expenditure – top ten countries, 2008–13	55
5.1	Sources of funds for health care in India, 2004–5	87
5.2	Selected health status outcomes in major Indian states	88
5.3	Net earned premium in health insurance, 2008–9	95
7.1	Number and percentage of seats won and valid vote percentage by party by Muslim population proportion (1989 parliamentary election in Bihar)	114
7.2	Percentage of valid vote by socialist parties by OBCs population proportion (state assembly election in Bihar: 1977–95)	120
7.3	Caste composition of Bihar state assembly (1967–2005)	121
7.4	Voting behaviour of upper castes in Bihar (1995–98)	123

Acknowledgments

This volume is the result of an interdisciplinary workshop on the theme of Human and International Security in India that was organised in January 2010 by the Graduate of School of African and Asian Studies at Kyoto University Japan. The editors wish to thank all those who were involved in these events and who supported this project. Special gratitude is reserved for Suranjan Das of Calcutta University, who provided expert guidance and financial support for the participants from India; for the funding provided by the INDAS project in Japan; and for support provided by the National Museum of Ethnology, Osaka. We would like to also extend our gratitude to Shinya Ishizaka, Kyouta Yamada, Takako Yoshikawa, Masako Akedo, and Ryoko Seto for their help in organising the event. Further thanks are due to the patient and indefatigable editors at Routledge, including Dorothea Schaefter and Jillian Morrison, and to Aya Ikegame for her vital role in liaising between the editors. Finally, the project could not have been accomplished without the careful copy-editing skills of Ben Thurman and Charlotte Thornton, to whom we are heavily indebted.

Contributors

Subho Basu is an Associate Professor, Department of History and Classical Studies, McGill University. He co-edited with Suranjan Das *Electoral Politics in South Asia* (Stylus Publishing, 2001) and has widely published on labour history and contemporary Indian politics. His publications include his monograph *Does Class Matter?: Colonial Capital and Workers' Resistance in Bengal, 1890–1937* (New Delhi, New York: Oxford University Press, 2004) and (with Ali Riaz) *Paradise Lost: State in Crisis in Nepal* (Plymouth: Lexington Press, 2007). His research focuses are modern South Asian history, labour history, the history of contemporary social movements, nationalism, and post-colonial politics.

Crispin Bates is a Professor of Modern and Contemporary South Asian History in the School of History, Classics and Archaeology and Director of the Centre for South Asian Studies at the University of Edinburgh. His publications include *Subalterns and Raj: South Asia since 1600* (London: Routledge, 2007); *Beyond Representation: Constructions of Identity in Colonial and Postcolonial India* (Oxford, New Delhi: Oxford University Press, 2005), and (with Subho Basu) *Rethinking Indian Political Institutions* (London: Anthem Press, 2005). He also edited (with Alpa Shah) *Savage Attack: Tribal Insurgency in India* (New Delhi: Social Science Press, 2014) and is the editor and principal contributor to *Mutiny at the Margins: New Perspectives on the Indian Uprising of 1857*, vols. 1–6 (New Delhi: Sage, 2013–14).

Sunil Chacko is Professor (adjunct) at the University of Alberta, Edmonton, Simon Fraser University, Vancouver, and Indira Gandhi National University, New Delhi. He holds degrees in medicine from Kerala University, an M.P.H. in public health from Harvard University, and an M.B.A. with concentration on finance from Columbia University. He has worked as a physician in hospitals and rural health centres in India, and was previously a Harvard University faculty member and Assistant Director of Harvard's International Health Research Commission, which first documented worldwide health capacity and research needs. He has worked as a senior official and advisor of both the World Bank Group and the Rockefeller Foundation.

Contributors xi

Ann Grodzins Gold is the Thomas J. Watson Professor of Religion at Syracuse University, New York. Gold has received fellowships from the American Institute of Indian Studies, the Fulbright Foundation, Fulbright-Hays, the National Endowment for the Humanities, the Social Science Research Council, and the Spencer Foundation. Her publications include numerous articles and four books: *Fruitful Journeys: The Ways of Rajasthani Pilgrims* (1988); *A Carnival of Parting: The Tales of King Bharthari and King Gopi Chand* (1992); *Listen to the Heron's Words: Reimagining Gender and Kinship in North India* (1994, co-authored with Gloria Raheja); and *In the Time of Trees and Sorrows: Nature, Power and Memory in Rajasthan* (2002, co-authored with Bhoju Ram Gujar), which in 2004 was awarded the Ananda Kentish Coomaraswamy Book Prize from the Association for Asian Studies.

Mushirul Hasan, formerly Vice-Chancellor of Jamia Millia Islamia and Director-General of the National Archives of India, is currently a Jawaharlal Nehru Fellow at the Jawaharlal Nehru Memorial Fund in New Delhi. A former President of the Indian History Congress, he is a renowned historian of Islam in South Asia. His numerous publications include *Legacy of a Divided Nation: India's Muslims since Independence* (Oxford, 1997), *The Nehrus: Personal Histories* (London, 2006), *Moderate or Militant? Images of India's Muslims* (Oxford, 2008), *Faith and Freedom: Gandhi and History* (India, 2013), and (edited) *From Ghalib's Dilli to Lutyen's New Delhi* (Oxford, 2013). In 2007 he was awarded the Padma Shri by the Government of India and the Ordre des Palmes Académiques by the French Government in 2010.

Takenori Horimoto is Project Professor at the Graduate School of Asian and African Area Studies at Kyoto University, specializing in international politics of South Asia and Asia. He has authored and edited twelve books in Japanese, including *India: The Big Elephant Globalizes* (Iwanami Shoten, 2007) and *India as a Rising Military Power* (Aki Shobo, 2010, co-edited with Masashi Nishihara), besides the English book *India-Japan Relations in Emerging Asia* (Manohar, 2013, co-edited with Lalima Varma). He has also given 170 India, South Asia, and Asia related lectures and presentations, as well as serving as a political commentator on NHK TV programmes more than thirty times.

James Manor is a Professor at the Institute of Commonwealth Studies, School of Advanced Study, University of London. He has authored several books, including *Broadening and Deepening Democracy: Political Innovation in Karnataka* (London, 2009), *Aid that Works: Successful Development in Fragile States* (Washington, 2007), *The Political Economy of Democratic Decentralization* (Washington, 1999), *Power, Poverty and Poison: Disaster and Response in an Indian City* (London, 1993), and (co-authored) *Against the Odds: Politicians, Institutions and the Struggle against Poverty* (London, 2011). He served as the editor of the *Journal of Commonwealth and Comparative Politics* from 1980 to 1988 and has also edited several volumes, including *Nehru to the Nineties: The Changing Office of Prime Minister in India* (London, 1994) and *Rethinking*

xii *Contributors*

Third World Politics (London, 1991). He has also acted as a consultant to international organisations, including the Ford Foundation, the World Bank, and the United Nations Development Programme.

Minoru Mio is an Associate Professor at the National Museum of Ethnology, Osaka, Japan (NME), and the Director of the Centre for Contemporary Indian Area Studies at NME. He has carried out extensive fieldwork on popular religious practices and social transformation in Rajasthan and Gujarat and has written several articles in Japanese and English, including 'Looking for Love and Miracles: Multivocal Composition and Conflicts among Believers in a Sufi Mausoleum Festival of Rajasthan, India', *Bulletin of the National Museum of Ethnology* (2004) Vol. 29, No. 1 and 'Young Men's Public Activities and Hindu Nationalism: Naviyuvak Mandals and the Sangh Parivar in a Western Indian Town', in David N. Gellner (ed.) *Ethnic Activism and Civil Society in South Asia* (New Delhi: Sage, 2009).

Kazuya Nakamizo is an Associate Professor at the Department of South Asian and Indian Ocean Studies, the Graduate School of Asian and African Area Studies, Kyoto University, Japan. He specialises in socio-political research of South Asia, with an emphasis on the relationship between poverty, violence, and democracy. Among his publications, he has authored *Democracy and Violence in India: The Collapse of One-Party Dominant Rule and Identity Politics* (in Japanese) (Tokyo: University of Tokyo Press, 2012), written 'The Weak and Democracy: The Practices of Sixty Years of Indian Democracy' (in Japanese) in the *Annual Bulletin of Japan Association for Comparative Politics* on 'Reconsidering Contemporary Democracy' (2012), and contributed 'Political Change in the Bihar – Riots and the Emergence of Democratic Revolution', in Sunita Lall & Shaibal Gupta (eds.) *Resurrection of the State: A Saga of Bihar – Essays in Memory of Papiya Ghosh* (New Delhi: Manak Publications, 2013).

Jayanta Kumar Ray is National Research Professor, Ministry of Human Resource Development, Government of India, and Honorary Professor, Institute of Foreign Policy Studies, University of Calcutta, Kolkata. His previous assignments include: Chairman, Maulana Abul Kalam Azad Institute of Asian Studies, Kolkata; National Fellow, Indian Council of Social Science Research, New Delhi; Centenary Professor of International Relations, and Founder-Director, Centre for South and Southeast Asian Studies, University of Calcutta. His publications include: *India's Foreign Relations, 1947–2007* (New Delhi: Routledge, 2011); *India: In Search of Good Governance* (London: Wimbledon Publishing, 2002), and *To Chase a Miracle: A Study of the Grameen Bank of Bangladesh* (1987).

Antonysamy Sagayaraj is an Associate Professor at Nanzan University, Nagoya, Japan. His research interests are socio-religious movements, caste, communalism, and gender in India. His publications include 'Christianity in India: A Focus on Inculturation' in *Research Series of Anthropological Institute* (Vol. 1 2013, Nanazan University), 'Language and Identity in Multilingual India' (in Japanese) in Takahiro Kato (ed.) *The Interconnection between a Nation and its Language* (Kohro-sha, 2012), 'The Role of Religious Institutions in Relief', in P. P. Karan and S. P. Subbiah (ed.) *The Indian Ocean Tsunami: The Global Response to a Natural Disaster* (University Press of Kentucky, 2011), 'Democracy and Development: A Case Study of Self Help Groups in Tamil Nadu' (in Japanese) in *Acculturation and Development in Asian Societies* (Toyo University Asian Cultures Research Institute, 2010), 'Collective Violence and Reconciliation: A South Asian Narrative' *Academia* (2007) Vol. 85, and 'The Contribution of European Missionaries to Tamil Language and Dravidian Consciousness' in L. Fernando and M. Mundadan (eds.) *Indian Church History Review* (2004) Vol. 38, No 1.

Takahiro Sato is a Professor at the Research Institute for Economics and Business Administration, Kobe University, Japan. His publications include *Economic Development: Structural Adjustment and Globalization in India* (in Japanese) (Kyoto: Sekaishisosha, 2002), 'Economic Relations between India and Japan' in *Eurasian Geography and Economics* (Vol. 53, No. 4, 2012), 'Growth and Employment in India: The Impact of Globalization on Employment in the Indian Manufacturing Industries' in *International Journal of South Asian Studies* (Vol. 3, 2010), as co-editor *India's Globalising Political Economy: New Challenges and Opportunities in the 21st Century* (Tokyo: The Sasakawa Peace Foundation, 2010), and as co-author 'The Effect of Corruption on the Manufacturing Sector in India' in *Economics of Governance* (Vol. 15, No. 2, 2014) and 'Recent Changes in Micro-Level Determinants of Fertility in India' in *Oxford Development Studies* (Vol. 42, No. 1, 2014).

Akio Tanabe is a Professor in South Asian Area Studies and Anthropology in the Graduate School of Asian and African Area Studies and Director of the Centre for the Study of Contemporary India at Kyoto University. He is also the Convener of the Contemporary India Area Studies (INDAS) project, which is conducted, in collaboration with the National Institutes for the Humanities, by the INDAS Network in Japan. His publications include *Caste and Equality: Historical Anthropology of Local Society and Vernacular Democracy in Eastern India* (in Japanese) (University of Tokyo Press, 2010) and as co-editor *Democratic Transformation and the Vernacular Public Arena in India* (London: Routledge, 2014), *The Tropical Humanosphere in Global History: Beyond the Temperate Paradigm* (in Japanese) (Kyoto University Press, 2012), *The State in India: Past and Present* (New Delhi: Oxford University Press, 2006), *Dislocating Nation-States: Globalization in Asia and Africa* (Kyoto University Press and Trans Pacific Press, 2005) and *Gender and Modernity: Perspectives from Asia and the Pacific* (Kyoto University Press and Trans Pacific Press, 2003).

Introduction
Looking back on human and international security in India since independence

Crispin Bates

In recent years there has been a paradigmatic shift in our notion of national security – a shift from the state-centric idea of national security based on military power or ideological and military confrontation to an understanding of security based on certain human concerns cutting across state frontiers, such as socio-economic development, human rights, gender equity, environmental degradation, terrorism, democracy, and governance. More importantly, it has been realised that human security and international security are inextricably interlinked. British Prime Minister John Major commented as follows in his opening remarks as president of the UN Security Council in New York in January 1992:

> It is of course true that without economic development and prosperity we cannot hope to achieve lasting peace and stability but it is every bit as true that only when conditions of security and peace are assured can sustained economic development take place; both are needed and only when we have both can resources be directed to where they are so urgently needed, towards the economic and social needs of the world's population.[1]

As a result of this new understanding, the people, instead of the state, have emerged as the central point in discourses on national and regional security. The United Nations Development Programme's Human Development Report 1994 pertinently underlined this trend when it noted:

> The concept of security has for too long been interpreted narrowly: as security of territory from external aggression, or as protection of national interests in foreign policy or as global security from the threat of nuclear holocaust. It has been related more to nation-states than to people. Forgotten were the legitimate concerns of ordinary people who sought security in their daily lives. For many of them, security symbolized protection from the threat of disease, hunger, unemployment, crime, social conflict, political repression and environmental hazards.[2]

We thus have an accumulating literature in the realm of global security studies which emphasises poverty, socio-economic underdevelopment, and the lack of good governance as lying at the root of national security in developing states, whilst socio-economic uplift and good governance are regarded as obligatory prerequisites for the achievement of real security. Security as it is usually defined cannot have 'enduring appeal for hungry masses'. 'Security, in the end, is freedom from threat to one's survival, and should, therefore, include concerns that are much more than the conventional issues of political independence, national defence and territorial integrity.'[3] Accordingly these concerns require us to focus on three key questions: whose security, what does security consist of in particular issue areas and contexts, and how in terms of strategies and instruments is security in these areas to be achieved?

With its common colonial experience, an overarching cultural unity despite apparent diversities, and issues of nation-building cutting across national frontiers, South Asia offers a critical site on which to develop a discourse on regional security that centres around the notion of human security. The debate on human security is ongoing and remains unresolved.[4] Human security is clearly related to international security: disturbances on the frontiers of the nation are used frequently by politicians in order to divert the attention of the electorate from the failure to achieve development targets at home. The demands of national defence are a constant drain on resources that might better be employed elsewhere in health, welfare, infrastructural, and educational schemes. At the same time, the remittances of Indians overseas, with whom the government has sought to reconnect, have become a major factor in India's foreign earnings. Foreign policy has itself become a hot domestic electoral issue since the Pokhran-II nuclear tests of May 1998 and the Mumbai terrorist attack of 2008 (Ogden, 2014: 157–8). Human and international security are thereby intimately related. The aim of this volume is to review the various challenges to strategic and international security that have faced India, the largest nation in South Asia, since independence. We will also summarise the progress that has been achieved since independence in multiple intersecting areas of human security development and consider the paradigms that might be brought to bear in future consideration and pursuance of these objectives.

Chapter 1 begins with Subho Basu and Crispin Bates discussing how historians and political scientists follow different tracks in interpreting Indian politics. Barring a few, historians tend to stop in 1947, and political scientists tend to pick up the story from this point onwards, albeit concentrating largely on the events of just the last 20 years. This predominance of political scientists in analysing Indian politics has reinforced the myth that politics in India, as seen from the assumptions of their discipline, is riddled with paradoxes. Thus the constitutional commitment to individualism is apparently constantly contradicted by the communitarian ethos of politics, the official policy of secularism is compromised by repeated occurrences of communal violence, and the emphasis on a universal adult franchise is undermined by the persistence of political dynasties. The top-heavy state, the politics of identities, the etiolating institutional capacity of the state to govern, and the degenerated condition of class politics are often used as critical templates by which to measure political dynamics in India. National security is a key term often referenced, but poorly defined, in such theoretical constructions of the Indian polity.

The chapter argues that a dialogue between historians and political scientists can provide for a far better comprehension of Indian politics than is offered by these functionalist templates. Rather than viewing Indian society and politics through ready-made theoretical lenses, the chapter argues for a more expansive, temporal view of the articulation of different forms of political practice in India. It argues that a temporal analysis can instead establish that the apparent paradoxes of Indian politics are no more than the expression of long-standing dialectical and dialogical processes of engagement by different actors in political society. These articulate complex but integrated patterns of political transaction that are by no means contradictory but have become established and clearly recognised by political actors over time. Politics in India, in other words, involves the working out of predictable and normative practices that are by no means as unstable and insecure as they might at first appear from a European perspective.

In the second chapter, Jayanata Kumar Ray discusses Indian foreign policy – or the lack thereof – before the year 1991 and contrasts this with foreign policy after this date, attempting to show how the failure or success of foreign policy impacts on human security in both the short and long term. Ray also explores the way in which hero worship and the power of dynastic rule have led foreign policy analysts to overrate the leadership of such iconic figures as Jawaharlal Nehru and Indira Gandhi and overlook the more tangible successes of less prominent premiers such as Narasimha Rao and Atal Behari Vajpayee.

In his critical analysis of foreign policy up until 1991, Ray discusses various issues such as the hurried passing of the Boundary Award in 1947, the mishandling by Indian leaders of the conflict in Jammu-Kashmir, and the so-called policy of nonalignment. The consequences of these blunders are examined, showing how their effects are still felt powerfully even today. Following this, there is an exploration of the situation post-1991, which Ray refers to as an 'era of pragmatism in India's foreign economic and political relations'. The chapter illustrates how the abandonment of the policy of nonalignment in favour of a strategy of constructive and flexible engagement, alignment, and partnership with countries such as the US led to a number of foreign policy successes, particularly in the realm of nuclear policy. Towards the end of the chapter, there is a brief discussion of the future foreign policy problems faced by India with regard to the situation in Afghanistan following the withdrawal of NATO and American troops, and how India might handle this effectively through the careful management of its relations with China and America. The thrust of Professor Ray's analysis is to chart a general shift from principled disengagement – an aloofness even in India's international policies – to one of pragmatic engagement, which hopefully will better serve India's relations with her neighbours in the years to come.

In Chapter 3, Takenori Horimoto discusses the relationship between India and China. He first addresses the significant attention that Indians, especially policy makers and scholars, direct towards China. This is demonstrated by the Center for Strategic and International Studies' report *Strategic Views on Asian Regionalism*, published in February 2009, which was based on an opinion survey conducted in the USA and eight Asian countries, including Japan and India, with 313 respondents. China was viewed as the strongest overall national power by 65.5 per cent of respondents. China was also considered to be the greatest threat to peace and stability over the previous decade (Gill et al., 2009). These concerns are mirrored in China itself. A 2013 Pew poll revealed that less than 23 per cent of the Chinese population have a positive view of India, while 62 per cent offer a negative opinion.[5]

It might be thought that the growing economic interaction between China and India could help resolve their differences. In fact, the opposite has happened, with trade itself becoming a source of friction as India's trade deficit with China soared from $1 billion in 2002 to $40 billion in 2013. Meanwhile India's increased defence expenditure is regarded with suspicion in China, especially in the light of India's 2008 civil nuclear agreement with the United States. Since 1998 – the year India tested nuclear weapons – border patrols by the People's Liberation Army began making routine forays across the disputed 2,400-mile-long LoAC (Line of Actual Control) in order to establish China's territorial claims, and in April 2013 there was a tense stand-off between the two countries when a Chinese platoon set up tents some 12 miles inside the border of Indian Kashmir. This territorial dispute is unlikely to be resolved soon, as the two countries have failed to even exchange maps showing each other's perception of where the border lies. Moreover it seems unlikely that either side wishes to do so, as unsettled border claims have become pawns within the much larger rivalries and disputes between the two countries.

Horimoto discusses the common features of the two countries that have led to them being regarded as competitors. These include their large populations, national areas, their history, and the unique way in which both have carried their ancient civilisations forward to the present day. China is considered the de facto Number 2 in the world, being three times larger than India in terms of GDP and military expenditure. India's foreign service is seriously underresourced and lacking in coherence and clear long-term objectives.[6] However, both countries are considered as major powers, with India dominating in South Asia, and China in East Asia. It is thus inevitable that each should have a keen interest in the other where their areas of influence overlap. Horimoto explores the mutual perceptions that have arisen from this rivalry and the evident gap in the relative economic and military powers of the two countries, and concludes by considering whether it is possible for them to maintain an amicable relationship in the future.

In Chapter 4, Takahiro Sato investigates India's macroeconomic performance since independence by tracking long-term trends and changes in macroeconomic policy and development strategy. First he discusses three major economic crises that stimulated long-term fundamental changes in India's development strategy: the serious droughts in the mid-1960s, the oil crisis in 1979, and the Gulf war in 1991. The response to each crisis is different, i.e. the tightening of regulations in the late 1960s, partial economic liberalisation in the 1980s, and full-fledged globalisation in the 1990s. Second, the chapter focuses on the Indian economy and how it has become less dependent on weather instability through a reduction in the GDP share of the agricultural sector and improvements in agricultural technologies and infrastructure. In particular, since the 1980s the Green Revolution has brought stability to the inflation rate and economic growth and has alleviated the balance of payments problem caused by food imports, which was a conspicuous feature of the Indian economy between 1947 and 1980. In the early 1980s the Indian economy reached a turning point after which it was able to achieve sustainable higher economic growth rates. This high growth, backed by the success of the Green Revolution, has alleviated India's absolute poverty slowly but steadily. In the late 1990s monetary policy became independent from fiscal policy. An independent monetary policy followed by the Reserve Bank of India during the 2000s ensured continuing economic growth and stable low inflation. India's economy has in consequence continued to grow steadily without falling into serious economic crisis since the 1990s. This is despite the Asian currency crisis of the late 1990s and the large increase in international oil prices during the period from 2003 to 2008. In other words, the Indian economy has become relatively independent from external shocks. Finally, Sato discusses how India's macroeconomic performance since the 1990s has been successful in terms of economic growth, inflation, and the balance of payments. Unfortunately, India failed to reduce its fiscal deficit during this period, and following the financial crisis of 2008 the fiscal deficit only increased further. This large fiscal deficit will be the most serious constraint on India's macroeconomic growth prospects in the future.

Sunil Chacko's contribution to this volume in Chapter 5 concerns the importance of access to health care as a means of attaining human security. The chapter describes the state of health care in India today, revealing it to be deeply iniquitous as a result of inadequate resources and insufficient coverage, combined with years of neglect of the public health system. The essay examines the measures already taken by the Indian government to tackle these issues – principally a huge recent increase in spending on health. However, despite the benefits brought about by this cash injection, Chacko argues that spending by itself is not sufficient, and a whole variety of additional measures are needed to secure universal health care coverage in India. Various suggestions are made for how the power of information technology (IT) could be harnessed to improve the quality, value for money, and effectiveness of health care services – for example, through monitoring and surveillance to ensure accountability and transparency in the medical system, thus augmenting the outreach of health care coverage to greater numbers of people. Finally, Chacko offers a comparison between the public health challenges faced on a daily basis in coastal Indian communities and those faced following a natural disaster such as the 2011 earthquake in Japan and the ensuing nuclear crisis, or the 2004 Indian Ocean tsunami. Parallels are drawn regarding the need for lifeline and infrastructure measures, such as decentralised power solutions, to ensure human security, and once again the potential for IT to help with regard to these issues is discussed.

In Chapter 6, Mushirul Hasan challenges the both two-nation theory of India's partition and the myth of a homogeneous 'Muslim India'. He emphasises the differences from region to region and class to class in Islamic religion and culture, which resulted from its gradual and varied paths of penetration into South and South East Asia. Thus, instead of a single unified Muslim identity and community set apart from the rest of India, Hasan argues that there exist multiple identities amongst India's Muslims, whose religious and cultural practices were often interwoven with local Hindu traditions. This interweaving resulted in a shared, not separate, perspective within their local communities, which tended to transcend religious difference.

Hasan traces the invented and imaginary sense of Muslim homogeneity and the ideological contours of Pakistan back beyond Jinnah's call for a Muslim nation to the colonial government, whose policy of separate electorates enforced a single defined identity and attempt to represent the Muslims of India as a distinct religio-political entity. Hasan considers the long-term repercussions of this and the response of South Asia's Muslims to their geographical and ideological separation in the formation of Pakistan. He writes that the reduction of Muslim identity to a 'mere rationalisation of normative Islamic discourse' and the privileged place assigned to Islamic religion has led to an us/them divide which conflates being a Muslim with being 'Islamist' or 'fundamentalist' and views Islamic religion as incompatible with Western ideals of democracy and secularism. In emphasising the disjunction between the formal ideology of Islam and the day-to-day practices of the many varied Islams throughout the subcontinent, Hasan seeks to dispel the myths surrounding South East Asia's Muslims, both past and present. He thus demonstrates the existence of a sound empirical basis for future communal harmony in India that is often pessimistically assumed to be absent.

In Chapter 7, Kazuya Nakamizo discusses the issues of democracy and violence within India, with particular attention to the state of Bihar. He considers how it is possible to understand violent conflicts within a stable democracy. India, the motherland of non-violence movements, has experienced numerous violent conflicts, such as religious riots, caste riots, and class struggles since independence. After the 1980s in particular, the extent of violence rose drastically following the Ayodhya incidents, the implementation of the Mandal Commission report, and the government's confrontation with the Maoist Naxalite insurgency in the tribal areas of central India. He asks how we can account for the apparent frequency of these violent conflicts in the 65-year experience of 'the world's largest democracy'.

Bihar is one of the most infamous states for violent conflicts in India. Apart from general 'law and order' problems, which critics of past state governments have emphasised, Bihar has experienced numerous riots. These include religious riots since before independence up to the 1980s, caste riots triggered by the Mandal agitation in 1990, and violent confrontations between left extremists and landlord private armies in the 1990s. From 1990, however, the situation started to change. First, religious riots have been contained with increasing success, and caste riots have been quickly settled, rendering them only temporary phenomena. Lastly, the activities of Ranvir Sena, the most brutal private landlord army in the history of Bihar, have been decreasing since 2000. Nakamizo asks how we can explain this change in the trajectory of violent conflicts in Bihar. In analysing political processes within the state, it becomes clear that in order to answer this complex question, the role played by the institution of elections must be considered. In short, elections have on the one hand prompted conflicts to become violent, yet paradoxically this same political practice has the ability to prevent and contain violent conflicts. Exploring the extreme case of Bihar, Nakamizo shows that within the very structure of its democracy lie the means in the long term to overcome the quotidian violence that formerly was imagined to be a normative aspect of life within the less developed states of India.

In Chapter 8, Antonysamy Sagayaraj discusses microfinance and gender with a specific focus on the state of Tamil Nadu. All individuals have a number of essential needs that they strive to satisfy. These essentials go beyond just food, clothing, and shelter. They include both physical and non-physical elements needed for human growth and development, as well as all those things humans are innately driven to attain. In a developing country such as India, society often fails to satisfy even the three basic needs for subsistence and survival. Unmet needs lead to feelings of insecurity. To meet unsatisfied and emergent needs, households in lower asset groups turn to non-institutional credit agencies and become increasingly dependent upon them thereafter. The high level of dependence of such groups on non-institutional sources leads to exploitation. Monopolistic moneylenders will sometimes charge exorbitant interest rates, extracting substantial profits. A variant of the monopolistic moneylender is the lender whose primary aim is to make the borrower default in order to gain his land, to force him into bonded labour, or to get him to sell the lender his produce at below market prices. By focusing on the Mahalir Thittam programme in Sharma Nagar, a suburb of Chennai, Sagayaraj discusses how the people of Tamil Nadu have sought microfinance in order to secure their daily lives. Initially such lending was poorly managed and was mostly between males, resulting in debt bondage and family indebtedness. However, since the 1990s there has been a gender shift, so that now both the lenders and borrowers are women, who have been more narrowly focused on the immediate needs of household expenditure. This has led to a gradual improvement in the economic security of low-income households. The positive results of this shift offer a paradigm for future work in this area, and in the future strategies of development projects.

While global flows and urban cultures may epitomise our imagination of the twenty-first century throughout the world, rural life remains of vital significance if we wish to characterise human security in India today. In Chapter 9, Ann Gold discusses rural lives and livelihoods based on ethnographic research spanning three decades in a village in Rajasthan. Her chapter discusses geophysical and material as well as social and moral transformations in this region. Her three main areas of focus are environmental change and practices of food production; domestic change including household labour, gender roles, and education; and intangible change: community, morality, aspiration. All of these are connected to human security in the broadest understanding of the term. Gold addresses significant enhancements in security and quality of life that people recognise and appreciate on a daily basis. She also notes some emergent forms of insecurity, both material and psychological, that leave little room for complacency.

In Chapter 10, James Manor examines certain key implications of a monumentally important trend, which is the declining acceptance of caste hierarchies across rural India. When so-called lower castes – especially Dalits (ex-untouchables) – begin to refuse to acknowledge and even challenge the principle of hierarchy, important consequences result. We might expect violence as 'higher' castes seek to enforce old injustices, and some instances of violence have occurred, taking even more savage forms than a generation ago. But such outrages are greatly outweighed by accommodations between Dalits and others when intercaste tensions arise. Those accommodations are based not on a change of heart among 'higher' castes, but a change of mind – on measured calculations by 'higher' caste leaders. James Manor seeks to explain in this chapter the logic of intercaste accommodations between Dalits and one set of 'higher' castes, the formerly dominant landowning groups. Manor focuses on the repertoire of actions that Dalits use to indicate their rejection of caste hierarchies, on the often difficult realities faced by landed castes, and on their perceptions of them. The chapter ends with an analysis of the negotiating processes that have led to important and new accommodations in intercaste relations in rural India, and the potential threats that still remain to the future improvement of these relationships.

Finally, in an epilogue, Akio Tanabe and Minoru Mio consider the growth in human capital resources, the flourishing of the informal sector, and the expansion of vernacular public life, which are neglected in most 'top-down' analyses of social and political change in Indian economy and society and which are poorly reflected in official government statistics. Mio and Tanabe will propose a very different view of social change that allows us to view India from 'the bottom up', from the point of view of rural society and the southern half of the subcontinent. They suggest that the structure of hierarchy and dominance that has characterised colonial and post-colonial India has become more relative today, as there is an ongoing process of redefinition of categories and relationships of caste, religion, class, and gender as well as the development of social networks that support socio-economic mobility. They suggest that the question of human and regional security has become pertinent in this new context, where the old national order is destabilised due to the rise of vibrant agency from below, accompanying new opportunities and risks. Here the main issue has shifted from the question of to what extent India succeeds in national development to a question of how India can provide better life chances to the multitudes of people in the glocal environment while minimising risks and securing an inclusive, sustainable, and peaceful path of development. They conclude with the view that in order to deal with the new agenda of risk and security, it is vital, besides improving the governance of power and capital, to further promote the capability, agency, and human capital of diverse sections of society through state-supported and human-centred forms of development.

Overall, it may be argued that the conditions to achieve human and international security in India are poised for dramatic change, building upon the solid and incremental improvements on both fronts that have been achieved in recent decades. However, the degree to which these changes have been the deliberate result of government policy remains open to debate. The move towards pragmatism in Indian foreign policy has resulted primarily from changing external circumstances rather than profound introspection and an ideological shift on the part of the government of India. The diplomatic rhetoric of the government of India indeed still often reflects the self-representations of the era of non-alignment, replete with references to Mahatma Gandhi and an imagined civilisational commitment to the ideals of *ahimsa* (non-violence) and the renunciation of self-interest. This rhetoric is employed even as India displays an increasing level of commitment and strategic pursuit of its self-interest in international affairs.[7] There thus remains a mismatch between self-perception and the careful pragmatism that is more likely to enhance India's standing in international relations in the future, and which has indeed come to characterise the country's foreign relations. This applies particularly in India's relationship with neighbouring China, the only Asian country with a seat on the Security Council and soon to be the world's largest economy. This is a relationship quite crucial to India's future and one that requires an intensely focused and realistic approach if it is to become anything more than a one-sided affair.

On the economic front, since the 1990s India has seen a flourishing of the IT and business process outsourcing (BPO) industries, located especially in Mumbai, Hyderabad, Chennai, and Bangalore. However, the IT-BPO sector benefited uniquely from diasporic networks. These industries were not amongst those specially targeted for growth in the liberalisation policies of the government of India after 1996. Growth has resulted most often from targeted and specific foreign inward investment rather than domestic saving. As a result, although tax revenues and foreign earnings have greatly improved, manufacturing and other sectors targeted for development have not achieved substantial profitable growth. Thus engineering goods still accounted for only 19.84 per cent of export commodity earnings in 2010–11, and the income from the export of gems and jewellery remains one of the largest items in India's foreign earnings.[8]

India's cities have been transformed by a building and construction boom, fuelled by easy credit and government spending, but bankruptcies from this property and construction bubble are mounting. At the same time, liberalisation combined with rising commodity prices has encouraged illegal mining on a vast scale within tribal areas: a 'resource war' generating huge profits for a few whilst adding to landlessness and the subsistence problems of the marginalised communities who live there (Padel & Das, 2010). Meanwhile, those directly employed within the flourishing IT and BPO sectors do not exceed 2.8 million (the most generous estimate for 2012),[9] and sustained economic growth has been achieved only in specific enclaves. When state-level statistics are compared for 2004–5 to 2009–10, those states with the highest net domestic product per capita or longest life expectancy remain those, such as the Punjab, that benefited most from the Green Revolution innovations of 30 years before, whose effects – although unequal – were spread far more widely.[10]

Whilst famine has long since been abolished, and the numbers enduring absolute poverty have significantly declined,[11] easy credit and high oil and food prices have fuelled inflation in contemporary India, which is making daily life extremely difficult for those struggling in the middle and even more so for those on the margins of society. Government statistics (the Gini coefficient of inequality) suggest that India remains economically amongst the more equal societies in the world, but these statistics need to be taken with a pinch of salt, as there is little differentiation amongst the poorer sections of society, and most wealth in India is undeclared (only 2.9 per cent of the population, or barely 35 million, paid income tax in 2013).[12] It is also evident that income inequality is on the increase. Thus the Gini coefficient of household consumption expenditure at the national level went up from 29.7 in 1994 to 36.8 in 2004, and the Gini coefficient of state per capita incomes has risen from 21 in 1980 to 29 in 2001 (Joshi, 2010). The transition from wearing cotton to nylon saris, the use of mobile phones, and the more widespread availability of consumption items such as luxury soap are amongst the trappings of modernity that have become more apparent in the urban suburbs and small towns of present-day India. Yet this is of little significance when large numbers still remain without access to decent education or a supply of clean ('improved') drinking water: optimistically estimated as 8 per cent of the population in 2012.[13]

Marked inequalities thus persist in India in terms of standards of living (broadly defined), and there are huge differences between the wealthier and poorer states. Yet there clearly has been a very great change in the overall health of the population, and especially in the levels of infant mortality. This has led to a veritable demographic revolution in the past three decades, with the average family size declining from figures in excess of 5 per couple in the 1960s to an estimated average of only 2.55 in 2013.[14] In neighbouring Bangladesh, there has been even more dramatic progress, with the average family size falling to just 2.2 children. Whilst the number of children within the population has been stabilising, the legacy of past population growth has created an unprecedented increase in the number of young adults of working age. In this respect, India differs markedly from China, Japan, and most other developed countries, where the population is rapidly ageing and those in the working age group are in decline. As a consequence, it is estimated that India's population will reach 1.5 billion by 2030, making it the most populous country in the world. Sixty-eight per cent of this population will be of a working age, i.e. between the ages of 15 and 65.[15]

Between 2005 and 2020 alone, it is estimated by India's Planning Commission that some 200 million will be added to the population in the 15–64 age group. This 'demographic dividend' is often described as a huge opportunity for India and the country's brightest and best hope for the future. Yet it also poses India's greatest challenge. Even as output growth accelerated in the 1990s, employment growth fell to less than half that of the preceding decade. Employment increases of only approximately 1 per cent per year from 1994 to 2000 earned this period the epithet of 'a decade of jobless growth'.[16] In the last ten years, total employment (organised plus unorganised) has just about kept pace with labour-force growth, but in the organised sector, employment has been largely stagnant. Most jobs were thus produced in the informal, unorganised sector, and these were often purely notional jobs of low quality. 'Unless large numbers of productive jobs are created,

India will remain an economy in which a significant part of the population is excluded from the benefits of growth' (Joshi, 2010).

Less than 10 per cent of India's relevant age group receives college education. Without improvements in the educational system, the majority of young adults will join the workforce in the decades to come with few skills and their prospects of finding employment may diminish still further. The only 'benefit' the economy will enjoy from their numbers will be the downward pressure this will put on wages and thereby the costs of manufacturers. That might produce job growth in some sectors, but for the moment China has cornered the market in low-cost labour combined with capital investment. Looking further into the future, it will be hard for Indian workers to compete with more skilled and even cheaper employees that are available elsewhere in Asia, such as in Indonesia.

Aside from the retail sector, where reform might unleash opportunities for agricultural producers, the need to educate India's burgeoning population is thus an urgent priority. In 2007, Prime Minister Manmohan Singh announced plans for the creation of as many as 30 new central-funded universities and 6,000 publicly funded high quality schools in every block of the country.[17] However, universities take a long time to establish and there has been no articulation of a strategy that might allow for the creation of such a large number of new secondary schools in rural areas. Fortunately, to fulfil the need for education, India need not look only to the establishment of formal, state-run institutions. India has a long history of private, indigenous educational enterprises, going back to even before the nineteenth century, and unregulated (mostly English-medium) schools are flourishing throughout the country. Although criticised for their standards, past experience suggests they are more likely to fulfil the needs of the bulk of the population.

Rather than aspire to becoming the world's next major low-wage export economy, slower yet more stable growth may be achieved through the development of India's internal economy and through an improved trading relationship with its immediate neighbours. An improved relationship with Pakistan, in particular, might add to the 'demographic dividend' a 'peace dividend' that it has been conservatively estimated could in the long run add, with improved trade relations, 0.42 per cent to annual real GDP growth in both India and Pakistan.[18] It could also help realise India's ambitions for a seat on the Security Council and a more equal partnership with China in international relations. However, perhaps the greatest hope for India's future security and stability does not lie straightforwardly in economic growth and the Faustian bargaining of wealth in exchange for social and political harmony (as in China). Instead it lies in the awakening of new ideas, an awareness of the wider world, and the recognition of the equal rights of individuals as citizens, the lack of which has been one of the greatest obstacles to development.

The awareness and implementation of fundamental democratic rights have been fostered by the Indian government since independence, backed by numerous legal innovations, beginning with the Untouchability Offenses Act of 1956. It has accelerated in recent years with the enactment of socially transformative legislation with the Scheduled Castes and Scheduled Tribes (Prevention of Atrocities)

Act of 1989, the extension of reservations for Dalits and women in 1991, the granting of coparcenary rights to daughters in 2005, the National Rural Employment Guarantee Act of 2005, and legislation aimed at opening up the business of government to democratic control, such as the Right to Information Act of 2005 and the Lokpal and Lokayuktas Act of 2014.[19] Quite apart from these top-down, state-led initiatives, there has been a wealth of grassroots initiatives and campaigns led by feminist and Dalit organisations, and numerous other activist groups and ordinary individuals, without which most state-led initiatives would never have been enacted. These developments have empowered the multitude and have led to a dramatic democratisation of public discourse that has become evident to most observers (see Tanabe, Neyazi, & Ishikaza, 2014). It is through the resulting burgeoning revolution in social consciousness (outlined by Gold, Manor, and the epilogue in this volume) – more than anything else – that India's aspirations towards security and social stability in the future are most likely to be fulfilled.

Notes

1 Opening Remarks by John Major to the UN Security Council, New York, 31 January 1992.
2 *Human Development Report 1994* (New York, UNDP: 1994).
3 Yezid Sayigh quoted in Das (2002), p. 146.
4 For further discussion on the many meanings of human security, see Special issue on 'What Is "Human Security"?' *Security Dialogue*, September 2004, 35(3): 345–346. See also the debate relating to the report *Human Security Now* (New York, Commission on Human Security: 2003); www.unocha.org/humansecurity/human-security-now [accessed 25/6/2014].
5 Pew Research Centre, *Growing Concerns in China about Inequality, Corruption* (2012), Chapter 2, 'China and the World', www.pewglobal.org/2012/10/16/chapter-2-china-and-the-world/ [accessed 20/02/2014].
6 On the underresourcing of India's Foreign Service, see 'India Abroad: No Frills', *The Economist*, 29 September 2012; http://www.economist.com/node/21563415 [accessed 18/2/2014].
7 Chacko (2013) provides a sympathetic historical account of Indian foreign-policy ideology since independence. A rather more critical perspective is available from Ray (in this volume). See also Malone (2011), who concludes that India is unlikely to develop a grand foreign-policy vision in the future but will continue to opt for pragmatism guided by economic interest.
8 The share of gems and jewellery in India's total commodities exports was 15.3 per cent in 1991–92, 12.64 per cent in 2006–07, and 16.14 per cent in 2010–11. However, this is a highly import-intensive industry requiring large amounts of imports of pearls and precious stones. Directorate General of Commercial Intelligence and Statistics Ministry of Commerce and Industry, Govt. of India, *Foreign Trade Performance* 2010–11. Overall India continues to run a large deficit in merchandise trade. www.dgciskol.nic.in/annual_report.asp [accessed 24/02/2014].
9 NASSCOM, *The IT-BPO Sector in India Strategic Review 2012*, 'Executive Summary', p. 5 at www.nasscom.in/sites/default/files/researchreports/SR_2012_Executive_Summary.pdf [accessed 21/07/2015]. NASSCOM estimates that the combined total of those directly and indirectly employed in 2012 could total 8.9 million.
10 The exception as always is Kerala, where very high literacy levels (94 per cent) are to be found in combination with an extended life expectancy of 74 years and an only slightly above average NDP per capita. The states which have seen the greatest increase

in per capita NDP between 2004–5 and 2009–10 have been Punjab, Haryana, Maharashtra, and Orissa (a centre for mining). The states with the highest levels of infant mortality per 1,000 live births (in 2008) and absolute poverty (in 2004–5) remained Orissa (69/57 per cent), Bihar (56/54 per cent), and Madhya Pradesh (70/49 per cent). By comparison only 21 per cent of the population of the Punjab were classified as below the poverty line. Tomlinson (2013), p. 195.

11 According to the Indian Planning Commission, in 2011–12 India had 270 million persons below the Tendulkar Poverty Line as compared with 407 million in 2004–5; that is a reduction of 137 million persons over the seven-year period. Government of India Planning Commission, *Press Note on Poverty Estimates 2011–12* (New Delhi: GOIPC Press Information, July 2013, p. 3). Critics have argued, however, that this reduction is mostly a result of changes in the definition of absolute poverty and that the estimates rely upon overly optimistic assumptions about the rate of inflation for items of household consumption as well as ignoring the large variation in prices between different states. Poverty in the states of North Eastern India, such Assam, Bihar, and West Bengal, is consequently underreported.

12 Sixty-nine per cent still live in rural areas where 60 per cent of agricultural holdings are classified as 'marginal'. Tomlinson (2013), p. 208; Charan Singh, 'Why India Should Reward Honest, Rich Taxpayers', *Economic Times*, 1 May 2013. http://articles.economictimes.indiatimes.com/2013-05-01/news/38958335_1_tax-compliance-tax-base-35-million-taxpayers [accessed 18/2/2014].

13 WHO/UNICEF Joint Monitoring Programme for Water Supply and Sanitation www.wssinfo.org/data-estimates/table/ [accessed 15/3/2014]. See also A. Shaheed, J. Orgill, M. A. Montgomery, M. A. Jeuland & J. Brown, 'Why "improved" water sources are not always safe', *Bulletin of the World Health Organization* 2014; 92: 283–289.

14 The Indian total fertility rate (TFR) was 3.3 as recently as 2000, indicating a fall of more than 19 per cent during the first decade of the 21st century alone. World Bank databank, Fertility Rates, http://data.worldbank.org/indicator/SP.DYN.TFRT.IN [accessed 18/2/2014]. By comparison, the TFR in Pakistan was a rather less favourable 3.3 in 2013.

15 UN Population Division (UNPD), *World Population Prospects: The 2012 Revision*. http://esa.un.org/wpp/ [accessed 18/02/2014].

16 See B. B. Bhattacharya and S. Sakthivel, 'Economics Reforms and Jobless Growth in India in the 1990s', Working Paper E/245/2004, cited in D. Narayan & Glinskaya (2006), p. 8.

17 PM's address at the 150th anniversary of the University of Mumbai, 22 June 2007. http://pib.nic.in/newsite/erelease.aspx?relid=28780 [accessed 18/02/2014].

18 See De, Raihan, & Ghani (2013), p. 14. At present South Asia has the lowest inter-regional trade in the world, at 1.5 per cent of the region's economic output, according to a report by Standard Chartered Bank, compared with 7 per cent in East Asia. www.bloomberg.com/news/2012-06-26/sons-of-partition-tragedy-seek-india-pakistan-peace-dividend.html [accessed 18/2/2014]. See also Batra (2012). Apart from the economic growth that might arise from interregional trade, lasting peace could allow defence budgets to be cut by 25 per cent, saving $550 billion over the next twenty years.

19 See Ghosh (2006), pp. 88–102. A further proposed progressive legal innovation of the UPA government (drafted by the National Advisory Council) was the Prevention of Communal Violence (Access to Justice and Reparations) Bill, tabled before the Indian Parliament in 2013, but abandoned after fierce debate in February 2014.

Bibliography

Batra, Amita (2012) *Regional Economic Integration in South Asia: Trapped in Conflict?* London: Routledge.

Chacko, Priya (2013) *Indian Foreign Policy: The Politics of Postcolonial Identity from 1947 to 2004*. London: Routledge.

Das, Suranjan (2002) 'Globalisation, Good Governance and Human Security', in P. R. Charic & Sonika Gupta (eds.) *Human Security in South Asia: Energy, Gender, Migration and Globalisation*. New Delhi: Social Science Press.

De, Prabir, Selim Raihan, & Ejaz Ghani (2013) *What Does MFN Trade Mean for India and Pakistan?* NewYork: World Bank Poverty Reduction & Economic Management Network.

Ghosh, Jayati (2006) 'The "Right to Work" and Recent Legislation in India'. *Social Scientist* 34(1/2): 88–102.

Gill, B., M. Green, K. Tusji, & W. Watts (2009) *Strategic Views on Asian Regionalism: Survey Results and Analysis*. Washington DC: Center for Strategic & International Studies.

Joshi, Vijay (2010) 'Economic Resurgence, Lopsided Reform and Jobless Growth', in Anthony F. Heath & Roger Jeffrey (eds.) *Diversity and Change in Modern India: Economic, Social and Political Approaches*. Proceedings of the British Academy 159, Oxford & New York: Oxford University Press.

Malone, David M. (2011) *Does the Elephant Dance? Contemporary Indian Foreign Policy*. Oxford: Oxford University Press.

Narayan, D. & E. Glinskaya (eds.) (2006) *Ending Poverty in South Asia: Ideas that Work*. Washington DC: World Bank.

Ogden, Chris (2014) *Hindu Nationalism and the Evolution of Contemporary Indian Security Policy*. New Delhi: Oxford University Press.

Padel, Felix & Samarendra Das (2010) *Out of This Earth: East India Adivasis and the Aluminium Cartel*. Delhi: Orient Black Swan.

Tanabe, Akio, Taberez Neyazi, & Shinya Ishizaka (eds.) (2014) *Democratic Transformation and the Vernacular Public Arena in India*. London: Routledge, New Horizons in South Asian Studies.

Tomlinson, B. R. (2013) *The Economy of Modern India: From 1860 to the 21st Century*. Cambridge: Cambridge University Press.

1 The paradoxes of Indian politics

A dialogue between political science and history

Subho Basu and Crispin Bates

On 15 August 1947, at the moment of the birth of the Indian republic, Premier Jawaharlal Nehru hyperbolically announced to the nation that India's dark past was over and India's assignation with nation-making had begun. Interestingly, Nehru's brilliant metaphor became a reality for scholars studying India. Barring a few exceptions, historians often stop at 1947, indicating the end of India's past and the nation's 'history'. Political scientists commence their analyses only in 1947, as if a line had been drawn in the flow of time, indicating the beginning of 'modern' India. This division of labour has been a convenient shorthand with which to hammer into shape the complicated flow of events.

Underlying the academic division of labour in 1947, there is a theoretical assumption common among historians that politics in post-colonial India was somehow radically different from that of the late colonial era. Post-colonial India was a sovereign democratic republic operating under a citizen's constitution. Under the provisions of this constitution, the state regularly held mass elections in order to provide opportunities for its citizens to determine the succession of governments. This is perceived to be a quantitative leap forward from the paternalistic despotic structure of the colonial state.

While there is no doubt that the assumption of a qualitative difference in the nature of pre- and post-independence governments is partially true, it is also evident that the first generation of politicians in post-colonial India were products of the late colonial era. India witnessed the rise of mass politics after the First World War. Many politicians who held high positions in the government of India after independence learnt their craft in the inter-war era. Political parties also matured their tactics of mass mobilisation during the high tides of the nationalist movement. Even many aspects of the constitutional edifice of the post-colonial polity were established in the late colonial period.

In the study of India post-1947, historians complain about methodological problems caused by the lack of access to archives that constitute the primary materials of the historian's craft. This is a result of the fact that after 1955 most government departments gave up the practice of regularly weeding and transferring records to state and national archives after a lapse of 20 or 30 years so that they might be available for public access (in itself an interesting departure from British colonial practice). All government records after 1955 are therefore a part of current departmental repositories, to which normally only government officers have access. This includes even reports on the debates of state legislative assemblies.[1] In the 1980s restrictions were also placed on access to any historical government files that related to communal or secessionist movements. The collections of private papers held at the Nehru Memorial Library in New Delhi offer one of the few opportunities to methodically and systematically chart the workings of government and society since 1947, but outside Teen Murti there is a dearth of repositories in which a complete run of regional newspapers are available. Yet historians can import methodologies from various social science disciplines to reconstruct a temporal framework approach for the post-independence period. More importantly, the Indian polity was and is embedded within wider societal structures characterised by divisions along lines of caste, class, region, religion, and gender. These social fault lines came to inform politics in a significant way over a period of nearly a century. Thus the state-society relationship that constitutes the critical bedrock of politics cannot be viewed in isolation from the longer temporal framework of social and economic transformations in India. Unfortunately, with a few exceptions, historians have tended to surrender the field and have failed to engage in a dialogue with political scientists, sociologists, and anthropologists that might allow for a thoroughly historicised understanding of post-independence developments.

It terms of methodology, political scientists have displayed a far more nuanced and interdisciplinary approach. Many have borrowed field survey techniques from anthropology that have enabled them to develop a more penetrating analysis of contemporary affairs. However, political scientists approach Indian politics with ready-made theoretical frameworks that are often grounded in Eurocentric notions of democracy and nation formation. Thus soon after independence, when political scientists looked at the complex ethno-social mosaic of Indian society, they developed deep doubts about the possible survival of the new nation-state. In Europe and North America, nation-states had identifiable commonalities in terms of language and ethnicity, but in India these were spectacularly absent. It was long held that democratic forms of governance are integrally related to the prosperity of industrialised societies. Yet India remained industrially underdeveloped, and poverty was endemic for many decades after independence. Scholars were often surprised by the continuation of democracy, let alone its growth, in such a poor nation. The sensational titles of many popular and even some academic publications on India, predicting catastrophe for the new nation, starkly reveal the widespread influence of this prejudice.

Confounded by the complexity of the Indian situation and influenced by the functionalist theory of modernisation dominant in American academe, many pioneering political scientists, such as Myron Weiner, Morris W. Jones, and Lloyd I. Rudolph and Susanne Rudolph, chose to look at Indian politics through the prism of culture. Within cultural contexts they reworked the notions of tradition and modernisation in a complex fashion. These pioneering analysts thus sought to understand how a democratic state can withstand the pressures of a transitional 'primordial society', which was characterised by a complex ethno-religious mosaic and emerging modern interest groups. Others, such as Rajni Kothari and Stanley Kochanek, used the same functionalist templates to understand the party political system and the links between the party political system and interest groups. Their initial focus was thus directed towards the Congress Party of India's preeminent political apparatus of governance.

With the decline of the Congress Party's political hegemony from the 1970s onwards, many scholars looked at the operation of factions to understand India's political dynamics. A giant figure among them was Paul Brass, who in his 1965 study *Factional Politics in an Indian State* proffered possibly one of the very best analyses of the operation of factions in a North Indian polity. Finally, as India progressed into seemingly endless political crises and supposedly spasmodic economic development, scholars turned their attention to the restricted capabilities of the state to deliver development and how the pressure from societal interest groups paralysed India's economic development. Borrowing from Samuel P. Huntington's *Political Order in Changing Societies* (1968) and *The Crisis of Democracy: On the Governability of Democracies* (1976), Atul Kohli (1987) explored the idea of India having an overloaded state within a hypermobilised society. Finally, with the demise of the dirigiste economy and the simultaneous rise of liberalisation, political scientists and political sociologists such as Rob Jenkins (1999) turned their attention to behavioural characteristics of actors within the corridors of power and the workings of institutions. Finally scholars such as Ashutosh Varshney (1995) brought society to the centre stage of politics and relocated the capacity of the state to prevent riots within the context of societal relationships between rival ethno-religious groups.

No doubt the development of new scholarly approaches after independence generated powerful insights that have helped us to better understand Indian politics. We selected these few scholars not because of their ideological predilections, but because their towering presence has in many ways substantially informed our understanding of Indian politics. Nonetheless, with a few exceptions, such as Varshney, these highly sophisticated and nuanced analyses, in general, ignored the resistance of subaltern groups and tended to view social movements as merely contributing to the complex problem of hyperpoliticisation within Indian society. Complex developments within local politics were reduced simply to the operation of patron-client relationships and political brokerage. Even Marxists such as Sudipto Kaviraj and Achin Vanaik preferred to view politics through the lens of passive revolution or used terms such as 'degenerated working class parties', thereby reducing the agency of popular movements and parties and imposing their own theoretical preferences onto their complex and seemingly unruly subject matter.

An alternative approach suggested here is that a dialogue between historians and political scientists can provide a far better comprehension of Indian politics than is offered by the functionalist templates that have been widely employed hitherto by Indian scholars. Rather than viewing Indian society and politics through ready-made theoretical lenses, a case can be made instead for a more expansive, temporal view of the articulation of different forms of political practice in India.

From this perspective it may be argued that the apparent paradoxes of Indian politics are no more than the expression of a long-standing dialectical and dialogical process of engagement by different actors in political society. These articulate complex but integrated patterns of political transaction that are by no means contradictory but have become established and clearly recognised by political actors over time, in many cases beginning even in preceding centuries and continuing up to the present day.

Tradition and the modern in the making of political culture

The most popular reworked version of tradition and modernity surfaced in the writings of Myron Weiner, who was possibly one of the most formidable intellectual influences studying South Asia in the second half of the twentieth century. Weiner's first monograph, published in 1957, analysed opposition politics in India. The study was based on detailed personal interviews with numerous opposition politicians, primarily from left and centre-left parties. But his theoretical considerations were rooted in an assumption that education was eroding earlier sources of social status based on caste or tribal loyalties, and that politics had become the new source of power (Weiner, 1957). However, political parties in India represented not simply political ideologies but also factions and personal loyalties to leaders. In a powerful monograph in 1962, Weiner studied Indian politics through an examination of West Bengal politics. His study of politics in West Bengal was deeply influenced by the approaches of functionalism and offered an input-output analysis of the political system. He was associated with Gabriel Almond and his colleagues on the Committee on Comparative Politics of the American Social Science Research Council, who dominated the study of comparative politics in the United States in the 1960s. Weiner wrote a classic text on how pressure groups sought to engage in bargaining with the state. He promoted the view that there were two kinds of interest groups: one based on modern associational politics, such as trade unions, student movements, and peasant associations, which were thus characterised by modern political rhetoric; whilst the other was that of tribes, castes, and organisational associations of the locality. He thought that both kinds of group were authentic and legitimate representatives of democratic aspirations and that the interests of both should be accommodated.

Soon after publishing *The Politics of Scarcity* (1962), Weiner wrote a powerful essay introducing the concepts of elite culture and mass culture to the study of Indian politics (Weiner, 1963). Both these cultures, Weiner argued, were permeated by a modernising ethos and traditional cultural values. For Weiner, mass political culture represented the attitudes of society towards governance at a local and state level where local politicians operated within the ambience of caste, tribe, ethnicity, and language. He argued that elite political culture could be located within the national capital, generate the discourse of development in the English language, and plug into globally dominant paradigms of development. Weiner claimed that these two cultures would be likely to clash as elite developmental culture operates within a utopian vision of development spawned by the governing elites, whilst mass political culture was demanding power and patronage for ethnic groups and tribes. Thus he feared that the governing elite would be likely to impose an increasingly authoritarian regime as their failure to control mass culture became evident. In other words, Indian politics was viewed through the prism of modernity and tradition but in a more sophisticated and nuanced manner than before. But whilst Weiner tended to view these groups as being motivated in completely opposite directions, it could be argued that historically such multiple interests groups and contradictory articulations of politics were merely a part of the usual rhetoric of bargaining and resistance exercised by political entrepreneurs arising from the subaltern classes. These were neither new nor diametrically opposite but were dialectically related to the logic of domination and hegemony.

The most important contribution in Weiner's work lay in his understanding of the functioning of the Congress Party of India. To understand the operation of the Congress Party, he studied politics in five states using two cities (Calcutta in West Bengal and Madurai in Tamil Nadu) and three rural-urban contexts (Belgaum in Karnataka, Khaira in Gujarat, and Guntur in Andhra Pradesh). His methods were anthropological, using detailed in-depth interviews. Weiner conducted this research for 18 months in 1961–62. Based on this detailed field research, he maintained that the success of the Congress within a competitive party political structure could be located in the way the party managed different interest groups at district level. He believed that districts had their unique social mosaics and cultural loyalties that could not transcend their geographical boundaries. Thus Congress's success lay in the successful management of caste, tribes, and linguistic pressure groups within districts. This sums up his understanding of Indian society as an aggregation of localised interest groups locked within their castes and linguistic identities, articulated by local political actors within the framework of the Congress Party machine. Congress was thus a supra-local alliance of political actors operating at grassroots level. This view obviously discounts ideologies and the abilities of local actors to make independent cross-district alliances. Politics was merely an aggregate of interest groups confined to their caste, language, and regional identities representing mass political culture, which were in dialogue with elite political culture focused on development and nation-building.

An understanding of India in terms of diverse and contrasting political cultures received further clarification in W. H. Morris-Jones's work on government and politics in India, published in 1964. Morris-Jones expounded the idea that there were three languages of politics in India: the modern Westernised language in which politicians talked about constitutions, law courts, and administration; the traditional language in which caste or jati, as it is understood in rural India, plays a dominant role; and the saintly language adopted by many politicians to prompt Indian people to demand better moral conduct from their governing elites. Morris-Jones claimed that the contrasting pulls of traditional culture and modern culture often created conflicts of loyalty among politicians. Village subcastes, argued Morris-Jones, thus play a critical role in shaping politics in India (Morris-Jones, 1964).

In *The Modernity of Tradition* (1984), Susanne and Lloyd Rudolph challenged the misplaced polarities between modernity and tradition in Indian society so fondly espoused by earlier functional theorists. They argued that modernity and tradition are inextricably interrelated in ways that are significant to modernisation. They applied this thesis to the development of caste associations, the traditional roots of Gandhi's charisma, and the functioning of British law courts and legal traditions in the country. They argued that caste functions as a para-community in India whereby mass media and the transportation system reinforce caste consciousness. This has transformed caste associations into collective entities through which people are mobilised into parliamentary democratic politics. Similarly, they presented Gandhi as a moderniser who selectively used Indian traditions to initiate the process of modernisation. Finally, they demonstrated how British judicial courts reinforced Brahminical law and thus combined elements of both British and Brahminical legal practices. They thereby effectively demonstrated that tradition and modernity are not antipodes but are intertwined in terms of their impact on Indian politics. The book, a collection of three essays, thus undermined the possibility of any simplistic reading of tradition versus modernity in understanding Indian politics.

Despite the sophistication of the Rudolphs' reinterpretation of the dialogue between tradition and modernisation, the theme of modernisation under the British and Indian parliamentary system remained central to the writings of a majority of political scientists. For example, nearly quarter of a century after independence, writing in 1970 in *Asian Survey*, an influential political scientist, Robert Hardgrave Jr., brilliantly posited these apparent contradictions in explaining the Marxist movement in Kerala:

> Kerala is a land of contradiction in a nation of contrasts. It is a miniature of India with all its varieties pushed to the extreme. . . . It has the highest literacy rate and the highest rate of unemployment. With the largest community of Christians, it has the Communist vote also. It is once a bastion of orthodox Hinduism, with the most elaborate caste ranking in India and a region deeply affected by social mobilization and change. With many of the "prerequisites" of political modernization, Kerala is regarded by the Communist Party of India (Marxist) – or CPM – as an advanced outpost of revolutionary struggle.
> (Hardgrave Jr., 1970)

The operative word here is modernisation. Interestingly, instead of viewing these contrasts as the product of a societal arrangement where domination and resistance constituted critical components of the same societal structure, even a scholar like Hardgrave juxtaposed them as contrasting examples of tradition and modernity. Even while engaging with history, in his illuminating study of the Nadar 'community' in Tamil Nadu, Hardgrave (1969) spoke of its transition from being a disjointed, low-caste, ritually poor social group to becoming a well-organised community under the impact of the modernising forces of Christianity and colonial rule; the community then again fragmented into social groups and divided along class lines under the impact of post-colonial democracy. The unifying theme of his entire thesis was the impact of forces of modernisation on community formation. Hardgrave thus subjected his materials to a theoretical straitjacket and almost avoided entirely the fundamental question of what constitutes a community. Can we really call Nadar a community? Or is it possible that various local, disjointed, oppressive groups merely self-mobilised by using this template in order to secure their interests? The Nadar community was thus possibly a rhetorical construct rather than a practical socio-political entity.

Using an approach similar to Hardgrave's, in an important study Marcus Franda (1971) ignored the growth of communist politics in Bengal as a manifestation of the elite assertion of regional identity and posited instead a theory of the acculturation of the Bengali bhadralok under Western impact as the reason for their infatuation with Marxism. Studying culture became another cryptic shorthand for the reassertion of the thesis of modernisation, albeit in a more historically nuanced manner. Again Franda simplified his rich empirical data in order to subject it to his theoretical framework. If he had not done so, he might have recognised that Marxism in Bengal not only had an impact on the high-caste bhadralok but was still more popular with rural, ritually low-caste communities, who produced some of the most effective peasant leaders of the CPI(M), such as Harekrishna Konar. No doubt Hardgrave and Franda provide us with rich examples of the dialogue between history and politics, as well as locating politics within the ambit of wider state-society relationships, but their continued regard for modernisation theory leads to the pruning of rich details of historical reality for the sake of theoretical coherence.

System and faction

In 1964 Rajni Kothari condensed his series of articles on the Indian party political system published in the journal *Economic and Political Weekly* into a single article on the Congress system published in *Asian Survey*. He argued here that the Congress Party had the ability and willingness to accommodate diverse and contradictory interest groups within its fold and at the same time could incorporate pressures from opposition leaders (Kothari, 1964). He demonstrated that inter-party competitions and inner party factionalism had a dynamic relationship within the Indian political system. Inter-party competitions were thus incorporated within inner party factional struggles and these factions in their turn created a democratic dialogue within the party for policy making and personal political relationships. In his monograph published in 1970, Rajni Kothari further explained the Congress system as a uniquely Indian system, which could be resilient and flexible enough to accommodate pressures from diverse groups, from secessionists to Marxists, and could thus create a stable political system in the midst of crisis (Kothari, 1970). While Kothari's model can be applied to explain high politics in the Nehruvian era, it seems such assertions ignore the complex realities of Indian politics. Different forms of regional social movements and resistance to Congress rule not only exposed the vulnerabilities of the Congress Party but also led to the death of the Nehru Congress, with Indira Gandhi forming her own Congress (the Requisitionists) in 1969. The new Congress was a radically different outfit with very little intention of absorbing factions and regional leaders. Accommodative politics was over. Nonetheless, rather than looking at the Congress as a supra-local alliance among different types of local actors operating within diverse and segregated localities, Kothari sought to provide a theory of the party political system in India in its totality which simply did not fit the historical facts.

The term 'one party democracy' that Kothari coined and used to explain the Congress system was again invoked by Stanley Kochanek in his study of the Congress Party published in 1968. Kochanek studied the relationship between the party Congress president and the prime minister, the role of the Congress central working committee and such related bodies as the parliamentary board, and finally the socio-economic background of the Congress leadership. Kochanek (1968) studied the relationship between the party executive and the government executive in terms of three time periods: the period of transition (1946–51), the period of centralisation and convergence (1951–63), and the period of divergence (1963–67). His basic argument highlights the success of the Congress under Nehru, during which period Nehru allowed the working committee to operate in a creative manner. The third phase, argues Kochanek, was the era of equilibrium between the central and state governments. Sadly, however, Kochanek provides us with little understanding of the operation of the entire political system of the country. It provides intricate details of the party political mechanism, but not the wider societal impetus and the forces of change that lay outside the party political mechanism and yet profoundly influenced the political process.

As the term 'the Congress system' gained popularity, ironically the very operation of the system was being explained in terms of factions and rivalries within the factions. Obviously Kothari used factions in terms of inter-party and inner party political competitions, but a more substantive lead came from Paul Brass. In a major study of Uttar Pradesh (UP) politics published in 1965, Brass argued that in the absence of external threats, the presence of an internal consensus on ideological issues, and the absence of authoritative leadership, the UP Congress was composed of factions stretching from villages to state level. Faction leaders exercised a tight control over their immediate followers, which often resembled guru-disciple-type relationships of intense quasi-religious devotion. He further asserted that in traditional society decisions about factional disputes are not resolved through institutional laws but by personal arbitration from a reputed neutral leader, and that such leaders are few and far between. In other words, factions immobilise the functioning of the decision-making process. But factions also enable the Congress Party to recruit new activists, as different factions engage in the process of recruiting new followers. More importantly, factions cut across caste, class, and regional boundaries. Paul Brass thus brilliantly introduced a new concept of functionalist discourse into the study of Indian politics, namely the role of factions. His theoretical apparatus remained the old theory of tradition and modernity, but it operated with a new analytical tool. Factions can certainly provide a useful critical tool to help explain the rise of social movements or new types of ideological templates based on caste, such as that proposed by the Jat leader from UP, Charan Singh. However, the concept of the faction tends to project a view of Indian society devoid of ideological clashes or the economic and cultural moorings of politics. Despite Paul Brass's brilliant engagement with politics, his original interpretation provides us with a largely reductionist view of Indian society. Later Brass moved away from factional analysis and concentrated on deeper theoretical explanations of regional politics.

Political economy: the state, dominant classes, and social movements

With the introduction of emergency rule by Prime Minister Indira Gandhi in 1975 and the increasing assertions of state power by the central government in every aspect of society, the 1970s saw a new focus on the state as a critical political arena in contemporary research on India. Scholars concentrated particularly on the analysis of the relationship between state and dominant proprietary classes. In 1973, Hamza Alavi, the noted Marxist scholar of South Asia, argued that in post-colonial societies where the indigenous bourgeoisie was weak, the military-bureaucratic axis that came into existence with the emergence of colonial rule would become an autonomous power and would subjugate the other 'exploiting classes', such as the landed classes and the indigenous and metropolitan bourgeoisie (Alavi, 1973). This thesis of the state as the playground of elite interest groups in the Indian context found more coherent shape in the neo-Marxist writings of Pranab Bardhan. Bardhan's *Political Economy of Development in India* (1985) identified three dominant proprietary classes: the industrial capitalists, rich farmers, and professional bureaucratic elites. Competition and conflict among these dominant classes influenced the ability of the state to act independently. Soon after independence, India's political elites enjoyed a substantial degree of autonomy because the dominant classes were not very organised. Increasingly, in the post-colonial era these classes became more mobilised and thus made demands on resources that were needed for public sector investments and long-term planning. This led to increasing corruption, with the state becoming a virtual patronage distribution mechanism by means of subsidies and inefficiently managed public enterprises of various sorts.

In contrast to Bardhan, Susanne and Lloyd Rudolph (1984) highlighted the paradox of a weak-strong state presiding over a rich-poor economy. The economy is described as rich-poor because of the highly developed industrial sector coexisting with subsistence-level agriculture. According to the Rudolphs, the state was weak-strong because despite having substantial bureaucratic personnel, it was unable to penetrate rural society effectively. The rising level of political mobilisation in rural society further survived to undermine state influence. The de-institutionalisation of the Congress Party under Indira Gandhi, growing agrarian conflicts along caste and class lines, and increasingly powerful religious nationalist movements in the 1980s constituted the final imposition of clear limits on the extent of state control.

Despite its weaknesses, the state, according to the Rudolphs, is nonetheless a critical player in politics. Social engineering initiated by the state brought into existence a powerful class whose interests are tied to its functioning. While this social class attempts to garner resources through the state in the name of socialism, ordinary citizens form pressure groups that the Rudolphs label 'demand groups'. These demand groups organise street-level agitations to achieve their goals. They do not seek to organise lobbies, influence patronage networks, or develop institutional networks to influence political power. They cite the campaigns of rich peasants in Uttar Pradesh and Maharashtra (a common demand being debt relief)[2] as examples of such one-issue movements.

Both these readings of Indian political economy provide powerful insights. Nonetheless, Bardhan's account of structural conflicts marginalises human agency in the unfolding rivalries of class and sector. It also ignores critical societal factors such as caste, region, and language that influence political decision-making processes. His structural approach provides us with a critical analytical apparatus to help understand the material bases of political power. But that structural analysis needs to be grounded in the historical reality of long-term processes leading to the formation and dismantling of social classes. More importantly, this model needs to incorporate resistance from subaltern social groups both at an everyday level and in terms of critical policy events. The Rudolphs' historically contingent model is arguably still more problematic when it comes to explaining the complexity of Indian politics. For example, they ignore the seminal role that agrarian class conflicts play in shaping politics in India. Such conflicts are articulated in diverse ways. The street-level agitations of rich peasants in Uttar Pradesh and Maharashtra thus had a deep impact on the policies of the state. They inserted themselves into political patronage networks, and important politicians such as Charan Singh and Devi Lal built their careers in Uttar Pradesh and Haryana on the basis of the articulation of these new agrarian interests. These rich peasant groups and their leaders transformed themselves into powerful power brokers. They very effectively illustrate the manner in which the apparent paradoxes and crises of Indian politics are no more than the expression of a long-standing dialectical and dialogical process of engagement by different actors in political society.

Atul Kohli's influential work *The State and Poverty in India* (1987) provides us with a nuanced model of the Indian polity. Kohli argues that in developing economies, propertied classes impose their demands on the state through their control over productive resources. States that could insulate themselves from the pressures of propertied interest groups were more likely to be able to reach their developmental goals. The nature of the state's ability to rule crucially hinges upon the types of regime that organise political rule. In a democratic society, party political configurations constitute regimes. According to Kohli, the nature of the leadership, ideology, and organisational structure of the ruling party critically influence the ability of a regime to implement developmental policies for the poor. By engaging in a comparative study of West Bengal under the CPI(M), Uttar Pradesh under the Janata Party, and Karnataka under Devraj Urs, he argues that the CPI(M) with its pro-poor political ideology, disciplined organisational structure, and stable leadership was able to penetrate the countryside more profoundly. It was therefore able to implement far more effectively pro-poor policies such as land reforms, central government-financed programmes for the improvement of the living standard of small farmers, and wage and employment schemes for landless workers. This was particularly so when their efforts were compared with those of the faction-ridden, rural elite-dominated Congress Party after the exit of Devraj Urs. Nonetheless, though Devraj Urs's Congress government shared with the CPI(M) government a pro-poor ideology, it had comparatively a far less impressive record in implementing pro-poor policies because of the weak organisational structure of the party. He thus concluded that the left-of-centre political parties could implement pro-poor policies far more effectively than others.

In a similar fashion, in a subsequent study on the gradual decline of the state's ability to govern and maintain the rule of law, entitled *Democracy and Discontent: India's Growing Crisis of Governability*, Kohli (1991) directed his investigations at three levels: the district, regional state, and nation, with a focus on leadership. In selecting districts, he deliberately followed Myron Weiner's earlier study, *Party Building in a New Nation* (1968), and thus looked at five districts (Belgaum in Karnataka, Khaira in Gujarat, Guntur in Andhra Pradesh, Madurai in Tamil Nadu, and Calcutta in West Bengal); he then looked at three states (West Bengal, Bihar, and Gujarat), and finally looked at the leadership of Rajiv Gandhi in terms of his failure to implement policies of liberalisation, organisational reform of the ruling party, and finally his handling of the Punjab crisis. According to Kohli, the systematic intervention by the state in the economy and its inclination to influence the allocation of resources led to competition among interest groups to influence the decision-making process of the state. The continuous erosion of social hierarchy has further increased collective demands and pressures upon the government. In response to this situation, leaders resorted to populism and mobilised social groups whose demands they knew they would not be in a position to satisfy. This populism undermined the long-term credibility and planning of political parties. Again Kohli's research indicated that the CPI(M) in West Bengal was far more successful in establishing a party organisation that could direct popular pressures into building new institutional infrastructures that would enable better governance.

Kohli provided a new analytical focus on the political party and its role in managing economics, providing stability in terms of law and order, and innovating new policies. Yet his highly sophisticated and nuanced interpretation of Indian politics ignores how a political party develops the capability to deliver such development goals. In Bengal the left movement developed such capabilities through participation in popular social movements and by translating this social capital into governance after accessing political power. Thus it is as important to see how political parties are embedded within longer-term changing social relationships as how they are produced by ideology and able leadership. Societal structures and human agency interact with each other in reshaping politics. Neither of these relationships is static, nor are they divorced from one another. State policies alone do not create demand groups, rather developments within society lead to the formation of social networks and alliances which seek to influence state policies, and state policies then further empower social groups.

So far the literature surveyed focuses on the role played by indigenous factors in shaping the Indian political economy. But a crucial study by Francine Frankel, *India's Green Revolution* (1971), demonstrated how developments within the Indian political economy were affected by influences from abroad. Francine Frankel's study of high politics in relation to economic policies presents us with a more nuanced picture of how the gradual abandoning of Nehruvian institutional reforms was informed by resistance from local elites as well as by international pressures. Frankel argued that during the first five-year plan, Nehru directed policies towards the development of agriculture. He promoted rural government bodies based on universal suffrage, multipurpose cooperative societies, and financial support for community self-help organisations. After the modest success of the first plan, and faced with resource constraints, the government moved in the direction of rapid industrialisation. But the low level of state investment in agriculture, the failure to implement land reforms, and the slow growth in productivity undermined the overall drive for industrialisation. Frankel here brilliantly brings forth the structural constraints built into India's constitution in relation to agriculture. Agriculture remained a state subject, and state governments were beholden towards landed elites who supplied resources and political muscle to the ruling party. According to Frankel, under Lal Bahadur Shastri the government of India increased investments in agriculture but concentrated on productivity. The power of the already feeble planning commission was trimmed, and the government invited private capital to play a significant role in industrial expansion. Frankel here identifies two key factors in policy change. First, the World Bank pressured the Shastri government (1964–65) to initiate economic reforms for higher food grain production. Meanwhile state leaders persuaded the central leaders to abandon land reforms as a goal for agricultural development. Soon US President Johnson's administration, using the leverage of American food aid, further pushed India into abandoning institutional reform projects in favour of technical solutions to raise agricultural production. Frankel's work provides a much-needed international dimension on the abandonment of India's redistributive development goals. Of course, recent research has further established that planners were not at all powerful under Nehru and that the Congress made historic compromises in 1948 by restraining labour and allowing conservative proprietary interests to dictate terms to the central government (Chibber, 2003: 85–98). However, this process clearly was profoundly reinforced due to international pressures in the 1960s.

Two subsequent works on political economy further provide us with a focus on rural society and the political economy of agricultural management. Ron Herring's *Land to the Tiller* (1984), for example, provided us with a detailed explanation as to why certain types of policies were designed and the reasons behind their lack of implementation. He focused his attention on land reform policies through an explanation of three different types of land reform: tenure reform policies, land-ceiling–based redistributive policies, and land to the tiller policies. Land reform in poor countries remained the cornerstone of agricultural development, with the aim of achieving both higher productivity and social justice. The latter provided regimes with political legitimacy in the eyes of the peasantry. According to Herring (1984), land reforms failed because the existing social structures and state organisations remained captured by the landed elites and reproduced social inequity. He further explained this by highlighting the concept of the 'embedded bureaucracy'. Bureaucrats, a privileged stratum in the society, were invariably tied to landed elites. Either they came from landholding social classes or they themselves aspired to become landed elites, as landholding provided security and social status in a predominantly agrarian society. The bureaucracy thus remained tied to landholding elites through shared economic interests and social aspirations, and sabotaged land reforms through corrupt practices. Like Atul Kohli, Herring argues that left-of-centre political parties can play a critical role in implementing redistributive reforms. In the case of Kerala the undivided CPI and later CPI(M) enacted the most radical land legislation which redefined the nature and formation of classes and the direction of rural class conflicts. He thus claims that legal enactments effectively transformed both the interests and actions of social groups. This is an interesting claim, but the fact remains that in most cases laws alone proved inadequate to the task of implementing land reform. Indeed, on the contrary, laws could become a radical force only when backed by democratising social movements headed by committed political parties.

Another important thesis that implicitly sought to provide an alternative to Bardhan's, Frankel's, Kohli's, and Herring's class-based reading of rural politics was provided by Ashutosh Varshney in *Democracy, Development, and the Countryside: Urban-Rural Struggles in India* (1995). Following Michael Lipton's (1968) notion of urban bias in the development process, Varshney highlights the sectoral struggle between rural and urban India. He assumes a hypothetical unity in rural interests and proceeds to analyse it in terms of the rural-urban divide in Indian politics. Between his chapters 2 and 5, he provides a history of India's agricultural policies: the shift in the agricultural policies in India in the mid-1960s, the growing government intervention in input and output markets, the birth and consolidation of the rural lobby, and the diverse types of party, non-party, and bureaucratic forums that played a critical role in effecting agricultural policy change. Thus Varshney's abiding concern was to explain why the rural sector did not become a predominant player in Indian politics. Following the famous assertion of Barrington Moore (1966) that democracies were established through the obliteration of the peasantry, he starts with the exceptional case of India's rise as a peasant democracy. But he attributes the failure of the rural sector to politicise itself to the urban bias of Marxist leaders such as Nehru.

The next section in Varshney's study examines the rise of rural sectoral politics in India from the late 1970s. He claims that this was exceptional in the history of industrial transformation. He further argues that despite the large-scale mobilisation of rural interests, the rural sector did not achieve much in terms of economic gains. This he attributed to the divergence between economic and political interests. Yet he claims that there did exist for some time a rural bias in India's economic policies, which led to the rural sector gaining in terms of subsidies for farm output in a situation of production surpluses, relatively low taxation, and even the benefit of substantial loan remissions during the Janata Dal regime in 1990. More importantly, rural food prices did not fall despite an increase in government stocks of surplus food grains. This obviously implied that through government food subsidies the richer segments amongst rural producers could resist falling prices and gain at the expense of poor rural workers (amounting to some 60 per cent of rural society) who depended on the market for access to food products.

The problem with Varshney's thesis is his construction of the notion of a single, unitary rural sector. The rural sector has always been divided in terms of class, caste, region, and religion. Varshney's final chapter pays inadequate attention to this. Indeed, to avoid the inevitable reality of class, caste, and regional fault lines in rural society, which constituted a fundamental axis of Indian politics, Varshney posits an entirely imagined reality of unified rural interests to simplify the task of analysis. He further omits to explain what constitutes urban interests and urban interest groups in India.

Conclusion

This survey of classics in the political science literature on India between the late 1950s and late 1990s establishes a clear pattern in the range of approaches used by political scientists to understand Indian politics. Political scientists have used ready-made theoretical lenses to understand Indian society. Politics, they often presumed, was based upon the single institutional edifice of society. Instead of viewing institutions as deeply embedded within Indian social structures, institutions were provided with a life of their own and were attributed with the ability to change society. Except for the writings of a few scholars, who used neo-Marxist templates, societal contradictions were presumed to be emanating entirely from state policies. When the modernisation of society through political institutions increasingly appeared to be untenable, political scientists sought to view India through paradoxes and even constructed homogeneous social entities such as 'the rural interest', in defiance of the evidence of empirical reality. India thus had to be invented and reinvented as diverse forms of political movements contesting for political power, with political formations emerging in one historical conjucture and then dissolving in the next when faced with the social contradictions that brought them into existence in the first place.

The fluidity perceived by political scientists is expressed in terms of the complexity of Indian society and its multiple forms of transition over nearly seven decades under the impact of global, local, social, economic, and cultural forces. It would certainly be a mistake to argue that there is a unidirectional flow in terms of societal change in India. Democracy in a predominantly agrarian society will be marked by resource constraints that generate diverse societal responses and can be shaped by these societal responses in a way that might not fit into existing theoretical lenses. But rather than using ready-made theoretical constructs, it should be possible instead to explore Indian politics in terms of the social analysis of the historical unfolding of events. Theories could then be used to interrogate historical processes, and historical evidence could be used to interrogate theories.

National security is a key term, often referenced but poorly defined, in many theoretical constructions of the Indian polity. It would arguably be better to redeploy the term to understand societal security. The processes that lead to the creation of a socially just, politically inclusive, and culturally tolerant society can only be understood through a nuanced historical interpretation of social changes within a temporal framework. Humans operate within structural constraints but they also impose their imprints on structures. The security desired by individuals needs to be understood in terms of their agency to engage with historically given structural constraints and their ability to transcend them. Dominance and hegemony, furthermore, cannot be understood without an examination of subaltern resistance and its imprints upon society as a whole. A dialogue between historians and political scientists, through the medium of contemporary history, could therefore potentially provide a superior instrument with which to understand the ability of citizens to mitigate and transform society and the politics that represents it.

The historian Ramachandra Guha has remarked that historians have a preference for writing about the colonial era, since this was a time when events within even the most isolated rural setting could easily be seen to be connected to global events and grand historical arguments about the development of colonialism, capitalism, and the national movement.[3] The history of politics post-1947 is, by contrast, at least until the era of globalisation takes off in the twenty-first century, an apparently more parochial affair. It may be argued, however, that this appearance is merely a consequence of the way in which post-independence politics has been represented in the writings of functionalist political analysts. By abandoning the study of politics in the late twentieth century through preference, and by citing the difficulties of writing history without access to the usual form of archival sources, historians have evaded the need for methodological innovation that has been more keenly felt by the social sciences. In the second decade of the twenty-first century, an era in which the post-independence 'post-colonial' political hegemony of the Indian National Congress seems finally to have stumbled to its end, the time is now ripe for historians to face up to the challenge of interpreting the last half-century of Indian history with the same acuity and depth with which they explored the colonial era. Rather more convincing explanations may then be forthcoming for the remarkable durability and stability of the Indian political system and for the ability of Indian democracy to satisfy the demands of its so many diverse constituents, despite its apparent contradictions.

***

Notes

1 A brave attempt was made to recommence the transfer of files from central government ministries to the National Archives following the rare appointment of a professional historian, Professor Mushirul Hasan, as director of the National Archives in 2010. The government's brief enthusiasm for transferring historical records was perhaps related to the passing of a Right to Information Act in 2005, which led to a growing number of

requests for access to specific historical documents. Thousands of files were allegedly transferred, and staff were recruited to catalogue them. However, this initiative ground to a halt upon Professor Hasan's voluntary retirement in May 2013. A controversy subsequently erupted concerning the destruction of old files at the direction of newly elected prime minister Narendra Modi – 1.5 lakh (150,000) Home Ministry files were allegedly destroyed, including documents recording discussions of a cabinet meeting held at the time of Mahatma Gandhi's assassination (*Times of India*, 23 June 2014).

2 The state-sponsored consolidation and elimination of rural indebtedness was, interestingly, an idea first introduced by the British colonial government in the 1930s, the memory of which, arguably, persists to this day.

3 Ramachandra Guha, 'The Challenge of Contemporary History', Plenary Address at the 37th Annual Conference on South Asia, Madison, Wisconsin, 17–19 October 2008.

Bibliography

Alavi, Hamza (1973) 'The State in Post-Colonial Societies', in Kathleen Gough & H. Sharma (eds.) *Imperialism and Revolution in South Asia*. New York: Monthly Review Press.

Bardhan, Pranab (1985, 1st edn; rprt 1999) *The Political Economy of Development in India*. Delhi: Oxford University Press.

Brass, Paul (1965) *Factional Politics in an Indian State: The Congress Party in Uttar Pradesh*. Berkeley: University of California Press.

Chibber, Vivek (2003) *Locked in Place: State Building and Late Industrialization in India*. Princeton, NJ: Princeton University Press.

Frankel, Francine (1971) *India's Green Revolution: Economic Gains and Political Costs*. Princeton, NJ: Princeton University Press.

Franda, Marcus (1971) *Radical Politics in West Bengal*. Cambridge, MA: MIT Press.

Jenkins, Rob (1999) *Democratic Politics and Economic Reform in India*. Cambridge: Cambridge University Press.

Hardgrave Jr., Robert L. (1969) *The Nadars of Tamilnad: The Political Culture of a Community in Change*. Berkeley: University of California Press.

Hardgrave Jr., Robert L. (1970) 'The Marxist Dilemma in Kerala: Administration and/or Struggle'. *Asian Survey* 10: 993–1003.

Herring, Ronald J. (1984) *Land to the Tiller: The Political Economy of Agrarian Reform in South Asia*. New Haven, CT: Yale University Press.

Huntington, Samuel P. (1968) *Political Order in Changing Societies*. New Haven, CT: Yale University Press.

Kochanek, Stanley (1968) *The Congress Party of India: The Dynamics of One Party Democracy*. Princeton, NJ: Princeton University Press.

Kohli, Atul (1987) *The State and Poverty in India: The Politics of Reform*. Cambridge: Cambridge University Press.

Kohli, Atul (1991) *Democracy and Discontent: India's Growing Crisis of Governability*. Cambridge: Cambridge University Press.

Kothari, Rajni (1964) 'The Congress "System" in India'. *Asian Survey* 4(12): 1161–1173.

Kothari, Rajni (1970) *Politics in India*. Boston: Little Brown & Company.

Lipton, Michael (1968) *Urban Bias and Agricultural Planning*. Brighton: Institute of Development Studies, University of Sussex.

Moore, Barrington (1966) *Social Origins of Dictatorship and Democracy: Lord and Peasant in the Making of the Modern World*. Boston: Beacon Press.

Morris-Jones, W. H. (1964) *The Government and Politics of India*. London: Hutchinson University Library.
Rudolph, Susanne & Lloyd Rudolph (1984). *The Modernity of Tradition: Political Development in India*. Chicago; London: University of Chicago Press.
Varshney, Ashutosh (1995) *Democracy, Development, and the Countryside: Urban-Rural Struggles in India*. Cambridge: Cambridge University Press.
Weiner, Myron (1957) *Party Politics in India*. Princeton, NJ: Princeton University Press.
Weiner, Myron (1962) *The Politics of Scarcity: Public Pressure and Political Response in India*. Chicago: University of Chicago Press.
Weiner, Myron (1963) 'India's Two Political Cultures', in Myron Weiner (ed.) *Political Change in South Asia*. Calcutta: Firma K. L. Mukhopadhaya.
Weiner, Myron (1968) *Party Building in a New Nation: The Indian National Congress*. Chicago; London: University of Chicago Press.

2 India's foreign relations
An overview

Jayanta Kumar Ray

It is the view of this essay that until at least 1991, India had nothing that could properly be called a policy with regard to foreign relations. Instead, sermons and shibboleths passed for policy, and these often had negative domestic implications. The fact that such an equation of shibboleth with policy was allowed to persist for so long can be explained by various factors, including an undercritical press, a bureaucracy that had descended into sycophantocracy, and the dominant mode of foreign policy analysis in India consisting of the persistent hero worship of a ruling dynasty in New Delhi. Any analyst seeking to remove the veil of slogans and discover the realities of India's foreign relations will soon realise that this entails sifting through a lot of rubbish. After which it becomes clear that two favourite aphorisms of the social sciences do not apply in the case of Indian foreign relations. The first of these is, 'Nothing succeeds like success'; the second, 'A people gets the government it deserves.'

A critical study of the history of India's foreign relations, especially up to 1991, negates both of these sayings. First, during his time in office, India's first prime minister, Jawaharlal Nehru, made several huge mistakes, for example in the way he conducted relations with Britain, Pakistan, and China, as well as his failure to strengthen the Indian economy, which only served to reinforce the failures in India's foreign relations. Thanks to the prevalence of hero worship masquerading as foreign policy analysis, however, Nehru is regarded as a great statesman. In the case of Jawaharlal Nehru, therefore, it is more apt to say 'Nothing succeeds like failure.' Second, the economic strength of a country is evidently the bedrock of its potential for success in foreign relations. However, with long tenures as prime minister, Nehru, and subsequently Indira Gandhi, made numerous decisions that damaged the Indian economy, pushing it to the brink of bankruptcy. In 1991, Prime Minister Narasimha Rao, assisted by Finance Minister Manmohan Singh and Commerce Minister P. Chidambaram, took bold and decisive measures to avert this bankruptcy and place India firmly on the road to fast economic development. Over the following decades, this development endowed India with a level of leverage in foreign relations such as had been undreamt of under either Nehru or Indira Gandhi. Despite their failings, however, Nehru and Gandhi (unlike Narasimha Rao) continue to be hero worshipped – even in the second decade of the twenty-first century – because of the weight of dynasty, which seems to overawe professional foreign policy analysts. Thus, one can argue, Indians did not deserve the governance they suffered during the regimes of Nehru and Indira Gandhi.

In March 1947, at the age of 46, Louis Mountbatten was appointed Viceroy of India with a mandate from London to transfer power by June 1948 (Ghosh, 1967: 198). It is important to stress that despite Mountbatten's announcement of Partition just three months later, on 3 June 1947, and of the subsequent Boundary Award, it would have been feasible – and prudent – to have put more time into the process of transferring power, completing the process closer to the originally scheduled date of June 1948. As M. H. Saiyid, secretary to M. A. Jinnah, wrote: 'As a direct result of the Award, a mass exodus of population began. Emigration from either side was no doubt the natural consequence of partition, but had the Boundary Award remained in abeyance for some time the much accelerated speed of mass movements would have been considerably checked and both the countries would have gained time to negotiate an agreement on a peaceful exchange of population'(Saiyid, n.d.: 333). A delayed implementation of the Award would have meant an opportunity for a far less disorderly and violent movement of the population, a partially planned and peaceful exchange of property, and a less irreversible feeling of animosity between Hindus and Muslims, thereby pre-empting the perpetuation over the following decades of various hatreds/conflicts between individuals/governments (Godbolet, 2006: 344–348). Stanley Wolpert made an important comment on this subject: 'I believe that the tragedy of Partition and its more than half century legacy of hatred, fear, and continued conflict – capped by the potential of nuclear war over South Asia – might well have been avoided, or at least mitigated, but for the arrogance and ignorance of a handful of British and Indian leaders. Those ten additional months of postwar talks might have helped all parties to agree that cooperation was much wiser than conflict, dialogue more sensible than division, words easier to cope with and pay for than perpetual warfare' (Wolpert, 2006: 2).

Further to the rushed implementation of the Boundary Award, Louis Mountbatten, as the first Governor General of free India, took advantage of Nehru's lack of realism (and the resultant capacity to seriously damage India's vital interests). In 1948, principally as a result of yielding to pressure from Mountbatten, Nehru committed two grievous errors that had calamitous consequences for India in the key area of the interface between domestic and foreign/defence affairs. The first error was to refer the Jammu-Kashmir issue to the United Nations without first evicting the occupying Pakistani forces from Indian territory. The second – and less forgivable – error was to stop military action against these invaders at a time when they were about to be evicted from Indian territory, which would have forced Pakistan to plead for a ceasefire. The long-term consequences of these errors continue to impact India even today (2013). It is not possible to go back and alter how events unfolded in 1947–48; rather one can only construct alternative scenarios, reflecting painfully on what was lost and what might have been gained had a different course of action been taken. Militarily, in 1947–48 Pakistan was incomparably weaker than India; this was admitted by Field Marshal Ayub Khan himself. Still, on account of the errors mentioned above, Pakistan emerged from the situation with a windfall gain of approximately one third of Jammu-Kashmir. Pakistani-occupied Kashmir was an invaluable strategic asset, and, having been snubbed by India, especially during the Korean War of 1950–53, in the 1950s the United States planned to recruit Pakistan as a military ally. Official and non-official sources in Pakistan leave no doubt that while Pakistan made a pretence of joining America in an anti-Communist alliance system, its real aim was to counteract the military superiority of India. The US, for its part, chose to be deceived by Pakistan.[1]

It must be acknowledged that this might not have happened were it not for some incredible lapses committed by Indian leaders, especially Nehru, in 1947–48. Nehru was the prime minister of India and its minister for external affairs for 17 years, and his failures handicapped his successors for decades. In the first week of September 1947, Prime Minister Jawaharlal Nehru and Deputy Prime Minister Ballabhbhai Patel confessed to unmitigated bankruptcy and begged Louis Mountbatten to govern India as its de facto supreme ruler. Mountbatten agreed only when Nehru and Patel vested nearly unchallengeable authority in him as chairman of the Emergency Committee of the Cabinet. These events were, and remain, shrouded in secrecy, as the relevant government documents have either been destroyed or have had access to them withheld. Nehru's pathetic surrender to Mountbatten – a prelude to his momentous failures in the management of the foreign relations of post-independence India – remains largely unknown, except by a few iconoclastic researchers (Collins & Lapierre, 2007: 396–398; 1984: 30–34).

The hallmark of India's foreign policy is often characterised as non-alignment – especially by those analysts who happen to be admirers of the ruling dynasty – but a few examples suffice to reveal non-alignment as a hollow, undefined, and undefinable shibboleth. Advocates of non-alignment claim its essence to be independence of opinion and action. Yet, in 1947–48, when non-alignment originated, such independence was emphatically not a feature of Indian foreign relations: Indian leaders virtually abdicated sovereignty to the British on account of the issues mentioned above, as well as several other factors to which we now turn. Nehru not only initiated the installation of Louis Mountbatten as the first Governor General of free India, but also made him the chairman of both the Emergency Committee of the Cabinet and the Defence Committee of the Cabinet. Moreover, Nehru ensured that the heads of all three armed services were British officers. The result of this was a virtual negation of independence of action by India in the conflict over Jammu-Kashmir during 1947–48, when (as noted above) Pakistani aggressors benefited immensely from the collusion of powerful Britons, including Governor General Mountbatten (Dasgupta, 2002).

When, in June 1950, 'Russian-trained North Korean troops, with the backing and support of China, invaded South Korea, involving the United States and its United Nations allies in a costly war' (Bowles, 1974: 4–7; Gould, 1992: 20–21), those Americans who shared the apocalyptic notion of an attempt by communist countries to conquer the world by instalments found concrete evidence in support of their view. If a country (for example, India) offered only limited support to the US/UN war against North Korea, or showed signs of ambiguity or vacillation, it was accused of being unethical (Heimsath & Mansingh, 1971: 351). When India agreed at the UN to accept North Korea as an aggressor but refused to supply troops to the UN contingent for military aggression, it was criticised by America for taking an unethical stand; the supply of a medical unit by India was seen as no substitute for the dispatch of combat troops. However, in this half-hearted support for the UN, India sought – albeit clumsily – to preserve its aspiration to secure the role of go-between in the Korean conflict.

Ultimately, the criticism of India by the US turned into antagonism because of the peculiar way in which Nehru's closest associate, and India's de facto external affairs minister, Krishna Menon, handled the Korean issue at the UN in New York. 'Krishna Menon's acid tongue and striking – almost diabolic – looks soon made him a media celebrity at the United Nations. Since his barbed verbal threats were more often than not aimed at the United States, Menon's presence added a new, and ultimately heavy, burden to Indo-American relations' (Kux, 1994: 75). In the course of the Korean War, it was only once the two sides had reached an equilibrium of military power that India was called upon to play the part of a so-called mediator and brought in to chair the Neutral Nations Repatriation Commission (De Russet, 1969: 114–115). Thus, the image that was held by admirers of Nehru or Krishna Menon of the achievement of India in world politics at the time of the Korean conflict 'was no more than a make-believe. It was not because of our persuasion that the USA and China sought a settlement in Korea. They only used our services as a go-between after they had decided to negotiate' (Lal, 1969: 320). In connection with this, it is extremely important to note that in around 1953, India made two grievous mistakes and – which was typical of Nehru – threw away the prospect of long-term gains in the realm of power politics. India rejected first the American offer of support for an 'Indian Monroe Doctrine' in South Asia, and second, the American proposal to have India replace Taiwan in the UN Security Council (Tharoor, 2003: 183). Had India accepted these two offers from the US, it would have been able to forestall many threats in coming years from neighbouring countries such as Pakistan and China.

Given the limited space of this chapter, it is possible to select only a few key issues through which to assess the capabilities of India's leaders in serving national interests and/or practising the principles they professed to hold. One such issue is the Suez Crisis. Following the nationalisation of the Suez Canal by Egypt in 1956, Anglo-French troops began military operations against Egypt. In his response to these operations, Nehru noted that the Anglo-French action was 'clear aggression and a violation of the United Nations Charter' and 'a reversion to a previous and unfortunate period of history when decisions were imposed by force of arms by Western Powers on Asian countries' (Gopal, 1989, Vol. 3: 286). At the UN General Assembly, the Anglo-French invasion of Egypt was debated almost simultaneously with the Soviet intervention in Hungary. India's role in the Hungarian case was widely criticised, since it was 'not possible to justify India's ambivalent and generally supportive stance of the Soviet invasion of Hungary on moral or normative political grounds' (Dixit, 1998: 66). The dissonance between India's stances on Suez and Hungary was glaring, and in order to explain this, it is important to make reference to the events of the Security Council on 14 February 1957, when Australia, Cuba, Britain, and America submitted a draft resolution that was generally supportive of Pakistan's proposal for the use of a temporary UN force in Jammu-Kashmir. The draft resolution received nine votes in favour; Sweden, the president of the Council, abstained. Nevertheless, the resolution was vetoed by the Soviet Union (Gopal, 1989, Vol. 3: 48). Bearing this in mind, it is clear how friendless India was (despite the much-publicised policy of non-alignment) and why it could not have voted any other way on the Hungarian issue at the UN a few weeks earlier. It was forced to all but join the Soviet camp as a result of its own actions in the 1947–48 Jammu-Kashmir conflict, in which it had succumbed to British manoeuvres and did not drive out Pakistani raiders from the whole of Jammu-Kashmir, despite enjoying incontestable military superiority over Pakistan. This is one example of how Pakistan was able to reduce India's policy of non-alignment to a farce.

The 1947–48 conflict with Pakistan constituted the first and probably the most important defining moment in Indian foreign policy. The second such moment was the 1962 conflict with China and the circumstances that led up to it. On 29 April 1954, India and China signed an agreement on 'trade and intercourse between the Tibet region of China and India'. The apparently simple title of the agreement was highly deceptive: the agreement was such that India gained virtually nothing and gave away a great deal; further, it clearly entailed Indian acceptance of Chinese sovereignty over Tibet, thus demolishing the buffer against China that had been maintained by British-ruled India. Further, India pressed to set the duration of the agreement at 25 years, but at the insistence of China, it was fixed at 8 years (Maxwell, 1971: 78–80; Khera, 1968: 155; Gopal, 1989, Vol. 2: 180–181).

In July 1954 – in complete contradiction of his conduct towards China up to that point – the Indian prime minister sent a highly confidential memorandum to the Union Ministries of Defence, External and Home, as well as to state governments in India. The memorandum contained the specific instruction that the government was to set up check posts along the whole of the northern frontier, with special attention to areas that were looked upon as disputed. It also stated that India's northern frontier was so definite and firm that it would not be necessary to discuss this move with anyone. Further, the memorandum insisted that in border regions and other areas, India's administrative machinery should be strengthened; in other words, military-administrative measures would be used to compensate for the diplomatic failure of 1954 (Gopal, 1989, Vol. 2: 181; Khera, 1968: 155; Maxwell, 1971: 80).

Such measures signified the adoption of a forward policy by India vis-à-vis China. To put it succinctly, Indian leaders failed to realise that without adequate military preparations, a forward policy might prove to be a trap and pave the way for disaster and humiliation (as did in fact occur in 1962). With India's unwarranted agreement that China wielded sovereign authority over Tibet, China had won – without firing a single shot against India. China scored another victory when it built the Tibet-Sinkiang (Xinjiang) road across Aksai Chin, and a climactic touch was provided in 1962 when Indian soldiers in summer uniform – without even the minimum infantry weapons or rations – were forced by Nehru and Defence Minister Krishna Menon to confront a considerably more powerful Chinese army. India's defeat was followed by a unilateral declaration of ceasefire by China – due largely to unpublicised American intervention in favour of India. India complied with the ceasefire without formally accepting it.[2] Finally, non-alignment lost the last of its artificial lustre when, on 19 November 1962, the US Ambassador to India, John Kenneth Galbraith, proposed that components of the United States Seventh Fleet be dispatched to the Bay of Bengal. Later, Galbraith reminisced, 'It is good that the Chinese cannot come by water into the Bay of Bengal' (Galbraith, 1969: 419, 423–425, 428). Nevertheless, as already noted, the Chinese were realistic enough to take the American response seriously and declare a unilateral ceasefire.

The disaster of 1962 could have been avoided. By 1957–58 China felt satisfied that it was able to establish its control over what had in the past been a no-man's land, and construct the Tibet-Xinjiang road across Aksai Chin in accordance with its geopolitical necessities. Similarly, by that time, India too had succeeded in establishing its administrative authority over the North East Frontier Agency (NEFA), which is to say the areas south of the McMahon Line, which marked the boundary. Therefore, in the late 1950s, India and China were in an ideal position to strike a bargain by each allowing the other to retain its strategic advantages in, respectively, the eastern and western sectors of India's northern frontier. Actually, as he had done earlier in 1954, 1956–57, and 1958 (albeit implicitly), when he came to New Delhi from Rangoon (Yangon) in April 1960, Chinese premier Zhou offered a compromise in which he would agree on a boundary accord consistent with the geographical prescription of the McMahon Line (Ranganathan & Khanna, 2000: 32–38; 43–45; Gopal, 1989, Vol. 3: 35–36; Maxwell, 1971: 89, 105–106, 124–125, 159–160). Indian decision makers did not share Zhou's pragmatism.

The next important episode in the history of Indian foreign relations was the war with Pakistan in September 1965. The serious – although not unusual, and perhaps chronic – deficiencies of the relevant decision makers vitiated the Indian response to Pakistani aggression. For example, even on occasions when, as in Lahore, India managed to surprised its enemy by moving as close as 12 miles from the city, the authorities in Delhi failed to take the resolute measures that could have led to its capture (Kaul, 1971: 67; Nayar, 1971: 181; 186–188, 191–192). After all, it was an open secret that Pakistan, in search of a quick victory over India (as the rhapsodic broadcasts over Pakistani radio attested) exhausted nearly all its ammunition – which had been gifted to it by America – in just three weeks (Singh, 1999: 78; Wolpert, 1993: 93). Yet, it was at this moment that Pakistan and India agreed to a ceasefire.

India should have persisted with its military operations in the war of 1965 and sought to occupy important locations such as Lahore and Sialkot, which could later have been bartered away against the evacuation of Pakistan-occupied Kashmir. Had Pakistan been brought to its knees in this way, it may have been possible to avoid the India-Pakistan arms race, concentrate on economic development, and even pre-empt what might be called the Pakistan-sponsored jihad that raged in the late twentieth and early twenty-first centuries. However, alongside the loss of these opportunities, the dangerous Pakistani view that Indians (Hindus) were proper targets for jihad persisted. General Mohammad Musa, who headed the Pakistani army during the 1965 war, was proud of nurturing a 'spirit of jihad' among Pakistani soldiers (Musa, 1983: 111). A young Pakistani officer, wounded in the war and captured by India, rejected the offer of a blood transfusion that was part of the usual course of medical treatment, because he preferred death to receiving blood donated by an infidel (Nayar, 1971: 186). The Tashkent Declaration of 1966 brought to a close the Pakistan-India War of 1965. Much to the annoyance of many Pakistanis, however, the Declaration did not contain any reference to Kashmir as a 'dispute', an 'issue', or even a 'problem' (Taheer, 1980: 69). In view of this, the Tashkent Declaration represents the best deal that India has so far obtained from Pakistan. But the author of this deal, Prime Minister Lal Bahadur Shastri, has seldom received due credit for this unparalleled achievement – presumably because he does not belong to the dynasty.

Indira Gandhi succeeded Shastri as the prime minister of India in 1966, and her visit to America from 27 March to 2 April 1966 deserves special attention. It took place within two months of her coming to power, when Lyndon B. Johnson was president of the United States. 'The Prime Ministerial visit had been a great success', wrote B. K. Nehru. He added: 'It was clear that LBJ had been completely bowled over by Indira Gandhi's charm while she too had been impressed by his warmth and understanding' (Nehru, 1997: 464–465). Unlike her father, Indira Gandhi did not try to lecture and annoy. Instead, she used her magnetic personality and well-drafted speeches to impress not only the president but also congressmen; at the time, the Indian Wheat Bill was being considered by Congress, and '[t]he Bill finally went through without too much difficulty' (ibid.: 465). However, by July 1966, the goodwill generated during Indira Gandhi's visit to America had already dissipated. This happened mainly because Gandhi succumbed to pressures from her own partymen (including the leftists) and from leftists outside her party; these pressures arose, for instance, from the issue of the role played by the US in Vietnam. Gandhi visited Moscow in July 1966, when, as Chester Bowles wrote, 'the joint press statement issued by Mrs Gandhi and Premier Kosygin at the end of her visit called for an end to our bombing of North Vietnam and also contained vague references to the imperialistic powers . . .' (Bowles, 1974: 139). What most Indian authors refuse to acknowledge fully is that this surrender to Soviet priorities – reflected subsequently in several statements by Indira Gandhi that were critical of the US bombardment of Vietnam (Ganguly, 1992: 67) – could probably have been avoided but for the inexcusable mismanagement of the 1947–48 Jammu-Kashmir War, which resulted in a chronic dependence on the Soviet Union at the UN, revealed again in the India-Pakistan War of 1971.

This essay will now turn to the India-Pakistan conflict of 1971, which was an offshoot of the internal political crisis faced by Pakistan at the time. To summarise, on 25 March 1971 the government of Pakistan launched a pogrom in East Pakistan, resulting in a sort of demographic aggression through the expulsion of 10 million refugees from Pakistan into India over a period of only a few months.

As East Pakistanis formed a Mukti Bahini (Liberation Force) to combat genocide and achieve independence, India had no option but to extend large-scale assistance to this Mukti Bahini (Mascarenhas, 1971; Van der Heijden, 1971). Pakistan procured ample support from America and China, and the president of Pakistan, Yahya Khan, was interested in internationalising an essentially internal matter by launching a war against India. India in turn invoked Soviet military support as a deterrent against the threat of probable Sino-American intervention in the East Pakistan crisis, thus sacrificing the principle of non-alignment. India took the initiative in signing a Treaty of Friendship and Peace with the USSR on 9 August 1971; regarding the treaty, the Soviet people 'may have been a little surprised but they did not hesitate' (Kaul, 1979: 196). Once a full-scale India-Pakistan war commenced in early December 1971, it would have been in the interests of India and the people of East Pakistan for India's military operations to continue until East Pakistan emerged as the independent country of Bangladesh. But the United States tried to terminate these military operations prematurely with actions taken through the UN Security Council. It was only the exercise of a veto by the Soviet Union that saved India from having to end its military advances before they had achieved victory (Dixit, 2005: 173).

Bangladesh emerged as an independent country on 16 December 1971, and the counterproductive diplomacy in the period following the surrender of Pakistani forces in Dhaka on that date resulted in an unmistakable failure, leading to the Shimla Pact of 2 July 1972 between India and Pakistan. Z. A. Bhutto, an extraordinarily resourceful diplomat, converted the utter defeat of Pakistan on the battlefield into a great victory at the conference table. In the terms of the Shimla Pact, India agreed to hand over nearly 93,000 Pakistani prisoners of war and 5,000 square miles of fertile West Pakistani land that was occupied by Indian troops, and did not gain anything in return – not even the evacuation of the portion of Jammu-Kashmir that was under Pakistani occupation.[3] Above all, at the Shimla conference India committed a massive error in formally recognising Jammu-Kashmir as a disputed territory and consenting to bilateral talks on the issue. This is particularly curious as previously, and also subsequently, official declarations have referred to Jammu-Kashmir as an integral part of India.[4]

The subterranean nuclear explosion (SNE) of 1974 constitutes another landmark in the diplomatic history of India. In order to provide a critical analysis of this event, one has to locate it in the evolution of India's nuclear policy. This author was the first Indian to publish a book in defence of a limited nuclear deterrent for India within the framework of regional and global developments (Ray, 1967); he regrets that he could not credit India's decision makers with realistic thinking on this vital matter, despite two nuclear tests carried out by China in October 1964 and May 1965 (Halperin, 1965: 130). To take only one instance, in 1965, Prime Minister Lal Bahadur Shastri made a number of casual comments that indicated the lack of thinking and prevalence of confusion on nuclear policy in government circles.[5] Shastri announced at a press conference that while his government had decided not to manufacture nuclear weapons at present, 'the present' meant 'a long period of time'. Regarding a nuclear shield for India, Shastri denied that he had asked for any nuclear umbrella; he further maintained (somewhat unconvincingly) that China's nuclear weapon was not an immediate threat to India, nor was India its main target. In actual fact, Shastri did try to secure a nuclear shield for India, but failed.[6]

From this perspective, the 1974 nuclear test appeared as a departure from the norm of a lack of realism set by the Indian political establishment in the realm of the foreign relations-defence interface; this norm had been amply illustrated in previous decades, especially regarding relations with Pakistan and China. Thus, it is probable that the 1974 departure proved too demanding for Indian political leaders. They failed to pay proper respect to the intentions and capabilities of the Indian scientists and technologists (in the Bhaba Atomic Research Centre or the Atomic Energy Commission, for instance), who desired what would have been logical orders to carry out a number of tests over the following years. Such orders were conspicuous by their absence. 'The lack of any systematic military, technical, or political strategy to guide subsequent Indian nuclear policy soon became apparent' (Perkovich, 1999: 187).

Despite this apparent lack of commitment on the part of the political leaders, it is possible to offer another interpretation of the 1974 nuclear test by India. It could be seen as a desperate attempt by Prime Minister Indira Gandhi to divert public attention away from the economic failures of her socialist policies and from the underhanded manoeuvres made by her to maximise her personal political power (Frank, 2001: 349, 351, 353). In order to enhance her own power – along with that of her son, Sanjay Gandhi – Indira Gandhi resorted to a limitless misuse of power (Thakur, 1978: 162); this became both a cause and a consequence of a corruption that was all-pervasive, so that 'by 1974, corruption stories had started bursting like chain-crackers' (Frank, 2001: 161). Students spearheaded successful large-scale protests against inflation and corruption, targeting the Congress Party – first in Gujarat, and then in Bihar (ibid.: 358–359). It was under these somewhat unpropitious circumstances that on 18 May 1974, New Delhi carried out a nuclear test. 'That this was motivated primarily by political rather than scientific or military reasons was clear from the fact that there was no follow-up to the explosion', wrote Ajit Bhattacharjee (1978: 185).

In the early morning of 26 June 1975, a Proclamation of Emergency was approved by the Union Cabinet; arguably it almost equated to a slaughter of democracy. On that day, the Cabinet, long used to endorsing Indira Gandhi's dictates without holding a vote and without debate, concluded the meeting in less than 30 minutes and confirmed the Proclamation of Emergency (Frank, 2001: 379–380). As expected, the Soviet Union expressed unequivocal support for Gandhi's proclamation (Kux, 1994: 337); throughout Indira Gandhi's tenure as prime minister, Indo-Soviet relations were extremely close. One indicator of this closeness was, ironically, the phenomenal expansion of KGB operations in India: Indira Gandhi permitted the Soviet Union to post as many intelligence agents in India as it wished. Further, both the ruling Congress Party and Gandhi's family (Albats, 1994: 223) received money from the KGB, with KGB financial support for the Congress running to millions of rupees (Andrew & Mitrokhin, 2005: 321–323).

In the mid-1970s, India suffered from socio-economic political unrest on account of food shortages and inflation; the impact of this unrest was aggravated by government corruption and general maladministration – for example, in Gujarat, where Indira Gandhi's Congress Party was in power. Gandhi attributed the unrest in Gujarat to a CIA plot (Frank, 2001: 358). However, this allegation was effectively refuted by Daniel Patrick Moynihan, the US Ambassador to India, who wrote: 'We had twice, but only twice, interfered in Indian politics to the extent of providing money to a political party. Both times this was done in the face of a prospective Communist victory in a state election, once in Kerala and once in West Bengal, where Calcutta is located. Both times the money was given to the Congress Party, which had asked for it. Once it was given to Mrs. Gandhi herself, who was then a party official' (Moynihan, 1979: 41).

If the KGB was much more successful than the CIA in its Indian operations, the Soviet government too was more capable than its American counterpart of influencing Indian foreign policy, especially on various issues in the Cold War period that could only serve to open India to the charge of succumbing to Soviet desires (if not dictates). On the issue of naval presence in the Indian Ocean, India subjected Britain and America, but not the Soviets, to severe criticism. Regarding the Soviet invasion of Afghanistan, as well as the Soviet-backed invasion of Kampuchea by Vietnam, critics were easily able to claim that India's policy of non-alignment could be reduced to what was essentially alignment with the Soviet Union. On the issue of the Soviet invasion of Afghanistan in particular, it was not sufficient to argue that 'India could not be too categorically critical of the Soviet Union because of the factors of major defence supplies and significant portion of oil supplies and technologies coming to India from the Soviet Union' (Dixit, 2005: 182; Frank, 2001: 460). This was the sort of morass into which India was dumped by its so-called non-aligned foreign policy, reinforced by its so-called socialist economic policy. India continued to wallow in this morass and by 1991 had drifted into bankruptcy. 'India was like the friend who is always touching you for a loan, but who also refuses to change his behaviour in order to become solvent' (Nilekani, 2009: 68). During 1990–91, India's foreign exchange reserves dwindled to a level that was barely high enough to support essential imports for one month.

In order to arrest this drift, it was clear that some firm measures in economic policy and foreign relations were necessary, and such measures were taken following the election of P. V. Narasimha Rao as prime minister of India in 1991. Through the bold adoption of the policies of liberalisation, privatisation, and globalisation (LPG) and of pragmatism in foreign relations in general, Rao proved himself to be a truly great prime minister of independent India, and these reforms undoubtedly spurred economic growth and facilitated the flow of foreign direct investment to India. 'The actions taken in the early 1990s were simultaneously visionary – informed by a clear long-run goal – and pragmatic – taking specific concrete incremental steps to make that vision a reality.'[7] As LPG policies rapidly boosted India's economic strength, Rao rose above domestic vote-bank politics – for example, extending belated formal diplomatic recognition to Israel, which had always been an ally of India. Thus, the stature and bargaining power held by India in world politics witnessed a gradual but significant rise.

One lapse during the tenure of Prime Minister Narasimha Rao relates to India's nuclear policy, and requires some background analysis. The pusillanimity of India's political leaders in acquiring a nuclear deterrent was in sharp contrast to the energy and determination of their counterparts in Pakistan, to say nothing of those in China. Up until 1965, India had been ahead of China in nuclear reactor technology, but after this point China rapidly overtook India. As for Pakistan, as early as 1972, the Pakistani scientist A. Q. Khan had secretly obtained the technology to manufacture uranium-based nuclear bomb material from a laboratory in the Netherlands. When the first Indian nuclear explosion took place in 1974, Pakistan's atom bomb programme was already quite advanced. India had one apparent advantage in that Pakistan could not surmount the obstacles put in place by a nuclear cartel called the London Club, which restricted the transfer of nuclear materials and technologies; Indian scientists and technologists were able to overcome these restrictions. However, Pakistan found a way around the problem by obtaining clandestine supplies from Europe and comprehensive assistance from China. In around 1980, a large number of countries (including the UK, USA, France, and Canada) became aware that the Pakistani nuclear bomb was almost finished (Menon, 2000: 86–91). One reaction of Indian leaders to this revelation was, typically, consistent with neither the moralistic claims of pursuing an independent foreign policy nor the immense natural/human resources of India. 'Prayers, entreaties, arguments, curses and accusations were flung at the United States to get them to stop Pakistan from doing whatever they were doing. . . . The Pakistani bomb programme never wavered' (ibid.: 91).

A non-aligned country such as India, despite having at its disposal the fourth largest community of scientists and technologists in the world, did not have independence of action. It could not afford to alienate nuclear weapon states (NWS) such as America by staging a series of nuclear tests. In contrast, the Pakistani policy of multiple and flexible alignment enabled it to enjoy independence in the interface between defence and foreign affairs. Two NWS – China and the United States – colluded with Pakistan (Kapur, 2000: 38): Pakistan was able to acquire nuclear weapons and missiles with extensive Chinese assistance (Kumar, 1998: 157–168; Beri, 1998: 188, 192–199), and America turned a blind eye because, since Christmas of 1979, it had been forced to treat Pakistan as a frontline state in the defence of Afghanistan against the Soviet invaders (Subrahmanyam, 1998: 41, 43, 46, 50; Beri, 1998: 201–202). Pakistan did not even have to test nuclear explosives on its own soil: China carried out such tests on its behalf (Menon, 2000: 96, 101). The startling truth was: 'In 1987 Pakistan had a weapon, while India was still scrambling towards one' (ibid.: 92, 99). Moreover, in the decade following 1987, Pakistan even attempted nuclear blackmail of India, although this was fortunately unsuccessful because of unpublicised American intervention (Subrahmanyam, 1998: 45).

This chapter now turns to the valiant attempt by Prime Minister Narasimha Rao to assert India's independence in the area of the defence–foreign relations overlap.

In late 1995, Rao decided to conduct a series of nuclear tests, but upon learning of his intentions, the US put pressure on India to abandon the plan, and the tests did not take place (ibid.: 51).[8] This constitutes another example of the failure of non-aligned India to exercise independence. Narasimha Rao was succeeded by three prime ministers who each headed fragile, short-lived coalitions. One of them, I. K. Gujral, was so devoid of foresight and knowledge of the diplomatic history of India that he propounded a doctrine of non-reciprocity in dealings with India's neighbours. He failed to remember that India had followed this doctrine since 1947 and that it had had deeply detrimental, self-destructive effects on the country – for example, vis-à-vis Pakistan (on Jammu-Kashmir) and China (on Tibet). In abolishing the Special Forces, he stabbed the country in the back, as without them it was impossible to counteract the relentless proxy war of Pakistan against India, especially after the end of Soviet intervention in Afghanistan. By the mid-1990s, India found itself in a humiliating situation, quite inconsistent with its immense human and material resources. Pakistan treated India as if the latter were a minor power, using its official (for example, ISI) and non-official (for example, LeT, or Lashkar-e-Taiyaba) Special Forces to carry out the proxy war, play havoc with the Indian economy, and threaten India's secular-democratic polity. With Chinese support and American acquiescence, Pakistan successfully used nuclear blackmail to forestall an Indian attack on the terrorist infrastructure that was in place within Pakistan.

On the economic front, as the result of a lack of access to the dual-use technologies in the possession of Americans and Europeans, many talented Indian entrepreneurs were unable to use the LPG policies (initiated in 1991) to maximum effect and take large strides forward. Some bold policy initiatives were essential to underline India's capacity and earnestness for the attainment of its deserved status as a great power. These initiatives were launched by the NDA (National Democratic Alliance) government headed by Prime Minister Atal Behari Vajpayee, who belonged to the Bharatiya Janata Party (BJP). Five underground nuclear tests took place in May 1998, when Vajpayee was in office. Ashok Kapur wrote: 'Nehru had talked about an independent policy, the BJP-led coalition was practising it' (2000: 43). These tests signalled India's determination to explore means of becoming a great power in tune with its abundant human and material resources. India was indeed subjected to sanctions by America (and others), but the sanctions were gradually – though not always publicly – relaxed, and, following the Islamist terrorist attacks on America on 11 September 2001, the post-1998 sanctions against India died an unlamentable death.

In addition to 9/11, on 1 October of the same year there was an attack on India's Jammu-Kashmir Assembly and on 13 December an attack was carried out on the Indian Parliament. These acts of international (Jihadi) terrorism changed the situation not only in South Asia but in the entire world. All the attacks carried the indelible Pakistani signature. The major finding of the 585-page final report of the United States – the 9/11 Commission Report, carried out by the US National Commission on Terrorist Attacks – was as follows, in the words of Arnaud de Borchgrave: 'The imprint of every major act of international Islamist terrorism invariably passes through Pakistan, right from 9/11 – where virtually all the participants had trained, resided or met in, coordinated with, or received funding from or through Pakistan.'[9] Pakistan had used American money and arms lavishly to rear Al-Qaeda and the Taliban in its war against the Soviets in Afghanistan (and afterwards). Moreover, Pakistani security services had ample knowledge about both Al-Qaeda and the Taliban. Pakistan used their services in Indian Jammu-Kashmir too, as attested by the 9/11 Commission Report.[10] Nevertheless, in order to launch and carry out a war on terrorism within Afghanistan, America had to use, among other resources, Pakistani air space and bases.

Pakistan's proxy war left India in a helpless situation. India could not retaliate against Pakistani training camps, even after attacks on the Jammu-Kashmir Legislative Assembly and the Indian Parliament by Pakistani terrorists. This was because of Pakistan's successful practice of nuclear blackmail, sustained by its well-tested policy of multiple/flexible alignment yielding steady support from America and China and leaving the non-alignment policy of India in a state beneath contempt and pity. India had to devise a way out of the Pakistan-China grip in which it was held. It became necessary to devise a strategy akin to alignment, so that the assurance of undeclared protection by America could be used to pre-empt the gradual devastation of India by Pakistan's ruthless proxy war. The Vajpayee government adopted the policy of building a strategic partnership with America largely because a number of influential Americans were in favour of helping India to become a great power and assume global responsibilities, in collaboration with America, for combating terrorism, protecting the environment, and promoting democracy. The partnership was indeed a highly successful – and of course rare – foreign policy move by India. In November 2001, the meeting of Prime Minister Atal Behari Vajpayee with US President George W. Bush represented a significant achievement. Vajpayee and Bush agreed that their respective countries should accelerate cooperation in regional security, scientific collaboration (for example, in space), and civilian nuclear safety, alongside a vast range of economic and other matters. This agreement was acted upon with great determination.[11]

In 2005, the Indian-American strategic partnership saw dramatic progress. In March 2005, US secretary of state Condoleezza Rice visited New Delhi. She offered a comprehensive strategic partnership with India, including large-scale cooperation in the civilian nuclear sector, subject to the exercise of adequate control by India over the exportation of nuclear materials. Despite showing some surprise at the offer, 'the Indian Prime Minister's Office quickly acted on this opportunity to engage the United States' (Mistry, 2006: 682). In 2005, again, the United States announced that it would 'help India become a major world power in the 21st century' and that it would 'play midwife to the birth of a new great power' (Twining, 2007: 82). Such announcements are indeed without a parallel in the history of international relations, and thus the stage was set for a momentous development in Indo-American relations. Further, on 18 December 2006, President Bush signed into law a historic act: the Henry J. Hyde United States–India Peaceful Atomic Energy Act of 2006. This act enabled the Bush administration to prepare jointly with India a peaceful nuclear cooperation agreement, which, again, would be submitted to the United States Congress for approval after – and only after – India succeeded in entering into an India-specific safeguards agreement with the International Atomic Energy Agency (IAEA) and in obtaining clearance from the Nuclear Suppliers Group (NSG). The agreement with the IAEA was concluded on 1 August 2008, and NSG clearance was obtained on 6 September 2008. On 10 October 2008, India and America signed the nuclear agreement, following approval by the US Congress.

The year 2008 marked an appropriate climax to the era of pragmatism in India's foreign economic and political relations (as in India's domestic policy) that had begun in 1991. In 1991 the choice had been forced, but this did not detract from its merits, which became apparent in 2008 when the great powers (for example, Britain, France, Russia) and the United States – the sole superpower – appeared ready to boost strategic partnerships with India. These partnerships embraced not only nuclear transactions but also access to dual-capability technologies in diverse fields (for example, in space research, agriculture, transportation, etc.), which would uplift the Indian economy to an unprecedentedly high level. In the pre-1991 era, India had had a peculiar penchant for damaging relations with countries, especially America, that were in a position to assist it in various ways (Tharoor, 2003: 185–186). Thus, the success of the 2008 agreement was largely dependent on the ability of India to develop good relations with America. The Indo-US deal was actually 'a multilateral initiative involving the endorsement of all the other major powers and the international community', and 'without the U.S. delivering the "passport", there was no way India could get a "nuclear visa" from Paris or Moscow'.[12] For India specifically, the era of sanctimonious and sterile non-alignment gave way to constructive, multiple, and flexible alignment/engagement/partnerships.

At present, and in the coming years, the gravest challenge to India's foreign policy is probably that relating to the situation in Pakistan and Afghanistan. If Pakistan continues to misuse the massive amount of aid it receives from America, fails to rid itself of its growing characterisation as a failed state, remains unable to rein in the Jihadi terrorists (created largely by Pakistan itself), and generates so much instability as to lead to breakaway provinces becoming independent countries (as Bangladesh did in 1971), America may have to use India to assist in finding a solution to the Pakistani problem.[13] The enormity of the problem is underlined by the following statement, made by Bruce Riedel, a former White House official: 'Pakistan has more terrorists per square mile than any place else on earth, and it has a nuclear weapons programme that is growing faster than any place else on earth.'[14] The bizarre nature of the problem can be illustrated further by the fact that Pakistan has managed to virtually blackmail America into bankrolling its nuclear enterprise: American officials are afraid of linking 'aid to greater transparency and accountability on the nuclear front' because 'Pakistan would rather forsake aid, go bankrupt and self-destruct – a dread some critics say Islamabad is capitalizing on'.[15] 'The government is paralysed. People generally feel that they are on their own. This is not only a disturbing sentiment, but a dangerous trend.'[16] Thus, in the not-too-distant future, America may have to avail itself of Indian help to emerge as the agent that brings an end to this unusual situation.

After the planned withdrawal of American and NATO forces from Afghanistan in 2014, India may find itself confronting a frighteningly complex situation in the Pakistan-Afghanistan region.[17] One way of coping with this complexity could be to reach an understanding with China in order to put an end to the decades-old India-baiting that it practises in collusion with Pakistan. Potentially, this understanding could be reached by refining Chinese premier Zhou's 1960 proposal for the resolution of the boundary question using the latest cartographical techniques (including satellite photography) to keep in view the dominant economic-strategic concerns of the two countries to potentially buttress a wholesome normalisation of Indo-Chinese relations (Ray, 2011: 317). Another manoeuvre to reach an understanding with China requires an awareness of the intricacies in the relationship between China and various rival groups of Islamist militants in Pakistan.[18] It is indeed interesting to reflect on how China became embroiled in the ever-apparent Shia-Sunni conflict in Pakistan.[19] It is well known that China provided military supplies to Iran, thus assisting Shias in their fight against Sunnis in neighbouring Iraq. As a result, Sunni Jihadists have carried out attacks on the Chinese population in Islamabad and Balochistan. Al-Qaeda has supplied assistance to anti-Beijing militants in the Xinjiang province of China, and Sunni Jihadists in Syria have also received support from Al-Qaeda, which has made China uneasy because it is not in its interest to dislodge the ruling circle in Damascus. Thus it is important that the Indian diplomatic establishment is able to keep these Chinese sensitivities in mind when plotting its course through the difficulties that may arise in the wake of the withdrawal of American and NATO forces from Afghanistan in 2014.

Finally, as Indian finance minister P. Chidambaram has recently argued, the prosperity and security of a country are integrally related.[20] In other words, foreign-defence-economic policies have to be synergised. This is where policy makers in India have failed miserably. From time to time, cases of corruption in defence procurement – touching even the highest and the mightiest – come to light.[21] The most shocking such case is a report by the Swiss Banking Association which estimates the amount of Indian black money in Switzerland at around US$1,456 billion – enough to alleviate India's poverty and minimise foreign debt;[22] despite this, no serious attempt appears to have ever been made by Indian authorities to recover this money. In the foreseeable future, therefore, it is doubtful that India's policy makers (including foreign-policy makers) will find a way out of this cesspool of corruption and mismanagement.

Notes

1 For an elaborate documentation on observations in this paragraph, see Ray (1977: Chapter 3). Also see: Bowles (1974: 94); Sen (1973: 242–3; 279–92; 295–6); Vas (1987: 155); and Krishna Rao (2001: 259).
2 For some interesting details about the 1962 India-China conflict, see Dalvi (1969: 45, 53–8, 61–63, 70–71, 79–81, 83–4, 219–24, 225–44); Nehru (1997: 267–68, 279–82,

287–89, 347–48); Galbraith (1969: 376–96, 413–16, 423–25, 427–28); and Dixit (1998: 75).
3   J. K. Dutt, *The Statesman*, Calcutta, 19 July 1997. Also see: Bloeria (2000: 93); Singh (1999: 186); and Jacob (1979: 10).
4   Sourin Guha, *The Statesman*, 27 July 1998.
5   See, for example, comments in *The Amrita Bazar Patrika*, Calcutta, 26 January 1965, and *Hindusthan Standard*, Calcutta, 20 February 1965.
6   See an article by a former foreign secretary of India, S. K. Singh, in *The Telegraph*, Calcutta, 15 January 1991; and a masterly analysis by Karnad (2002: 259–263).
7   World Bank (July 2006) *India Development Policy Review*. New Delhi, p. 30.
8   Also see Pranab Dhal Samanta, *The Indian Express*, Calcutta, 26 February 2013.
9   http://davinci.dilykos.com/story/2004/7/25/164937/572 [accessed 15/3/13].
10 *The 9/11 Commission Report: Final Report of the National Commission on Terrorist Attacks upon the United States*, US Government Printing Office, Washington DC, 2004, Executive Summary, p. 7.
11 K. Alan Kronstadt (July–August 2007) *CRS Report for Congress: India-U.S. Relations*, Congressional Research Service, Washington, p. 5.
12 Editorial, *The Indian Express*, 2 October 2008.
13 Stephen Philip Cohen (2002) 'Nuclear Weapons and Nuclear War in South Asia: An Unknowable Future'. Paper presented to the United Nations University Conference on South Asia, Tokyo, May 2002, p. 11. Also see Kurt Jacobsen and Sayeed Hasan Khan, *The Statesman*, 10 March 2013.
14 Quoted by Chidananda Rajghatta, *The Times of India*, Kolkata (Calcutta), 19 May 2009.
15 Ibid.
16 Sayeed Hasan Khan and Kurt Jacobsen, *The Statesman*, 13 August 2009. Also see PTI report, *The Statesman*, 10 March 2013.
17 Take, for instance, the statement of US General Joseph Dunford, who took over command of NATO forces in Afghanistan on 10 February 2013: AFP report, *The Statesman*, 11 February 2013. Also see, AFP report, *The Statesman*, 10 March 2013, and Editorial, *Frontier*, Kolkata, 45 (34) (3–9 March 2013), pp. 1–2.
18 For an analysis of these intricacies, see Rajinder Puri, *The Statesman*, 31 October 2012.
19 For just some of the innumerable instances of recent deaths resulting from this conflict, see PTI report, *The Statesman*, 9 February 2013; Ruchika Talwar, *The Indian Express*, 23 February 2013.
20 *The Indian Express*, 8 February 2013.
21 For the latest example, see reports in *The Indian Express*, 13–19 February 2013; Rajinder Puri, *The Statesman*, 16, 19, 22 February 2013.
22 http://myeconomist.wordpress.com/indias-black-money-in-swiss-bank/ [accessed 15/3/13].

Bibliography

Albats, Yevgenia (1994) *The State within a State*. New York: Farrar, Straus and Giroux.
Andrew, Christopher & Vasili Mitrokhin (2005) *The Mitrokhin Archive II*. London: Allen Lane.
Beri, Ruchita (1998) 'Pakistan's Missile Programme', in Jasjit Singh (ed.) *Nuclear India*. New Delhi: Knowledge World.
Bhattacharjee, Ajit (1978) *Jayaprakash Narayan: A Political Biography*. Delhi: Vikas/Bell Books.
Bloeria, Sudhir S. (2000) *Pakistan's Insurgency vs. India's Security*. New Delhi: Manas.
Bowles, Chester (1974) *Mission to India*. Bombay: BI Publications.

Collins, Larry & Dominique Lapierre (1984) *Mountbatten and Independent India.* New Delhi: Vikas.
Collins, Larry & Dominique Lapierre (2007) *Freedom at Midnight.* New Delhi: Vikas.
Dalvi, J. P. (1969) *Himalayan Blunder.* Delhi: Orient Paperbacks.
Dasgupta, C. (2002) *War and Diplomacy in Kashmir 1947–48.* New Delhi: Sage Publications.
De Russet, Alan (1969) 'On Understanding Indian Foreign Policy', in K. P. Mishra (ed.) *Studies in Indian Foreign Policy.* Delhi: Vikas.
Dixit, J. N. (1998) *Across Borders: Fifty Years of India's Foreign Policy.* New Delhi: Picus Books.
Dixit, J. N. (2005) *The Indian Foreign Service: History and Challenge.* Delhi: Konark.
Frank, Katherine (2001) *Indira: The Life of Indira Gandhi.* London: Harper Collins.
Galbraith, John Kenneth (1969) *Ambassador's Journal.* New York: Signet Books.
Ganguly, Sumit (1992) 'US-Indian Relations During the Lyndon Johnson Era', in Harold A. Gould & Sumit Ganguly (eds.) *The Hope and the Reality: US-Indian Relations from Roosevelt to Reagan.* Boulder, CO.: Westview Press.
Ghosh, Sudhir (1967) *Gandhi's Emissary.* London: Cresset Press.
Godbole, Madhave (2006) *The Holocaust of Indian Partition: An Inquest.* New Delhi: Rupa.
Gopal, Sarvepalli (1989) *Jawaharlal Nehru: A Biography, 1956–1964,* Vols. 2–3. New Delhi: Oxford University Press.
Gould, Harold A. (1992) 'US-Indian Relations: The Early Phase', in Harold A. Gould & Sumit Ganguly (eds.) *The Hope and the Reality: US-Indian Relations from Roosevelt to Reagan.* Boulder, CO: Westview Press.
Halperin, M. H. (1965) *China and the Bomb.* London: Pall Mall.
Heimsath, Charles H. & Surjit Mansingh (1971) *A Diplomatic History of Modern India.* New Delhi: Allied Publishers.
Jacob, Lt. Gen. J.F.R. (1979) *Surrender at Dacca: Birth of a Nation.* New Delhi: Manohar.
Kamad, Bharat (2002) *Nuclear Weapons and India's Security.* New Delhi: Macmillan.
Kapur, Ashok (2000) 'India's Nuclear Weapons Capability: Convincing or Confusing?', in M. L. Sondhi (ed.) *Nuclear Weapons and India's Nuclear Security.* New Delhi: Har Anand.
Kaul, B. M. (1971) *Confrontation with Pakistan.* Delhi: Vikas.
Kaul, T. N. (1979) *Diplomacy in Peace and War.* Delhi: Vikas.
Khera, S. S. (1968) *India's Defence Problem.* Bombay: Orient Longman.
Krishna Rao, K. V. (2001) *In the Service of the Nation: Reminiscences.* New Delhi: Viking/Penguin.
Kumar, Sumita (1998) 'Pakistan's Nuclear Weapon Programme', in Jasjit Singh (ed.) *Nuclear India.* New Delhi: Knowledge World.
Kux, Dennis (1994) *Estranged Democracies: India and the United States 1941–1991.* New Delhi: Sage Publications.
Lal, Sham (1969) 'National Scene and Foreign Policy', in K. P. Mishra (ed.) *Studies in Indian Foreign Policy.* Delhi: Vikas.
Mascarenhas, Anthony (1971) *The Rape of Bangladesh.* New Delhi: Vikas.
Maxwell, Neville (1971) *India's China War.* Bombay: Jaico.
Menon, Raja (2000) *A Nuclear Strategy for India.* New Delhi: Sage Publications.
Mistry, Dinshaw (2006) 'Diplomacy, Domestic Politics, and the US-India Nuclear Agreement'. *Asian Survey* 46(5): 675–698.
Moynihan, Daniel Patrick (1979) *A Dangerous Place.* Bombay: Allied.

Musa, Gen. Mohammad (1983) *My Version: India-Pakistan War 1965*. New Delhi: ABC Publishing House.
Nayar, Kuldip (1971) *India: The Critical Years*. Delhi: Vikas.
Nehru, B. K. (1997) *Nice Guys Finish Second*. New Delhi: Penguin Books India/Viking.
Nilekani, Nandan (2009) *Imagining India*. New Delhi: Penguin.
Perkovich, George (1999) *India's Nuclear Bomb*. New Delhi: Oxford University Press.
Ranganathan, C. V. & V. C. Khanna (2000) *India and China*. New Delhi: Har Anand.
Ray, Jayanta Kumar (1967) *Security in the Missile Age*. Bombay: Allied.
Ray, Jayanta Kumar (1977) *Public Policy and Global Reality: Some Aspects of American Alliance Policy*. New Delhi: Radiant.
Ray, Jayanta Kumar (2011) *India's Foreign Relations 1947–2007*. New Delhi: Routledge.
Saiyid, M. H. (n.d.) *The Sound of Fury: A Political Study of M. A. Jinnah*. New Delhi: Akbar Publishing House.
Sen, L. P. (1973) *Slender Was the Thread*. New Delhi: Sangham/Orient Longman.
Singh, Jaswant (1999) *Defending India*. Bangalore: Macmillan.
Subrahmanyam, K. (1998) 'Indian Nuclear Policy, 1964–98', in Jasjit Singh (ed.) *Nuclear India*. New Delhi: Knowledge World.
Taheer, Salman (1980) *Bhutto: A Political Biography*. New Delhi: Vikas.
Thakur, Janardan (1978) *All the Prime Minister's Men*. New Delhi: Vikas/Bell.
Tharoor, Shashi (2003) *Nehru: The Invention of India*. New Delhi: Penguin/Viking.
Twining, Daniel (2007) 'America's Grand Design in Asia'. *Washington Quarterly* 30(3): 79–94.
Van der Heijden, Hendrik (1971) *Thousand My Lais: World Bank Study on Bangladesh*. Dacca (Dhaka): Society for Human Rights.
Vas, Lt. Gen. E. A. (1987) *Without Baggage: A Personal Account of the Jammu & Kashmir Operations, October 1947–January 1949*. Dehradun: Natraj Publishers.
Wolpert, Stanley (1993) *Zulfi Bhutto of Pakistan: His Life and Times*. Delhi: Oxford University Press.
Wolpert, Stanley (2006) *Shameful Flight*. New York: Oxford University Press.

3 The transformation of India's external posture and its relationship with China

Takenori Horimoto

One of the most conspicuous changes India has shown since the 1990s is its external posture as a major world power. In the period from independence to the 1980s India made claims to major power status but was considered by the international community to be at best a regional power in South Asia. High economic growth over the past two decades, however, has altered this view. According to the latest data from the International Monetary Fund, India's gross domestic product (GDP) in 2009 was the eleventh highest in the world, with expectations that it would become one of the top ten biggest economies. This remarkable economic development has given India the financial resources to allocate much-needed funds to expand its military powers, particularly its navy. India is aiming to become a sea power whilst maintaining its basic character of a land (continental) power.

There are various definitions of a major power, but since this essay does not intend to go into semantic discussions, here the term will be used to refer to countries that have the continuous capability to play a decisive role in international politics as a result of their military, economic, political, and cultural attributes. During the Cold War period, the US and the Soviet Union were the two main major powers; after this period, the US remained the only such power. However, since the start of the twenty-first century China has also gradually begun to show signs of becoming a major world power; historically speaking, it might be referred to as a great power. Assuming that a minimum condition of a major power is a country having preeminent national power in terms of economy and military strength, India can be said to be undergoing a rapid process of transformation. The basic requirements of a major power, such as a large geographical area and population size, are already intrinsic to it, and the additional growth of its economic and military power suggests that India's long-cherished aspiration of becoming a 'major power' will also soon be realised.

In its transformative stage, India is trying to speak and act as a major power with regard to international issues in a completely different manner from the posture it adopted during the Cold War. Other countries, such as the main European countries, appear to be accommodative of India's changing attitude. One example of this accommodation is the US's policy initiative towards India when it established Next Steps in Strategic Partnership in 2004, which was then followed by a nuclear deal. Others have more or less followed the lead of the US – for example, by admitting India as a member of the G20. However, China has not been wholeheartedly forthcoming with regard to India's changing international position; the apparently excellent bilateral relationship between the two countries is in reality a facade, as will be made evident below.

India and China are located in close geographical proximity and have a combined population of 2.4 billion people, which accounts for two-fifths of the total world population. On the surface, the two countries have been gaining their rightful positions in the world given their sizes and populations coupled with their long histories. In fact, 'of the great world civilizations, only India and China embody a civilization in a single great nation-state' (Cohen, 2002: 51). Arguably, China is now one of the major global powers, while India's journey towards major power status is well under way, although not yet complete. Simply put, they are rivals. Naturally, in examinations of India's foreign policy, its relationship with China holds great importance. In addition, the Indo-Chinese relationship has a massive impact on various international developments. Their bilateral relationship and the international circumstances that surround them have a mutual cause-and-effect influence.

The basic aim of this essay is to demonstrate how India will tackle the issues it is currently facing and chart its possible foreign policy course in the future. It will discuss the changing nature of Indian foreign policy orientations and then Indo-US and Indo-China bilateral relationships.

India's external posture

India's foreign policy has demonstrated one noticeable characteristic, namely, *partnership orientation* – forming closely united relationships, multilaterally and bilaterally. This feature could be observed in the period between independence in 1947 and the 1980s in the form of non-alignment and then the Indo-Soviet alliance; in some respects it has also been visible since the 1990s.

Non-alignment and the Indo-Soviet alliance

India's post-independence political history can be divided into two phases. The first phase, between 1947 and the 1980s, coincided roughly with the Cold War. In this phase, the policy of non-alignment was the basic tenet of India's foreign policy. This policy has been discussed repeatedly and wearisomely, and its essence can be summarised as India choosing not to join either of the Cold War blocs in order to retain its strategic autonomy. However, this definition is only half true. Another aspect of non-alignment could be the formation of a partnership among non-aligned countries in order that they could voice their demands and complaints *en bloc*. Put another way, such non-aligned countries wanted to raise their objections to the then prevailing international order but did not have sufficient capability to do so alone respectively. India thus teamed up with other non-aligned countries such as (former) Yugoslavia, Egypt, and Indonesia to attempt this.

Although politicians and mandarins of the External Affairs Ministry refer to India's foreign policy as one of non-alignment even today, their statements are somewhat rhetorical. Since the early 1990s, the Indian National Congress and Bharatiya Janata Party have all but stopped carrying 'non-alignment' in their manifestos. Non-alignment policy was a valid line during the Cold War period of the 1950s and 1960s and during that period did produce certain tangible results. However, structural changes that took place around the early 1970s – particularly the new international formation of US-China-Pakistan relations in Asia – prompted India and the then Soviet Union to unite in order to cope with the new situation. This unity materialised as the Indo-Soviet Treaty of Friendship and Cooperation signed in August 1971. Though the title of the treaty refers to friendship and cooperation, its real essence was that of a security treaty, as demonstrated by Article 9, which stipulated as follows:

> Each High Contracting Party undertakes to abstain from providing any assistance to any third country that engages in armed conflict with the other Party. In the event of either being subjected to an attack or a threat thereof, the High Contracting Parties shall immediately enter into mutual consultations in order to remove such threat and to take appropriate effective measures to ensure peace and the security of their countries.

This stipulation aimed at protecting each party against threats created by any third party. This was clearly therefore a mutual security treaty. If we take the definition of alliance as the 'formal associations of states for the use (or non-use) of military force, in specified circumstance, against states outside their own membership'(Snyder, 1997: 4) and look back at the South Asian situation in August 1971 when the third Indo-Pakistan War was imminent, the Indo-Soviet treaty represented the changed nature of the bilateral relationship into alliance, although India maintained its figurehead of non-alignment. The 'alliance' with the Soviet Union was a useful foreign relationship for India. For example, when an inconvenient subject was brought up at the United Nations Security Council, India could rely on the Soviet Union to negate it using its veto; a typical example of this was the Kashmir issue.

The Indo-Soviet alliance signified the second phase of India's partnership orientation in its foreign relationships. During the partnership orientation period of non-alignment and the Indo-Soviet alliance, India had less of a need to rely upon other countries and be obsequiously sensitive to Western countries – including the US – because of the closed economic system that it had adopted.

India's new foreign policy

When faced with the new and dramatically different situation brought about by the end of the Cold War, the demise of the Soviet Union, and the breakdown of its economy, India had no option but to both alter its foreign policy and change its economic policy to one of liberalisation. India had to consider the pros and cons of the Indo-Soviet relationship, which it had had to pay a heavy price to maintain. A significant example of this is the Afghanistan War during the 1980s, in which India was unable to be critical of the Soviet invasion of Afghanistan even though its approach towards other countries was characterised by fighting for autonomy and defending non-interference.

When India initiated its policy of economic liberalisation, it adopted a multilateral or multidimensional foreign policy which emphasised an inclination toward closer relations with the US. However, when this policy is examined carefully, its overall characteristics could be summarised as a kind of partnership policy: one of strategic partnership (SP). India established SP with Russia in October 2000, preceded by South Africa (1997) and France (1998). Interestingly, the SP with Russia occurred only seven months after President Clinton's visit to India. This SP was followed by a partnership with the US in January 2004 and then further SPs with Germany, Britain, the EU, China, Japan, and so on. India was seemingly trying to simultaneously strengthen its relationship with the US and Japan and with China and Russia. Through such foreign policy moves and avoiding being caught in a dilemma as to which approach was preferred, India sought to gain maximum benefits. In other words, India was resilient and tough in utilising simultaneously its close relationships with the US and Japan, and China and Russia.

The metamorphosis of India's external posture

In addition to the transformation of India's foreign policy since the 1990s, another conspicuous change was India's ever-greater external posture as a major power.

India's orientation towards becoming a major power

In present-day South Asia, India occupies approximately three-quarters of the total population, territory, and GDP. Moreover, India is located in the centre of South Asia, and although the surrounding countries are all geographically connected to India, they lack mutual connectivity with each other. Its national size and geographic position make India an overwhelming presence in the region: a *de facto* hegemon. Harish Kapur, who has examined India's foreign policies from Prime Minister Nehru to present-day Manmohan Singh, has termed India's hegemonic diplomacy as *giantism* (Kapur, 2009: 410).

Is India evolving from South Asian regional power to a global major power? Certainly this has been the case historically. Almost 200 years ago, India matched China in terms of economic size and population. According to one estimate (Sugihara, 2003: 65), India shared 15.3 per cent of the world's total GDP (China's share was 31.6 per cent) and 19.6 per cent of the world's total population (1.068 billion; China's share was 35.5 per cent). Without claiming that history will inevitably repeat itself, it appears that India is moving towards becoming an economic giant. In 2006 India surpassed the Republic of Korea as the number three economy in Asia (according to GDP) and is now one of three major economic powers in Asia.

India turning into a military power

Throughout history it has been a universal phenomenon that when a country is emerging as an economic power, it simultaneously seeks to become a military power through expansion of its military, especially its navy. The oldest example would be the Roman empire using its enormous military power to maintain the Pax Romana in the surrounding Mediterranean area. In later centuries this was seen once more in the Pax Britannica; between the mid-nineteenth century and the beginning of the twentieth century, the British Royal Navy constituted the most powerful naval force in the world. Under the 1889 Naval Defence Act, Britain even sought to achieve the two-power standard: strength equivalent to that of the combined forces of the next two biggest navies in the world (those of France and Russia). After the Meiji Restoration, Japan also embarked upon military expansion in line with its economic development.

In the contemporary world, the US is an excellent example of this phenomenon. The US has become the number one industrial power in the world, having launched its naval build-up in the 1890s based on the sea power theory advocated by Alfred T. Mahan. The US enjoyed a Pax Americana in the twentieth century and even now continues to account for a 40 per cent share of global defence expenditure. The most recent example, however, is China. When China experienced high economic development in the 1990s, Beijing began to modernise and expand its military power. In particular China's navy has been a focus of expansion through submarines and aircraft carriers, transforming it from a land power to a land-sea power.

India is now following China's example, aiming to achieve the status of a nation that is both wealthy and powerful. Although India is generally noted as an emerging major economic power, another emerging aspect is a rising military capability. India is enjoying a military spending spree, purchasing 126 new fighter jets costing a total of US$10 billion, developing Agni III and V, and embarking on the joint production of a supersonic cruising missile with Russia, along with the production of the Chandrayaan moon explorer (convertible to missile technology). India has also purchased a Russian aircraft carrier, the Admiral Gorshkov – to be inducted in 2012 – and started building an Indian-made carrier in 2009 in addition to the incumbent Viraat. As Brian K. Hedrick points out, India is working to 'become a regional power across the Indian Ocean basin and secure agreements from partners in this region that support this goal, while building up expeditionary navy and air force capabilities' (Hedrick, 2009: 49).

Is India a major power?

As discussed above, India has been endeavouring to develop its economy and military power since the early 1990s. Is it therefore possible to consider India as a major power? Arvind Virmani points out that the present world is a unipolar world with a multipolar fringe and that India is currently merely a regional power. It is likely, however, to become bipolar in the next 20 years, which may induce certain policy reactions that result in the creation of a tripolar or even multipolar world that includes India (Virmani, 2005). George Perkovich (2003–4) has given a slightly different evaluation of India's status. Basing his claim on Kenneth Waltz's definition of a major power, he says, 'A state's power can thus be understood as a combination of its capacity to influence others to behave as it wants them and, conversely, to resist the unwelcome influence of others.' He argues that India is equipped with the latter but not the former. A significant factor in this might be the insufficient total national power of India. In terms of its GDP and military expenditure, India is still far behind the US and China in each category. Between 2008 and 2010, Indian military expenditure significantly increased in a growing spirit of competition with the rapid rise of Chinese military spending. However, assuming that economic size and military capability is the minimum *sine qua non* of a major power, India remains incomparable to countries in the following list.

Table 3.1 Global GDP – top ten countries, 2008–13

	2008	2009	2010	2011	2012	2013
USA	14.72	14.42	14.96	15.52	16.16	16.77
China	4.52	4.99	5.93	7.32	8.23	9.24
Japan	4.85	5.04	5.50	5.91	5.95	4.92
Germany	3.75	3.41	3.41	3.75	3.53	3.73
France	2.92	2.69	2.65	2.86	2.69	2.81
UK	2.79	2.31	2.41	2.59	2.61	2.68
Brazil	1.65	1.62	2.14	2.48	2.25	2.25
Italy	2.39	2.19	2.13	2.28	2.09	2.15
Russia	1.66	1.22	1.52	1.90	2.02	2.10
India	**1.22**	**1.37**	**1.71**	**1.88**	**1.86**	**1.88**

Source: World Bank *World Development Indicators Database*.
http://data.worldbank.org/indicator/NY.GDP.MKTP.CD [last accessed 7/2/15]

Table 3.2 Global military expenditure – top ten countries, 2008–13

USD (million)	2008	2009	2010	2011	2012	2013
USA	621.13	668.57	698.18	711.33	684.78	640.22
China	91.66	111.79	123.34	147.27	127.71	188.46
Russia	56.18	51.53	58.72	70.24	81.08	87.84
Saudi Arabia	38.22	41.27	45.25	48.53	56.50	67.00
France	66.01	66.87	61.79	64.63	60.06	61.23
UK	65.62	57.91	58.10	60.28	58.50	57.89
Germany	48.08	47.46	46.26	48.16	46.49	48.79
Japan	46.76	51.46	53.80	60.45	59.56	48.60
India	**33.00**	**38.72**	**46.09**	**49.63**	**47.21**	**47.40**
South Korea	26.07	24.41	27.57	30.88	31.66	33.94

Source: Stockholm International Peace Research Institute *SIPRI Military Expenditure Database*.
www.sipri.org/research/armaments/milex/milex_database [last accessed 7/2/15]

International order: creating capability and metamorphosis of India's foreign policy

Today the US and China are tussling over their roles in world leadership. Since the last century the US has been a major power and has played a leading role in the creation of a new international order. During the First World War, it advocated the founding of a new international conflict management and peacekeeping machinery, and since then the League of Nations and other organs have been established. After the Second World War, when the European countries were showing obvious signs of exhaustion, the US, as the sole superpower, occupying one-half of aggregated global GDP and with the greatest military power, was able to successfully form systems to deal with potential crises. Among these systems are the United Nations, the World Bank, and the International Monetary Fund. Thus the US has displayed its capacity to create international order since the twentieth century.

Despite these achievements, the predominance of the US has nonetheless started to diminish, although it is still the largest country, with one-quarter of the world's GDP and more than 40 per cent of the total global defence expenditure. Even now the US claims to maintain such capability; as the *National Security Strategy of 2010* says, 'Just as America helped to determine the course of the 20th century, we must now build the sources of American strength and influence, and *shape an international order capable of overcoming the challenges of the 21st century*' (emphasis added).[1] With its reduced status in the world, the US is now a major power for the status quo, whereas China is a power that is pro-change. Such a fundamental alteration of the international configuration may well have brought about the strategic tussle between the US and China that is evident today.

Today, India is moving to conduct its foreign policy as a pro-change country. During the Cold War period, India criticised the then prevailing world order and tried to improve its level of equality, but it could not. This was predominantly due to the massive head-on collision between the US and the Soviet Union, against which other countries did not have the scope to act, to say nothing of India's feeble national power. India now has embarked upon a process of adapting to and revising the current international order. This is a significant metamorphosis of India's foreign policy orientation. India envisions two phases to cope with the current international structure.

In the first phase (the present phase), India has been emphasising and advocating the multipolarity of the world and has aligned itself with China and Russia and the Shanghai Cooperation Organization (SCO) as a key organ of promotion. India may intend to gain leverage with the US as a member of the SCO, expressing its desire to be fully fledged. India has been trying to secure a leading position in other international organisations and has initiated various additional regional organisations such as IOR-ARC (Indian Ocean Rim Association for Regional Cooperation). India hopes to become an influential nation within the present international structure by making efforts to stymie any unfavourable international developments and facilitate developments to its advantage, which is typified in global warming debates such as the Conferences of the Parties (CoP).

The second phase that India aspires to bring about is that in which it becomes a creator of the international order. In this phase India would be much more influential than in the first phase. The most logical step towards this would be to become a permanent member of the United Nations Security Council. From 2004 onwards India, Germany, Brazil, and Japan have made concerted efforts to become permanent members, but this initiative has thus far been unsuccessful. Of these four countries, only India has consistently persevered in promoting its eligibility as a member of the council. Undoubtedly, permanent membership would provide powerful leverage over international affairs and stave off policies that are to the disadvantage of India.

India–China relationship and the US

Viewed from the Indian standpoint, the market, capital, and technology of the US are indispensable to its higher economic growth. Closer relations with the US are also effective with regard to keeping China and Russia in check. At the same time, India's closer relationship with China and Russia is useful in preventing overdependence on the US and could be utilised as an effective card to play against the US on issues such as climate change, where the US and India clash. Today's India is 'Asia's France' – France too has friendly relations with the US, sharing its interests and perceptions, but views the world in terms of its own prism and national interests (Horimoto, 2006). In the current international situation, the most important issue in Indian foreign policy is how to deal with China and the US. As far as South Asia and the Indian Ocean are concerned, there is a triangular relationship between India, China, and the US.[2]

There was an analogous triangle in East Asia during the Cold War. East Asia was a targeted area for the US, and there the US, China, and Japan were – and remain – the main players constituting the 'triangle' (Vogel et al., 2002) where the horizontal mechanism was not institutionalised and the US played a pivotal role. However, with the increasing tempo of China's emergence on the international stage since the early 1990s, such a *de facto* mechanism has ceased to be operational. The 'engagement policy' of the US has given greater importance to China. The China issue has in fact been the main driving factor in US Asian policy. Ever since the Second World War, US Asian policy has been almost synonymous with its policy towards China, especially in East Asia and more or less in Asia as a whole. The emphasis on China has become much clearer since the demise of the Soviet Union. After all, as noted in 2004, 'the most important bilateral relationship of the 21st Century is likely to be that between China and the US'.[3]

The US was forced to treat South Asia as a peripheral area in comparison to East Asia in terms of its global strategic policy during the Cold War period and up to the mid-1990s. With the rapid emergence of China and the active policies it pursues in the area, in addition to the gradual rise of India, the spread of terrorism, and the importance of protecting the Indian Ocean sea lane, however, the US can no longer remain a bystander.

India's relationship with China

The Indo-China relationship after the end of the Cold War could be characterised as 'bonhomie with ambivalence' (see Horimoto, 2010). A major turning point was the official visit of the Indian Prime Minister Rajiv Gandhi to China in 1988 – the first prime ministerial visit between the two countries since Prime Minister Nehru's visit in 1954. Shortly afterwards, his visit was reciprocated by Chinese premier Li Peng, who visited India in 1991 – the first visit in 31 years, since Zhōu Ēnlái visited India in 1960.

In 1993, during Indian Prime Minister Rao's visit to China, an epoch-making bilateral measure between India and China was arranged under the agreement 'Maintenance of Peace and Tranquillity in the Line of Control Area' (followed by a similar agreement in 1996). The main thrust of the arrangement was to improve bilateral economic relations while leaving the difficult issue of border settlement to be negotiated at a later date – effectively shelving it. Through the agreement, the two nations were able to create a new mutual confidence-building framework which still exists today.

While the Indo-China relationship cooled noticeably following India's successful atomic tests in 1998, the bilateral framework remained intact and the two countries were prompted to further bury animosities during the visit of Indian President Narayanan to China in 2000. Since then, the bilateral relationship has shown a dramatic improvement, although India has never lowered its vigilance against China, keeping its feet simultaneously on the brake and the accelerator. Although the Indian policy towards China could be termed an operation on two fronts, engagement and hedging, the latter is prevailing against the backdrop of a long-held wariness of China.[4] In essence, the bilateral relationship has been affected by both positive and negative factors.

Among the positive factors, bilateral trade is the most conspicuous. China is India's largest trading partner. During President Hu Jintao's India visit in November 2006, the projected trade amount was increased to $40 billion by 2010. Hu declared that 'if India and China take the necessary steps to strengthen trade and business, the 21st century will be Asia's'. The amount of total trade was further upgraded to $60 billion during Prime Minister Singh's China visit in January 2008. In comparison with a total trade between the countries of $0.38 billion in 1992, this evolution is quite remarkable. The bilateral relationship could certainly be termed as 'not rivals but partners' in this regard.[5] Yet India remains somewhat wary of the Chinese economy – for example, signing a foreign trade protocol or economic partnership agreement seems an unlikely prospect.[6] The Indian government has also maintained its half-hearted stance in contrast to its active signing of trade agreements with other countries, starting with Singapore in 2005.

Other factors include concerted cooperation in multilateral fields, most evidently in the field of global warming. Both India and China are deploying 'developing country diplomacy' in the fields of trade and the environment, alongside their pursuit of 'major power diplomacy'. China in particular tends to show off its presence as a major power in the Six-Party Talks on de-nuclearisation of the

Democratic People's Republic of Korea and peacekeeping operations in strife-ridden areas, but in economy-related organisations such as the World Trade Organization and CoP it holds fast to its status as a 'developing' nation. India is more or less the same, providing obvious reasons for cooperation. Both countries are also similarly oriented towards a multipolar world order, as discussed above.

Conversely, there are various negative factors jeopardising further improvement in relations. The biggest threat is the boundary issue. The two countries have formed consultation mechanisms to solve the border disputes.[7] One is a joint working group (JWG), established in 1988 when Rajiv Gandhi visited China; the JWG has met 15 times as of 2005. To aid the JWG, special representatives were appointed in 2003 to take a political view of the border dispute during Prime Minister Vajpayee's China visit; from 2003 to August 2009 they met 13 times. Both mechanisms have failed to produce concrete results. In the background, Tibet remains as a major latent and negative factor, in part due to a security buffer zone and the source of Indian rivers such as the Indus and the Brahmaputra.

The second negative factor for India is China's South Asian Policy, exemplified by China's all-weather relationship with Pakistan. Moreover, China's so-called String of Pearls operation has deepened apprehensions within India's strategic community.[8] For example, the Chief of Naval Staff, Admiral Sureesh Mehta, has said he opposes the bids of Chinese firms for the construction of the proposed Deep Water International Trans-Shipment Terminal at Vizhinjam, Kerala. He pointed out that China is developing good relations with Myanmar, Sri Lanka, Pakistan, and Bangladesh, with a view to enhancing the operational capabilities of its navy. He says that India will face the danger of being 'ringed by countries that have a favorable disposition toward China'.[9] A more extreme opinion has also been voiced. When Hu's India visit was imminent, Rinder Puri argued 'China must first get out of its defence and security arrangements with Pakistan and Bangladesh if it wants serious talks. . . . After the Chinese ambassador claimed Arunachal Pradesh as part of China, further dialogue is pointless.'[10]

One of India's ripostes to Chinese encirclement was its involvement in the so-called quadrilateral (quad) approach. From around 2005 onwards, there was a move to build a quad framework among the US, Japan, Australia, and possibly India. At the Sydney Asia-Pacific Economic Cooperation (APEC) summit in September 2007, the heads of the US, Japan, and Australia held a summit meeting for the first time. An Indian newspaper reported it, quoting the Japanese press secretary's statement that India had been requested to participate in such a meeting as a country with the same concerns of democracy and freedom.[11] *The Defense of Japan 2007* (Japan's White Paper on Defence) has dedicated Japan to enhancing its partnership with India and Australia. A Japanese newspaper reported that Japan is aiming to both contain the military rise of China and the threat of North Korea and maintain a security balance in the region by enhancing security cooperation with India and Australia.[12] Similarly, in August 2007 the Center for Strategic and International Studies brought out its *US-Japan-India Report*, in collaboration with the Japan Institute of International Affairs and the Confederation of Indian Industry. It said that since all three countries have common values and are aiming for a stable and open international system, they should cooperate in the fields of security, energy, the environment, and the economy.[13] The report emphasised that its recommendations should not be taken as targeting China, but in reality it did carry this nuance.

A concrete example of a quad approach took place in September 2007 at the Bay of Bengal in the form of a joint naval exercise by the US, India, Japan, Australia, and Singapore – '*Malabar 2007–2*'. This exercise, the largest to ever be held, was conducted in the middle of the Bay and Coco Islands, with 20,000 personnel, plus 28 ships and 150 airplanes. Its salient feature was a multilateral exercise, which was different from previous *Malabars* that had been conducted between India and the US. While the five participating countries hoped to boost their naval interoperability during this exercise, they were all at pains to emphasise that their war games were not an attempt to build an axis of democracy in the Asia-Pacific region in order to contain China.[14] But the view expressed by the Kyodo News Service of Japan hit the nail on the head. It said 'the exercise aims to strengthen the partnership among the countries in the field of sea lane defense such as oil transportation between the Indian Ocean and the Pacific. Its substance is to restrain China, which is expanding its network of military cooperation by assisting the littoral countries of the Ocean.' For Japan, it was a part of what Prime Minister Abe has been advocating as a quad dialogue.[15]

The quad approach died a natural death after the exits of Prime Minister Abe and Australian Prime Minister Howard, coupled with fierce criticism from China. But it is still alive in the form of bilateral arrangements as part of a policy of engagement. These are the Indo-US Defence Agreement (June 2005), India-Australia Defense memorandum of understanding (March 2006), and Joint Declaration of Security Cooperation (January 2009). There is also the Japan-India Joint Declaration on Security Cooperation (October 2008), released during the visit of Prime Minister Dr Singh to Japan. This was only the third such agreement Japan has made, after those with the US and Australia. The Japanese Prime Minister Aso and Dr Singh stressed that security cooperation should not target a third country, with Singh particularly keen to stress this point. Dr Singh made it clear that the Indo-Japanese economic partnership and security cooperation 'are not at the cost of any third country, least of all China'. Although the quad process is on the backburner, 'Japan's alliance with the U.S. and its new security ties, no matter how loose, with Australia and India sends the signal of a new security order in the region.'[16] In China, there has also been a great deal of criticism of the joint declaration as a policy for the containment of China.[17]

India–China relations and the US

China's perception towards India underwent a sea change in around the mid-1990s. To put it simply, its perception has changed from a country to which it pays only mediocre attention to a country that requires serious attention.[18] There are several factors which have prompted this shift of perception. The first is the closer relationship of India and the US. A detailed discussion of the accelerating close relations between India and the US will not be presented here (for details, see Horimoto, 2005), but it can be noted that there are close Indo-China and Indo-US interrelations. Garver (2001: 389) points out: 'The evolution of Sino-India relations will also be deeply influenced by China's relations with the U.S. and Japan.' As the Indo-US relationship has grown since 2000, China has also expressed an ever-greater interest in India. This is the strategic corollary of Chinese diplomacy, since the biggest strategic issue in Chinese foreign policy is how to deal with the US (Tagaki, 2007: 16).

The US altered its policy towards India during the second Clinton administration (1997–2001). Even though efforts by the US to improve its relationship with India were dampened by the Indian atomic tests in 1998, a big turning point came about in March 2000 when President Clinton visited India. The change prompted China to also increase its engagements with India, and since 2000 several high-level visits between India and China have been made. This is not at all coincidental; the Indo-US relationship is the other side of the coin of India-China relations as far as South Asia and the Indian Ocean are concerned.

The second factor to consider is the rapid growth of India's national economic and military power. China may be pursuing India in its diplomacy in order to prevent India from joining one of the China encirclement networks, or to prevent it from becoming too close to the US. For India too, China's courtship offers some real benefits. However, needless to say, China does not desire that India also become a major power. For example, there is the issue of permanent membership on the UN Security Council. In the past, Chinese high officials have repeatedly shown their support for India's membership by saying that they have acknowledged India's aspirations to play a greater role in the UN. During Dr Singh's visit in January 2008, in *A Shared Vision for the 21st Century* of the two countries, a new phrase was inserted for the first time after 'the UN' – 'including in the Security Council'. Certainly this inclusion might meet Indian requirements half way, although belatedly: it is a well-known fact that China tried to sabotage the possibility of a UN Security Council seat for India and other countries behind the so-called Coffee Club of Pakistan, Italy, Egypt, and Argentina.[19]

A similar Chinese stance – positive but wary – is evident in the Chinese response to the Indo-US Nuclear Deal of 2008. China took a rather forward-looking stance on Indian nuclear development, as can be seen in the Joint Declaration issued on 21 November 2006 during Hu's visit to India, which stated: 'international civilian nuclear cooperation should be advanced through innovative and forward-looking approaches, while safeguarding the effectiveness of international non-proliferation principles'. The reference to innovative and forward-looking approaches has been construed as confirming the evolution of the Chinese view on the Indo-US deal from negative to positive. Thus, the Indian foreign minister Pranab Mukherjee showed guarded optimism in his interview with IBN-CNN TV on 26 November 2006. In reality, however, China basically opposed the deal, and at the crucial Nuclear Suppliers Group meeting in September 2008 it tried from behind the scenes to block the deal.[20] China would in all likelihood not like India to emerge as a hegemon in Asia. As the Chinese proverb states: two tigers are unnecessary in one mountain. Beijing believes there should be only one tiger in the Asian mountain: China.

Future development of the Indo-China relationship

How will the Indian and Chinese relationship develop in the future? The most salient feature of Indian foreign policy is to thoroughly maintain its strategic autonomy. Such a feature has become even stronger since the 1990s, partly due to its reliance on the Soviet Union in the 1970s and 1980s, which severely limited its strategic autonomy, as discussed earlier; India learned a lesson from its relationship with a world superpower. Therefore, it is unlikely that India will establish an alliance relationship with the US in the foreseeable future, though it may maintain a closer relationship to the US than other powers. One Indian writer argued: 'India should not be seen as an American client state. Delhi will have to strike a balance – maintain close ties with the U.S.A and yet pursue an independent foreign policy.'[21] Similarly, an alliance with China is out of the question (Cohen, 2002: 262).[22]

In the diplomatic arena, India and China have continued to stress their mutual friendship, but the current reality is that both regard each other as rivals in Asia. As discussed earlier, their close relationship in the economic field is offset by a propensity to be wary in the fields of security and strategy. In other words, India has been unfolding a policy of engagement and hedging. This operation on two fronts has also been conducted by the US and Japan towards China. On 27 October 2007, during her China visit, the Congress president Sonia Gandhi stated publicly that India and China have different perspectives on both bilateral and global issues and that 'pragmatism and mutual interest' offered a sound basis for the future development of the relationship. This phrase is the most realistic characterisation of the mutual relationship; no doubt it was suggested by India's Foreign Office mandarins.

Conclusion

India is in the process of metamorphosing to a major power, which has brought about a subsequent metamorphosis of its external posture. Although India is prone to repel external pressures and influences, as in the Cold War period, there is a fundamental difference in the means it employs today. Previously, India displayed such an attitude as a result of its independent foreign policy orientation; now it does so due to its efforts to acquire major power status, even in a globalising world where mutual interdependence among countries is not at all comparable to the Cold War period. However, India cannot influence other countries to the extent it would like. Influencing others would be another characteristic of a major power, and one that India probably aspires to obtain. Thus, India has been deploying partnership diplomacy as a temporary measure, and it appears that the US has been making use of India's transitional foreign policy and that China may be trying to ward off India's emergence.

The international situation in which India must operate from now on will be interesting to watch, particularly with regard to how successfully India is able to manage its developing major power foreign policy.

Notes

1. The White House, *National Security Strategy*, May 2010, p. 1.
2. It could be a four-sided relationship if Pakistan were added.
3. James A. Leach, Chairman, Subcommittee on Asia and Pacific, *Hearing on the U.S. and Asia: Continuity, Stability and Transition*, 17 March 2004.
4. A classic example of India's perception of China as a threat is Prime Minister Vajpayee's letter to President Clinton immediately after India's atomic explosions in 1998. It hinted at a 'threat from a neighboring country' as a major factor behind the decision for India to conduct the test. This provides the world a glimpse of India's perception of China.
5. Editorial in *The Hindu*, 23 November 2006.
6. The Federation of Indian Chambers of Commerce and Industry (FICCI) has strongly opposed making the arrangements with China that it wants to have with India. FICCI's October 2007 study report *Granting Market Economy Status to China: Views from Corporate India* contended that the Chinese industrial sector enjoys an 'unfair advantage' over its Indian counterpart due to an array of exemptions by its government and an artificially undervalued Chinese currency. FICCI fears the inundation of cheap Chinese goods into the Indian market (*The Economic Times*, 29 October 2007).
7. Kondapalli, Srikanth. 'Mending Fences: Sonia's Visit to China', www.rediff.com/news/2007/oct/30guest.htm (28 October 2006) [accessed 15/3/14].
8. India may have vexed feelings towards China, which is expanding its presence in South Asia. To cope with this presence, India may increase its presence in East Asia in the future, but presently it is still negligible and at the inchoate stage, and is limited to participation in East Asian Community discussions and its successful launch of the Agni 3 (with a range of 3000 km, covering Beijing).
9. *The Statesman*, 3 December 2006. In addition he has said the Chinese firms would collect hydrological information about the coastal areas, which would hamper and endanger the operations of Indian submarines.
10. Puri, Rajinder. 'Ekla chalo!', *The Statesman*, 15 November 2006.
11. *The Economic Times*, 7 September 2007.
12. *Nikkei Evening Edition*, 6 September 2007.
13. Center for Strategic and International Studies, *US-Japan-India Report*, 16 August 2007.
14. *Indian Express*, 4 September 2007.
15. *Kyodo News Service*, 4 September 2007.
16. Purnendra Jain, 'Tokyo's Nexus with India Deepens', *Asia Times*, 25 October 2008.
17. Hayoun Ryou, 'India-Japan Security Cooperation, Chinese Perceptions', *IPCS Issue Brief*, No. 89 (January 2009).
18. According to the latest survey conducted by Horizon Research, Beijing, most Chinese people still perceive India, along with the US and Japan, as the countries that most pose a threat to China (*The Hindu*, 16 May 2010).
19. For example, N. V. Subramanian, 'Bridging the China-India Gap', *The Japan Times*, 2 November 2008.
20. For a detailed account, see Siddharth Varadarajan, 'China "Overestimated" the Strength of India's Critics at NSG', *The Hindu*, 8 September 2008. According to him, the main aim was to teach the US a lesson not to neglect them.
21. Ranjan Gupta, 'US Elections & India: Delhi Must Pursue a Flexible Foreign Policy', *The Statesman*, 25 October 2008.

22 Cohen (2002: 262) has pointed out: 'In the realm of speculation, developing a strategic relationship with China has its attractions for India but risks alienating the US. . . . [A]n alliance with China directed against Washington would still leave Delhi at the mercy of Beijing, since India would only be able to fend off the pressures of the US and the West with China's assistance.'

Bibliography

Cohen, Stephen P. (2002) *India: Emerging Power.* Washington DC: Brookings.
Garver, John W. (2001) *Protracted Contest: Sino-Indian Rivalry in the Twentieth Century.* Seattle & London: University of Washington Press.
Hedrick, Brian K. (2009) *India's Strategic Defense Transformation: Expanding Global Relationships.* Carlisle, PA: Strategic Studies Institute.
Kapur, Harish (2009) *Foreign Policies of India's Prime Ministers.* New Delhi: Lancer.
Horimoto, Takenori (2005) 'The US Asian Policy: A Strategic Perspective toward China and India', in Isabelle Saint-Mazard & James K. Chin (eds.) *China and India Political and Strategic Perspective.* Hong Kong: University of Hong Kong.
Horimoto, Takenori (2006) 'The World as India Sees It'. *Gaiko Forum* 6(3): 4–5.
Horimoto, Takenori (2010) 'India-China Relations: Bonhomie with Ambivalence', in Srikanth Kondapalli & Emi Mifune (eds.) *China and Its Neighbours.* New Delhi: Pentagon Press.
Perkovich, George (2003–4) 'Is India a Major Power?' *The Washington Quarterly* 27: 137.
Snyder, Glenn (1997) *Alliance Politics.* Ithaca & London: Cornell University Press.
Sugihara, Kaoru (2003, in Japanese) 'European Industrialization from the Standpoint of East Asia', in Shinozuka, N., A. Ishizaka, & H. Takahasi (eds.), *Chiikikogyoka no Hikakushi Kenkyu* [Comparative Studies of Regional Industrialization]. Hokkaido University Press.
Tagaki, Seiichiro (2007, in Japanese) 'Mutual Assessment in the External Strategy of the US and China', in Seiichiro Tagaki (ed.) *Structure and Development of the US and China after the Cold War.* Tokyo: The Japan Institute of International Affairs.
Virmani, Arvind (2005) *Global Power from the 18th to 21st Century: Power Potential (VIP2), Strategic Assets and Actual Power (VIP).* Working Paper No. 175, Indian Council for Research on International Economic Relations.
Vogel, Ezra F. et al. (eds.) (2002) *The Golden Age of the US-China-Japan Triangle, 1972–1989.* Cambridge & London: Harvard University Press.

4 India's macroeconomic performance in the long run

Takahiro Sato

Introduction

In 1947 India became independent from the British Raj, and for almost half a century after independence, its development strategy was oriented towards state-led import-substituting industrialisation (ISI). In 1991, when India faced its most serious economic crisis after independence, it gave up state-led ISI and launched a globalisation of the economy as a new development strategy. Following this globalisation, the Indian economy has maintained a high performance level. Goldman Sachs's BRICs (Brazil, Russia, India, and China) report in 2003 (Wilson and Purushothaman, 2003) projected the future emergence of India as the third largest economy, next to only China and the United States of America; in fact, after 2003, India's growth rate accelerated, seeming to prove the correctness of the predictions in the BRICs report. Further, the high performance of the Indian economy dramatically heightens interest from the global community.

This essay tries to investigate India's macroeconomic performance since independence from a long-term perspective. It will trace the long-term trends and changes in Indian macroeconomic policy and development strategy. By maintaining a historical perspective, it is able to find structural features of the Indian economy that have been overlooked in rapid and superficial changes in recent years. The chapter is structured as follows: the next section sketches the historical evolution of development strategy; then, India's long-term macroeconomic performance is investigated by showing the macroeconomic time series. I conclude with some remarks about the findings in this essay.

Development strategy in the long run

This section offers a brief description of the history of development strategy in India from independence to the present.[1] The period from 1947 to 1950 can be considered a transitional one, geared towards building a new, politically independent nation. This transitional period witnessed, among other significant events, the making of the Constitution of India, the settling of the political turmoil over partition, and the territorial integration of princely states into India. An end was finally brought to the transitional period by the monumentally important event that was the launch of the First Five Year Plan (1951–55). In 1951, the Industries

(Development and Regulation) Act (IDRA) was enacted in order to regulate private sector investments. IDRA established the legal basis for government intervention into private economic activities, which is widely known as 'Licence Raj'.

Fully fledged development planning was first introduced as the Second Five Year Plan (1956–61) under the strong political leadership of Jawaharlal Nehru and was based on the mathematical economic model constructed by P. C. Mahalanobis. This economic model proposed the prioritisation of heavy industry to facilitate high economic growth in the long run. The main framework of the Second Plan was followed by the Third Plan (1961–66). Thus, the Second and Third Plans are jointly referred to as the 'Nehru-Mahalanobis model' of development strategy for building the national economy. In 1956, the Industrial Policy Resolution (IPR) was adopted in the Indian parliament. IPR supported the mixed economy by clarifying the roles of the public and private sectors in the economic development of India. Another institutionally important incident was the State Reorganisation Act, passed in 1956 in order to deal with state language problems and restructure the framework of the federal system of post-independent India. The Second and Third Five Year Plans contributed significantly to ISI in India.

Two successive years of drought in 1965 and 1966 triggered a serious economic crisis, which, with the balance-of-payments crisis in particular, resulted in the postponement of the launch of the Fourth Plan. In 1966, in exchange for promises of economic aid from the United States and the World Bank, India implemented economic liberalisation measures, including trade liberalisation and substantial devaluation, in order to overcome this economic crisis. India thus embarked on economic liberalisation a quarter-century before the globalisation of 1991. It should be noted that in the same period Asian newly industrialised economies such as Korea shifted from the ISI strategy to a strategy of export-oriented industrialisation (EOI). However, the liberalisation of India was failed by the suspension of promised economic aid to India by the World Bank and the United States, due to the complex international political dynamics at the time. After the failure of economic liberalisation, India abandoned the policy and began to strengthen economic regulation under the administration of Indira Gandhi. From that point on, India's strategy of development was directed away from rational elitism and towards radical populism.

It can be said that India's three plans had two major flaws. The first was to neglect the development of the agricultural sector in comparison with the industrial sector, to which the Nehru-Mahalanobis model gave preferential treatment. In fact, the internal terms of trade for agricultural and industrial products were against the agricultural sector. In addition, the industrial sector was given priority over the agricultural sector in the allocation of public investment. These issues are a reflection of the emphasis of the Nehru-Mahalanobis model on the development of the industrial sector rather than the agricultural sector to promote long-term high economic growth. Such a development strategy in favour of heavy industry ultimately resulted in a serious economic crisis in the mid-1960s, as the underdevelopment of agriculture was the underlying cause of the successive droughts of 1965 and 1966. The droughts caused serious food shortages, as well as the balance-of-payments crisis that arose from severe inflation and a surge in imports of food. The second is the satiation of the expansion of the industrial sector in the mid-1960s. Once the import demand for industrial products is met by domestic production, industrial growth becomes constrained by the size of domestic markets unless the export market is open. In other words, unless there is a sustained expansion of domestic markets through the development of the agricultural sector, the industrial sector cannot be expected to grow sustainably.

The aim of economic liberalisation and the Green Revolution of the mid-1960s was to break the bottleneck of the ISI strategy created by the Nehru-Mahalanobis model. The 1966 liberalisation intended to resolve the market problem through exports to world markets. But it failed. India responded to the crisis that followed this failure by introducing stronger regulations and continuing to promote the Green Revolution. The Green Revolution succeeded in bringing about a dramatic increase in food production in the central and north-western area, i.e. Punjab and Haryana. It also achieved food self-sufficiency in the late 1970s, in the sense that there was no longer a constant need for food imports.

Since the late 1960s, the economic regulations have been tightened. The Monopolies and Restrictive Trade Practice (MRTP) Act of 1969, the nationalisation of 14 large commercial banks in 1969, the Patent Act of 1970, the Industrial and Licensing Policy of 1970, and the Foreign Exchange Regulation Act (FERA) of 1973, are famous examples of such tightening regulations. There is an often told anecdote about the exit of IBM and Coca-Cola from the Indian market as a result of their avoiding the limit of 40 per cent foreign ownership share imposed by FERA. As will be explained below, the partial economic liberalisation that occurred during the 1980s aimed at a gradual relaxation of the strong regulations that had accumulated after the late 1960s, without attacking the core ideas of the ISI strategy that had been followed since independence.

The second oil crisis of 1979 triggered the Indian balance-of-payments crisis. In order to prevent the impending crisis, the Indian government negotiated a large loan from the International Monetary Fund (IMF), and in 1981 the IMF agreed to provide a loan amount of 5 billion Special Drawing Rights to India on condition that the latter implement economic liberalisation. Thus, it can be seen that economic liberalisation began in the early 1980s. In particular, Prime Minister Rajeev Gandhi, who took over from Indira Gandhi in 1984, pushed for further liberalisation from 1985. The economic liberalisation was constituted by a partial relaxation and the flexible operation of strong regulations within the framework of the ISI strategy. The framework of development strategy itself was never tackled. However, in spite of the limitations of liberalisation in the 1980s, the blueprint for the globalisation seen in 1991 was prepared by various reports from government committees on economic reforms established during the late 1970s and the 1980s.

In the 1980s, when India's economic liberalisation had progressed to some degree, the average economic growth rate was about 6 per cent. It can thus be said that India achieved high economic growth. However, the fiscal deficit and current account deficit increased simultaneously. Such macroeconomic imbalance resulted in the huge accumulation of public and external debt. In fact, in 1990

India became the third largest of the developing countries in terms of external debt stock. Moreover, macro imbalances combined with high growth in the 1980s contributed to high, persistent inflation. Thus, India's economic growth in the 1980s ultimately faced a deadlock at the time of the most serious balance-of-payments crisis since independence.

In 1990 and 1991, India fell into the most serious political and economic crisis it had faced since independence. In early 1991, foreign exchange reserves dropped to a level sufficient to meet import bills for only two weeks; it was the first possible crisis of external debt default in the history of post-independence India. The main cause of the balance-of-payments crisis was the oil price hike of 1990 and 1991, triggered by Iraq's invasion of Kuwait. Along with an increase in the trade deficit due to drastic increases in the price of oil imports, macro imbalances such as large external debt, huge fiscal deficit, and a high rate of inflation gave rise to doubts about India's solvency to foreign investors. As a result, the capital flight by non-resident Indians (NRIs) who had until then contributed to finance the balance of payments via NRI deposits was decisive for the balance-of-payments crisis. To survive in the economic crisis, the Narasimha Rao government – which had been formed in June 1991 after the general election that followed the political crisis of the assassination of former prime minister Rajeev Gandhi during the election campaign – launched globalisation and economic reforms in the form of the implementation of the IMF conditionality.

The economic reform started with a 20 per cent devaluation in early July of 1991. The economic reforms drastically converted India's ISI development strategy into globalisation with a package of trade liberalisation, capital account liberalisation, privatisation, and deregulation, such as elimination of industrial licensing policy. It is noted that although both the leftist government of the United Front and the rightist government of the National Democratic Alliance won general elections after the Narasimha Rao government, globalisation as economic reform has been maintained in all administrations, including the current government of the United Progress Alliance.

Macroeconomic performance in the long run

This section investigates India's long-term macroeconomic performance by focusing on (1) economic growth rate, (2) per capita income, (3) rate of inflation, (4) agriculture, (5) fiscal balance, (6) current account balance, and (7) exchange rate. It uses several charts in order to examine the long-term trends and changes in the key macroeconomic variables mentioned above. It is noted that economic statistics for India are available from 1950 onwards. Therefore, the macroeconomic variables used below generally start from the year 1950.

Economic growth rate

Figure 4.1 shows the annual GDP growth rate during the period 1951–2008 and it is clear from this that the annual variation of growth rate was excessive until the

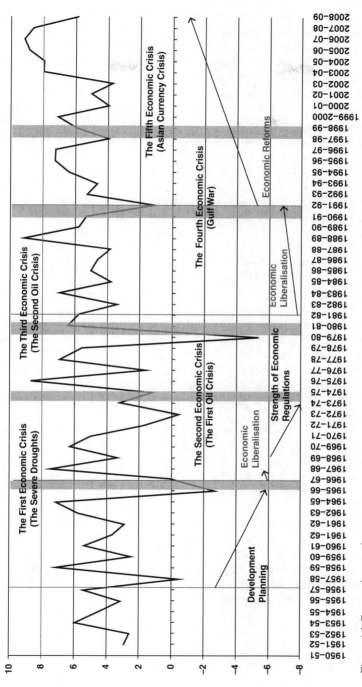

Figure 4.1 Economic growth rate

1980s. This means that before the 1980s, in addition to the two oil crises, annual fluctuation in agricultural production that resulted from changes in the monsoon and other weather conditions had a tremendous impact on economic growth. Since the 1980s, the Indian economy has come to be relatively disconnected from weather changes. As one of the most important underlying factors contributing to long-term changes in the economic performance of India, the decreased dependence of economic growth on weather conditions cannot be dismissed.

Furthermore, in Figure 4.1 five major economic growth crises can be identified as follows: (1) the crisis of 1965 and 1966, caused by severe droughts, (2) the first oil crisis of 1973, (3) the second oil crisis of 1979, (4) the crisis of 1991, triggered by the Gulf War, (5) the Asian currency crisis from mid-1997 to 1999. Of course, the growth rate declined significantly at times of economic crisis.

In addition to the identification of economic growth crises, Figure 4.1 shows the intuitive direction of change in development strategy described in the previous section by depicting the directing arrows. In the case of the development strategy towards economic liberalisation, the direction of the arrow is upwards. In case of strengthened regulations, its direction is downwards. Looking at the directing arrows, the overlap of the growth crisis and significant changes in development strategies that occur in some cases is clear. In the crisis of the mid-1960s, economic liberalisation was tried and it failed. After this failure, development strategy was switched from economic liberalisation to a radical tightening of economic regulations in the late 1960s and the early 1970s. Partial economic liberalisation in the 1980s followed the growth crisis of 1979. The economic crisis of 1991 stimulated the launch of globalisation from the 1990s onwards. Therefore, it can be said that – historically speaking – although all of the economic crises do not necessarily provide stimulus impacts on the change in development strategy, every transformation of development strategy was triggered by an economic growth crisis.

Since the 1980s, India's economic growth rate and per capita income have increased. However, it is not easy to read structural change in growth rates in Figure 4.1. This point is considered in the next subsection.

Per capita income

Figure 4.2 shows the per capita GDP from 1950 to the present. While the annual growth rate shown in Figure 4.1 did not explicitly express the long-term trends in per capita income level, the per capita income of Figure 4.2 clearly indicates that the Indian economy entered a phase of high growth around 1980. The low growth rate of India's economy had been derisively called the 'Hindu Rate of Growth', referring to the stagnancy that India experienced for a long time. This essay refers to the period during 1950–80 as the 'Hindu Growth Phase', and the period from 1980 onwards as the 'High Growth Phase', as two distinguished categories for understanding the long-term performance of the Indian economy. Moreover, it is noted that in the high growth phase, the growth has been accelerating since 2003.

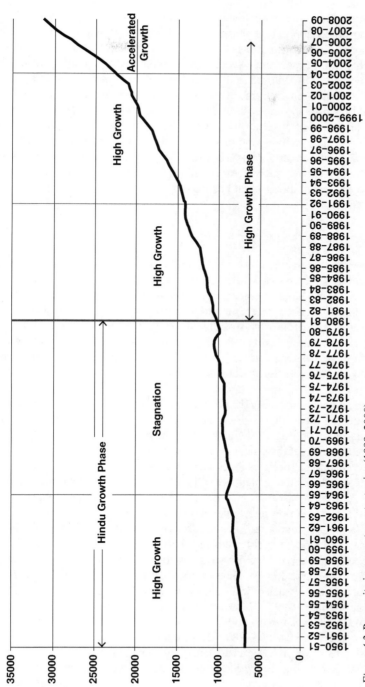

Figure 4.2 Per capita income at constant price (1999–2000)

As far as the long-term trend of economic growth is concerned, rapid growth in India started not in the 1990s of the full-fledged globalisation era, but in the 1980s of the partial economic liberalisation period. India's growth is modest compared with the rapid growth experienced in East Asian economies. However, Figure 4.2 shows that India experienced steady and stable growth without a drastic decline in income levels. It could be said that if East Asian economies were tigers, India would be an elephant, in terms of its slow but stable growth.

A stable and steady increase in per capita income level has contributed to the alleviation of India's absolute poverty problems since the 1970s. According to the estimates of the Planning Commission, as shown in Figure 4.3, the head count ratio of absolute poverty decreased from 55 per cent in 1973 to 22 per cent in 2004. Of course, absolute poverty is still a serious problem in India, but it should be noted that economic growth has played an important role in the reduction in absolute poverty.

Inflation rate

India is an exceptional country in Asia in the sense that it has maintained parliamentary democracy based on free and fair elections since it won independence. Being the world's largest democracy is a proud feature of the Indian political system. In this respect, it is interesting to note that there is a tentative law of politics that says that the incumbent government will be defeated in an election when the rate of inflation in the year before the general election is more than two digits. Of course, it is hard to consider it as a 'law' in the strict sense; however, this tentative law is an important factor in considering the economic influences of democracy in India.

Indian people – especially the poor, who are damaged by the short-term decline in real income levels due to price increases in food – are politically sensitive to inflation. Indian politicians facing a competitive political environment are unable to ignore the voice of the poor, and as a result, there is political support for restrictive macroeconomic policies for moderate inflation.

Figure 4.4 shows the annual rate of inflation. Bearing in mind the political law mentioned above, this section makes several comments on the long-term trends and changes in inflation rate since 1950 shown in Figure 4.4. There is structural change in annual fluctuations of the inflation rate around 1980; since then fluctuations of inflation have been reduced. This is coincident with the change in the stability of annual economic growth rates shown in Figure 4.1, which means the process of economic independence from weather conditions in India. It is also clear that the annual rates of inflation have reduced with the stable annual fluctuation since the late 1990s. Therefore, it is possible to identify three phases of the history of Indian inflation, as follows: (1) low level of inflation with high variability during the period 1950–1980, (2) high level of inflation with low variability during the period from 1980 to the late 1990s, and (3) low level of inflation with low variability during the period from the late-1990s onwards. The third phase can be referred to as the moderate inflation phase. The institutional background

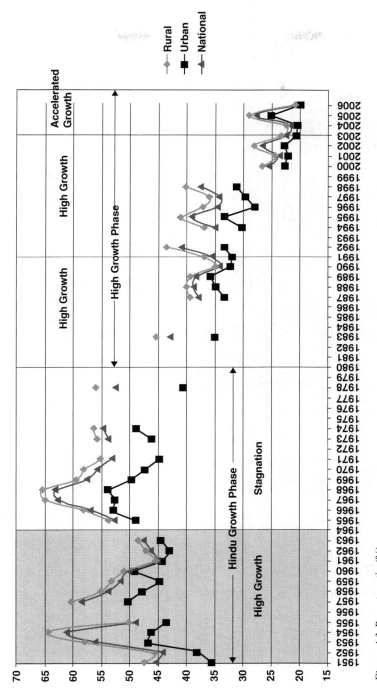

Figure 4.3 Poverty ratio (%)

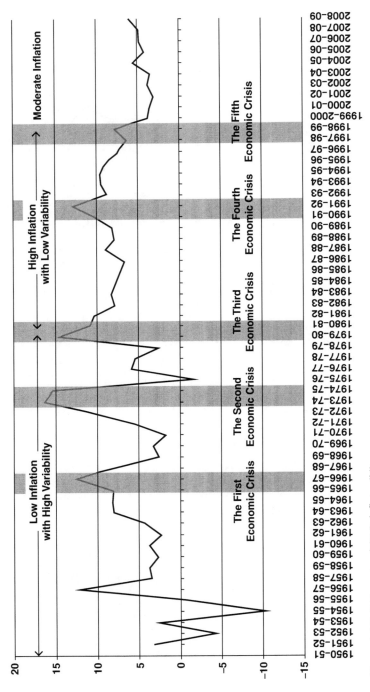

Figure 4.4 Inflation rate of GDP deflator (%)

of the moderate inflation phase is the independent monetary policy conducted by the Reserve Bank of India. It is noted that the Reserve Bank of India has gradually become independent from the Indian government, especially the Ministry of Finance, since the late 1990s.

According to Figure 4.4, in all of the economic crises except the Asian currency crisis, the inflation rate was in double figures. In other words, economic crisis in India generally signifies not only the depression and balance-of-payments crisis but also the crisis of high inflation. Furthermore, it is noted that the economic crisis caused by high inflation raises the level of discontent among the people and ultimately results in political crisis.

In the economic crisis of the mid-1960s high inflation was triggered by serious droughts, and in the economic crises in the 1970s and in 1991 high inflation was caused by the surge in oil prices. In this sense, two-digit inflation rates were due to exogenous internal and external shocks from the supply side rather than the demand side. In contrast, the increase in base money supplied by the Reserve Bank of India via automatic accommodation of the expanded fiscal deficit basically contributed to persistently high inflation from the 1980s to the mid-1990s. In that sense, the major cause of persistently high inflation from the 1980s to the mid-1990s was from the demand side. The dependent monetary policy to finance fiscal deficits was changed towards a more autonomous monetary policy from 1994 until 1997, when the Reserve Bank of India and the Ministry of Finance agreed to restrict automatic monetisation. Therefore, it should again be noted that progress in the autonomy of monetary policy since the mid-1990s is one of the most important institutional factors of moderate inflation in recent years.

From 2003 to mid-2008, oil prices rose more than four-fold. The price of oil per barrel in mid-2008 recorded the highest values of more than 130 US dollars. Over time this proved to be comparable to the previous two oil shocks. In order to deal with a huge increase in oil price, since 2003 the Reserve Bank of India conducted restrictive monetary policy. As a result, the average rate of 5 per cent inflation was kept during the recent oil price surge. From the international perspective, India's long-term inflation rate is relatively low compared with East Asian economies in the high growth period and Latin America. This can be accounted for by India's parliamentary democracy based on free and fair elections and the socio-political structure that the majority of people – the poor – are sensitive to inflation. It is noted again that relatively low inflation is one of the features of the Indian economy.

Agriculture

Figure 4.5 shows long-term trends and changes in the agricultural sector in terms of its share of GDP, net food grain imports, and ratio of non-irrigated land to total land. In 1950, the agriculture share of GDP was more than 50 per cent, and had fallen to less than 20 per cent in 2008. Along with economic development, the GDP share accounted for by the agriculture sector is shrinking gradually and steadily. This means that in the past the economic performance of the agricultural

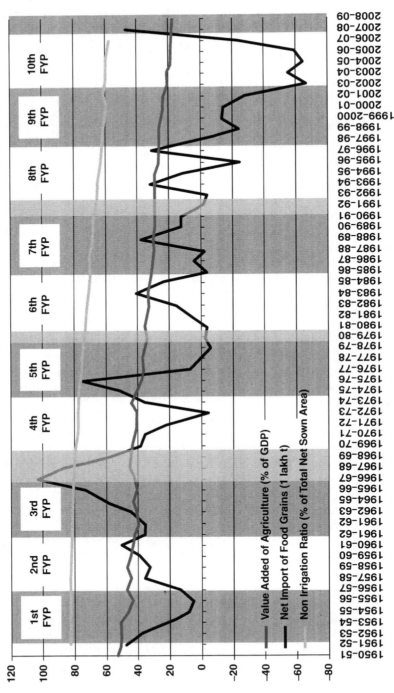

Figure 4.5 Agriculture

sector was the key factor for India's economic growth and fluctuation, but now the influence of the agricultural sector on the economy is undoubtedly smaller because of the substantial decline of GDP share.

The non-irrigation ratio was reduced from more than 80 per cent to less than 60 per cent from 1951 to 2006. For a long time, rain-fed agriculture in India had been likened to gambling, but now the validity of this analogy can be questioned. The spread of irrigated areas is an important factor behind the independence of Indian agriculture from weather conditions.

India was an agricultural exporting country, but it was a permanent net food importing country until the late 1970s. The decline in agricultural production caused by drought triggered increased food imports from abroad and this certainly made the balance-of-payments problem difficult. The achievement of self-sufficiency of food grains at the end of the 1970s was the decisive change in the situation. The Green Revolution from the mid-1960s achieved a dramatic increase in food production and saw the realisation of self-sufficiency of food in the sense of balancing of food trade. Figure 4.5 shows the net importation of food in units of 1 lakh. According to Figure 4.5, net food grains imports were more than 10 million tons in the drought years of 1965 and 1966. Huge food importation triggered the balance-of-payments crisis at that time. After the mid-1960s, a gradual decrease can be seen in the net amount of food imports. Net food imports were zero over several years in the late 1970s. In the 1980s, the net import of food peaked at 4 million, but it never caused a balance-of-payments crisis as it had before. India has also held sufficient food stock to stabilise food prices since the 1980s. In addition, during the period from the late-1990s to 2007, when international natural resource prices soared, India appeared to the world market as a net exporter of food. In fact, the net export of food grains was 6 million tons at the peak in that time. The development of agriculture over the long term was the driving force behind independence from weather conditions, and a fundamentally determinant factor on key macroeconomic variables such as economic growth, per capita income level, and inflation.

As supplementary information, Figure 4.5 shows the time periods of various Five Year Plans; thus far no Five Year Plan has actually been conducted for five years. This 'plan holiday' can be found in the years 1966–1968, one year in 1979, and two years in 1990 and 1991. Needless to say, these plan holidays were forced by the economic crisis and thus, since 1951, have indicated a serious economic crisis in India.

Fiscal balance

Before discussing the long-term fiscal balance, the definition of fiscal balance should be clarified. Here, fiscal balance is defined as the investment-saving (IS) balance of the public sector, which includes not only general governments but also public enterprises. Therefore, it is a broader concept than the usual fiscal balance. This essay uses this broader concept as fiscal balance because of long-term availability of the public sector IS balance.

Figure 4.6 shows the fiscal balance and indicates that India's fiscal balance has been consistently negative. Moreover, the fiscal deficit has worsened in the long

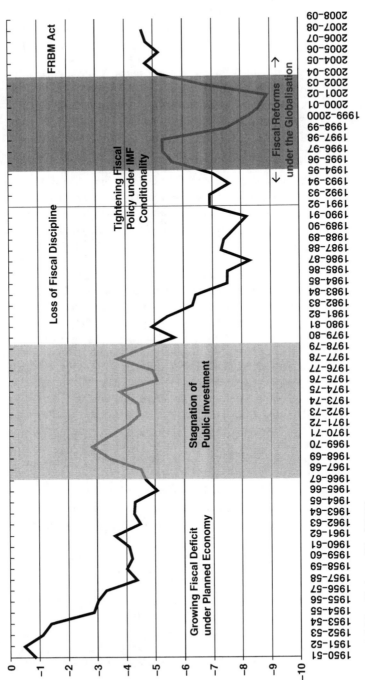

Figure 4.6 Fiscal balance (% of GDP)

term. In 1950 the fiscal balance was roughly in balance, and it then fell to 8 per cent of GDP in the late 1980s. The fiscal deficit reached its peak at 9 per cent of GDP in 2001.

Here the long-term fluctuations of fiscal deficit from 1950 to 2008 are divided into the four distinguished phases as follows: (1) the first phase, from early 1950 until the mid-1960s, will be referred to as 'planned economy'; (2) the second phase, during the 1960s and late 1970s, as the stagnation of public investment; (3) the third phase, from the late 1980s to 1990, as the loss of fiscal discipline; and (4) the fourth phase, since 1991, under the economic reforms.

In the first phase, as part of the first three Five Year Plans, the Indian government implemented the ISI development strategy by utilising public enterprises as leverage for rapid industrialisation. While public investment was allocated aggressively to public enterprises and infrastructure, tax revenues were not sufficiently raised, and this was a main factor of the worsening fiscal deficit. After the serious economic crisis in the mid-1960s, the expansion of the fiscal deficit was restricted in order to overcome the balance-of-payments crisis and high inflation. In particular, until the late 1970s, public investment was significantly suppressed. This compression of public investment accounted for the stagnation of the industrial sector during the period from the mid-1960s to 1980. In other words, this second phase overlapped with the stagnation period of the Indian industries. After the end of the 1970s, public debt accumulated massively as various subsidies, such as those for food and fertilisers, increased. At the same time, contemporary government expenditure, which consisted of interest payments and recurring expenses, primarily the wages and salaries of public servants, was not met by the revenue – which came mainly from taxes. Until this point the Indian government had kept the account surplus as an 'iron law' of fiscal policy; it can be said that this iron law was lost and broken in the early 1980s. India had fallen into a 'debt trap', meaning that existing debt created more debt in the third phase of fiscal policy. Loss of fiscal discipline and high economic growth were coincident in the 1980s. Therefore, it can be noted that high economic growth was supported by the demand side of the expanding fiscal deficit.

The fourth phase of globalisation, since 1991, can be classified further into three subperiods as follows: (1) the first subperiod of 1991–94 under the IMF conditionality, (2) the second subperiod of 1994–2002 as the transition, and (3) the third subperiod after the Fiscal Responsibility and Budget Management Act (FRBMA) of 2003 was passed. The reduction of the fiscal deficit has been the most important item on the agenda of economic reform since 1991. Not only the IMF and World Bank but also the Indian government considered the reduction of the fiscal deficit as the cornerstone for correcting the macroeconomic imbalances.

Figure 4.6 indicates that the fiscal deficit was restricted by an austere fiscal policy in the first subperiod. After graduating from the IMF conditionality of 1994, the Indian government accepted a larger fiscal deficit in order to prevent a serious recession and the contagion caused by the Asian currency crisis. This second transitional subperiod was terminated by the introduction of the FRBMA of 2003. The FRBMA obligates the Indian government to reduce the fiscal deficit sequentially and constitutes a landmark law in India's macroeconomic history. In addition to the high growth of tax revenues, mainly attributed to cyclical economic factors, the FRBMA will offer a significant contribution to the long-term reduction in the fiscal deficit.

Current account balance

This section discusses the long-term trends and changes in the current account balance in Figure 4.7. In Figure 4.7, the current account balance shows a different pattern of movement compared with other macroeconomic variables such as economic growth, per capita income, inflation rate, and fiscal balance. A cyclical movement from surplus to deficit of the current account balance is apparent. The cycle has been completed twice in the 60 years since independence. Looking at both Figures 4.6 and 4.7 simultaneously, it can be seen that the worsening of the fiscal deficit and current account deficit was coincident in the 1950s, 1960s, and the mid-1980s.

Figure 4.7 shows the four balance-of-payments crises. The first crisis happened in 1956; the exhaustion of sterling balances in London that had been accumulated during the Second World War was the backbone of the crisis. In order to manage the balance-of-payments crisis, the Indian government obtained foreign economic assistance and was able to start the Second Five Year Plan successfully. Thus, the first balance of payments crisis did not develop into an economic crisis.

The second balance-of-payments crisis, as already argued in the previous section, was triggered by two successive severe droughts in 1965 and 1966. The huge increase in food imports that resulted from the drastic decline in agricultural production made the management of the balance of payments highly difficult. In order to receive the agreed economic assistance from the World Bank and the US, the Indian government implemented economic liberalisation in 1966 as the conditionality.

The third crisis was caused by the second oil crisis of 1979. This crisis also stimulated the introduction of economic liberalisation in the 1980s. Interestingly, the first oil crisis of 1973 did not necessarily trigger the balance-of-payments crisis. In the mid-1970s, there was a strong exports boom and increases in remittances from the migrant Indian workers in the Middle East; these factors contributed to prevent a balance-of-payments crisis.

The fourth crisis was triggered by the Gulf Crisis of 1990, via the surge in international oil prices. As mentioned in the previous section, in order to overcome the balance-of-payments crisis, the Indian government received a loan from the IMF and began globalisation as the IMF conditionality. Figure 4.7 shows that there was a large current account deficit at the time of each of the four balance-of-payments crises. It should be noted that when the current account deficit to GDP ratio reached 3 per cent, a balance-of-payments crisis occurred. In fact, as Figure 4.7 shows, at the time of the Asian currency crisis in the late 1990s, India's current account deficit was between 1 and 2 per cent, and the Asian currency crisis did not create an Indian balance-of-payments crisis.

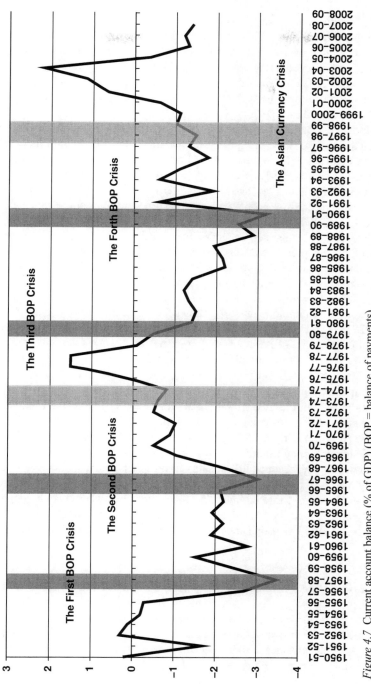

Figure 4.7 Current account balance (% of GDP) (BOP = balance of payments)

Exchange rate and external finance

This section discusses India's exchange rate and balance-of-payments management in the long run. Figure 4.8 shows the nominal exchange rate against the US dollar from 1948 onwards. According to Figure 4.8, under the Bretton Woods System, India had adopted a fixed exchange rate regime during the period from 1948 to 1971, with the exception of the 50 per cent devaluation of 1966. Even after the collapse of the Bretton Woods System in 1973, the Indian exchange rate moved in a narrow band until the 1980s.

The Indian exchange rate policy was changed in around 1980. Since 1980, India had adopted an exchange rate policy to devalue the exchange rate gradually, as shown in Figure 4.8. Despite several important reforms on exchange rate policy since globalisation in 1991, an exchange rate policy to devalue the exchange rate gradually was maintained as far as the long-term trend of the exchange rate is concerned. The long-term trend of depreciation turned into an appreciation trend in 2002. In around 2000 India's exchange rate regime became more flexible and market oriented, and India has adopted a flexible exchange rate regime up to the present.

Finally, this chapter offers a brief comment on the management of the balance of payment. Three different types of sources of external finance can be identified: aid, debt finance, and equity finance. Here debt finance is regarded as external commercial borrowings and NRI deposits, and equity finance as foreign direct and portfolio investments. Figure 4.9 shows the net capital inflow of aid, debt, and equity from 1950 to 2008. According to Figure 4.9, public aid from international financial organisations and developed countries in the period from the 1950s to the 1970s, external commercial borrowings and NRI deposits in the 1980s, and foreign direct and portfolio investments since the 1990s constitute the principal sources of external finance.

Synchronised with its financial globalisation, India began capital account liberalisation after 1991. As a symbolic event, it is noted that IBM and Coca-Cola, which withdrew from India in the 1970s, returned to the country in the 1990s. From the point of view of policy trilemma or impossible trinity – meaning a fixed exchange rate regime, capital account liberalisation, and independent monetary policy are mutually inconsistent – since 2000 India has chosen a consistent policy option such as a flexible exchange rate regime, capital account liberalisation, and independent monetary policy. It can be argued that the recent good macroeconomic performance in India is supported by sound and consistent macroeconomic policy management.[2]

Concluding remarks

In this essay, India's macroeconomic performance since independence has been investigated by tracking the long-term trends and changes in development strategy. Our findings are as follows: first, three major economic crises – serious droughts in the mid-1960s, an oil crisis in 1979, and the Gulf War in 1991 – stimulated long-term fundamental changes in India's development strategy. The crisis response was different each time, i.e. the tightening of regulations in the late 1960s, the partial economic liberalisation in the 1980s, and the full-fledged globalisation in the 1990s. Second, the Indian economy has become relatively independent of weather

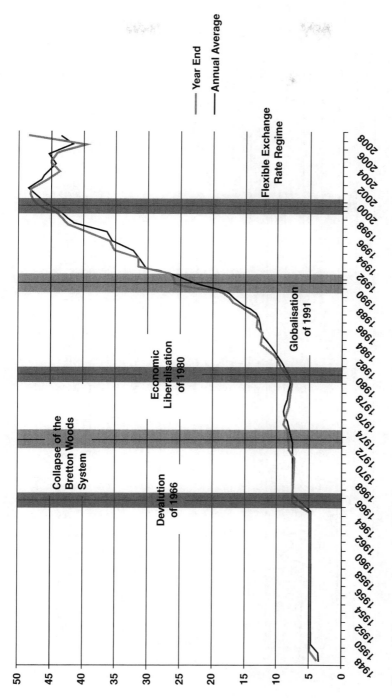

Figure 4.8 Exchange rate against US dollar

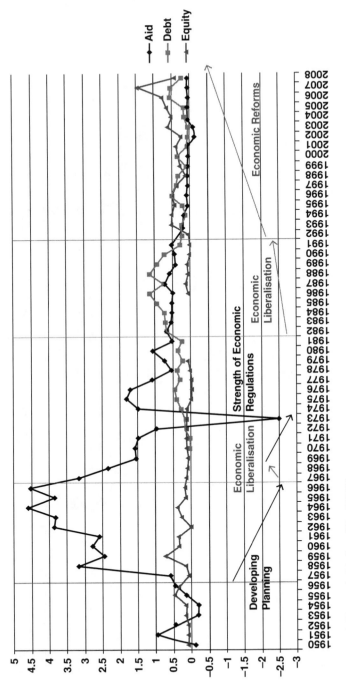

Figure 4.9 Net capital inflow (% of GDP)

instability as a result of a reduction in GDP share of the agricultural sector and an improvement in agricultural technologies and infrastructures. In particular, since the 1980s the Green Revolution has contributed to the stability in the inflation rate and economic growth and has alleviated the balance-of-payments problem caused by food imports. Third, in the early 1980s the Indian economy reached a turning point of a high economic growth phase. This high growth was backed up by the success of the Green Revolution. It has alleviated India's absolute poverty slowly but steadily. Fourth, in the late 1990s monetary policy became independent of fiscal policy. An independent monetary policy implemented by the Reserve Bank of India during the 2000s ensures sustainable high economic growth and stable low inflation. Fifth, since the 1990s India's economy has continued to grow steadily without falling into a serious economic crisis, although events such as the Asian currency crisis in the late 1990s and the international oil price hike during the period from 2003 to mid-2008 hit the Indian economy significantly. In other words, the Indian economy has become relatively independent of external shocks. Finally, the macroeconomic performance since the 1990s has been successful in terms of economic growth, inflation, and the balance of payments. However, India has failed to reduce its fiscal deficit, and this deficit will be a serious constraint on India's macro economy in the future.

Notes

1 Historical events in this section basically follow Chandra, Mukherjee, and Mukhrjee (2008); Joshi and Little (1994, 1996); and Panagariya (2008). However, we do not necessarily follow the economic interpretation of the existing studies.
2 On the details of India's macroeconomic policy under the capital account liberalisation, please see Sato (2002, 2009), and Esho and Sato (2009: Chapter 4).

Bibliography

Chandra, Bipan, Mridula Mukherjee, & Aditya Mukhrjee (2008) *India since Independence* [revised and updated]. New Delhi: Penguin Books.
Esho, Hideki & Takahiro Sato (eds.) (2009) *India's Globalising Political Economy: New Challenges and Opportunities in the 21st Century*. Tokyo: The Sasakawa Peace Foundation.
Joshi, Vijay & I.M.D. Little (1994) *India: Macroeconomics and Political Economy, 1964–91*. New Delhi: Oxford University Press.
Joshi, Vijay & I.M.D Little (1996) *India's Economic Reforms, 1991–2001*. New Delhi: Oxford University Press.
Panagariya, Arvind (2008) *India: The Emerging Giant*. New York: Oxford University Press.
Sato, Takahiro (2002, in Japanese) *Development Economics: India's Economic Reforms in the Era of Globalization*. Kyoto: Sekaishisosha.
Sato, Takahiro (ed.) (2009, in Japanese) *Macroeconomic Analysis of the Indian Economy*. Kyoto: Sekaishisosha.
Wilson, D. and R. Purushothaman (2003) 'Dreaming with BRICs: The Path to 2050'. *Global Economics Paper*, No. 99, October: Goldman Sachs.

5 Public health and human security in India
Poised for positive change

Sunil Chacko

This chapter concerns the increasing focus of the Indian government on improving its health care provision. The current system is deeply iniquitous, giving little security to much of the population, but government is working towards a system that would provide universal coverage and thereby a degree of security in health care provision for the people. Its main initiative is to increase spending on health care from its current level of around 1 per cent GDP to around 2.5 per cent by 2017, increasing its outlay annually regardless of the fiscal deficit in the economy.[1] However, such an increase in spending (2.5 per cent of a $2 trillion economy that is experiencing an annual growth rate of 5–8 per cent) requires a high level of management, as well as tools and training; alongside these, procedures, processes, and logistic chains need to be established. To secure universal access to health care for all, it is essential that the process receives adequate supervision, oversight, and regulation and that these are based on empirical evidence.

State of public health in India: public and private

At present, public health in India is deeply iniquitous, two central problems being that the available resources are inadequate and that coverage is insufficient. Alongside the rest of the population, the poor have increasingly been seeking a range of medical and public health services from any source available to them, leading to a major growth in medical care, especially in the private sector. The Planning Commission estimated India's total spending on health in 2012 at around 5 per cent of GDP, but of this, 4 per cent of GDP is constituted by private spending on health. This private spending includes direct spending by consumers, as well as companies reimbursing medical costs or paying out on insurance. In other words, the primary means of financing health care for people in India is through non-government sources.

Given the vast sums spent on private health care by individuals and families, there has thus been a massive growth in private health care facilities of all kinds as they race to keep up with demand.

It is estimated there are 1.37 million hospital beds in India, of which 833,000 belong to the private sector and 540,000 to public health facilities; given that the population of India is 1.2 billion, this averages out as 1 bed per thousand people.

Table 5.1 Sources of funds for health care in India, 2004–5

	Per cent
Households	71.13
State government	11.97
Central government	6.78
Firms	5.73
External flow	2.28
Social insurance funds	1.13
NGOs	0.07
Local bodies	0.92

Source: Government of India, 2009, *National Health Accounts 2004–05*, New Delhi: National Health Accounts Cell, Ministry of Health and Family Welfare

This figure is well below the beds-per-person average in the US, where the figure is 3.1 beds per thousand; the UK, with 3.9 beds per thousand; and Japan, where the figure stands significantly higher at 15 beds per thousand. Of course, in making such comparisons it is important to bear in mind the relative populations of these countries: the US has a population of around 300 million, while the population of the UK is approximately 62 million. This means that were the UK to have the same number of beds as India – 1.37 million – it would yield a ratio of 22 beds per thousand people. Thus, the denominator is critically important when trying to form a fair assessment of the tasks being undertaken in relation to this issue, as well as those that are in the pipeline. However, if one delves further into figures regarding hospital beds in India, it becomes apparent that of those 1.37 million beds, 520,000 are effectively non-functional as a result of shortfalls in human resources, among other constraints.[2]

Regarding the number of hospital beds in India, there are also major regional differences that must be taken into account. In urban areas there is an average of one hospital bed per 422 people. However, this ratio is notably lower in rural locations, which also vary significantly by region: in rural areas in central India there is one bed per 4,500 people; in rural southern India there is one bed per 1,650 people. In addition to this, health indicators vary greatly between states, as shown in Table 5.2.

Recent progress

In terms of the progress that has already been made in providing better health care to its citizens, since 2005 the Indian government has spent $15 billion on the National Rural Health Mission (NRHM). This scheme has augmented India's public health system, which had faced years of neglect, and has made contributions to the discernible and steady decline in maternal and child mortality, fertility, and overall mortality rates. From funds allocated for new construction and

Table 5.2 Selected health status outcomes in major Indian states

	Life Expectancy	Neonatal Mortality Rate per 1000 Live Births	Infant Mortality Rate per 1000 Live Births	Under-Five Mortality Rate per 1000 Live Births	Total Fertility Rate	Underweight Children, %
India	**62.5**	**39**	**50**	**74.3**	**2.6**	**48**
Andhra Pradesh	63.5	40.3	49	63.2	1.8	42.7
Assam	57.9	45.5	61	85.0	2.6	46.5
Bihar	60.8	39.8	52	84.8	3.9	55.6
Gujarat	63.4	33.5	48	60.9	2.5	51.7
Haryana	65.2	23.6	51	52.3	2.5	45.7
Karnataka	64.5	28.9	41	54.7	2.0	43.7
Kerala	**73.5**	**11.5**	**12**	**16.3**	**1.7**	**24.5**
Madhya Pradesh	56.9	44.9	67	94.2	3.3	50.0
Maharashtra	66.2	31.8	31	46.7	2.0	46.3
Odisha	**58.5**	**45.4**	**65**	**90.6**	**2.4**	**45**
Punjab	68.5	28.0	38	52.0	1.9	36.7
Rajasthan	61.1	43.9	59	85.4	3.3	43.7
Tamil Nadu	65.2	19.1	28	35.5	1.7	30.9
Uttar Pradesh	59.1	47.6	63	96.4	3.8	56.8
West Bengal	63.9	37.6	33	59.6	1.9	44.6

Source: Indian Health Statistics Report 2012[3]

renovation, NRHM has funded the refurbishment of 594 district hospitals, 27,732 community health centres, 5,459 primary health centres, and 31,001 health sub-centres. In addition to this, NRHM has overseen the recruitment of more than 100,000 doctors, nurses, specialists, and paramedics, along with around 850,000 accredited social health personnel. Finally, under NRHM, 518 districts have each been provided with a mobile medical unit.[4]

In addition to NRHM, the Indian government has introduced various other health programmes and initiatives to improve the provision of health care to the people. In the past three and a half years, new initiatives have been introduced concerning safe motherhood. These initiatives provide cash assistance to pregnant women to encourage them to give birth in a medical institution; over 11 million women have participated each year since the start of the scheme. The programme ensures that each woman can have a cost-free delivery in a government facility, with the costs of food, medicines, and other essentials also being covered. Other health care measures include the introduction of a new bivalent oral polio vaccine, which, combined with a stepped-up vaccination programme, has resulted in a massive decline in new polio cases from 741 in 2009 to 42 in 2010. A more comprehensive immunisation programme is also under way, providing second doses of the measles and hepatitis B (Hep-B) vaccines throughout the country. In two states, pentavalent, a combination vaccine which includes diphtheria pertussis tetanus (DPT), Hep-B, and haemophilus influenza type B, has been available since December 2011, covering 1.5 million children. The pentavalent scheme has led to savings on logistics costs, as well as allowing greater convenience for mothers; given its success, the programme will undoubtedly be rolled out – in phases – across the rest of the country. In the areas of medical education and training too, in the past two years alone the government has founded 46 new medical colleges, as well as providing 8,577 more medical seats and 8,181 advanced training seats.

A current focus of the health system is to build a range of partnerships aimed at reaching out to sectors of society that are underserved, or even unserved in the field of medical care, as well as striving to improve the overall quality of care. One example of this is a programme to improve menstrual hygiene, especially among tribal and rural adolescent girls; this can be achieved through the simple provision of sanitary towels, which are very inexpensive, costing only 1 rupee (less than 2 yen or 2 US cents) per piece. This programme has its roots in the voluntary sector: N. Balagopal, executive chairman of the Confederation of NGOs of Rural India, was the first to meet the need for sanitary products, and in doing so he was able to generate employment for disadvantaged young women, who manufacture the sanitary towels in micro-enterprises. This enterprise was later picked up by government programme managers.

India is also seeking to build international collaborations in several areas, including medical research, academic collaborations, telemedicine, and skill building. Towards this, the Indian government has encouraged foreign direct investment (FDI) in the opening of hospitals by placing such investments on the automatic route. It has favoured public–private partnerships, and there have been proposals for the computerisation and electronic networking of health facilities which have come out of collaborations with non-resident Indians and their companies, and which have done a great deal to bring Indian computer skills up to world standards.

Regulation in health and medicine: cost-control measurement

The spectacular growth of medical care in India is undeniable, but it has been accompanied by hushed and not-so-hushed rumours of unethical practices. There have been accusations regarding the alleged inappropriate use of medical procedures to get money from insurance companies, the individual's employer, or other payers. Given the growth in private medical care and the massive government spending in an attempt to reverse the relative decline in state care, even in the midst of the ballooning fiscal deficit, perhaps there is a middle ground that has not been given due consideration. This middle way entails having private provision of medical care, but in a properly regulated framework where unethical or excessive billing practices are curbed.

The reality of the predominance of the private sector as a source of health care funding in India presents formidable challenges to attempts to control costs. The huge gap in access to health care in terms of hospital beds between rural and urban communities, especially those Indians in rural central India, also serves to highlight the underlying trend towards health care inflation. While the overall cost of private health care in India has not yet reached the levels seen in the US, unless an intervention mechanism is put in place to control costs, the predominance of private health care will seriously hamper the drive towards universal coverage embarked on by the new India.

At the root of the desire to ensure that cost recovery is as rapid as possible is the high cost of capital required to implement the latest technologies and equipment in medical institutions, alongside the recurring costs of associated high-wage providers, including teams of doctors, nurses, and technicians. This issue is exacerbated by the fact that the current interest rates for bank financing in India, at around 13 per cent, are astonishingly high. These concerns add to the pressure to bill insurance companies etc. and to carry out procedures that, whilst not illegal or necessarily harmful, are not necessary; this is something of a grey area in medicine in India (but also in many other countries). To regulate this sort of problem is particularly difficult, because of information asymmetry between provider and customer/patient, and entities such as the Medical Council of India and other professional bodies have no practical means by which to do so. Even the high rate of interest is surprising: given that the world is fast becoming a global marketplace and that there are many institutions that create monetary policy – some of those policies being tighter than others – it seems strange that this has not played out to provide a reasonable interest rate. Finally, in an increasingly sensitive financial marketplace, there is constant pressure to add to net income in order to placate providers of capital, the financial market, and indeed the ownership; this all adds to the pressure to recover costs and increase income by whatever means necessary. This leads to a scramble to increase the revenue of hospitals by charging for every possible procedure, diagnostic test, and even slightly justifiable hospital stay, among other means. The majority of those belonging to the higher social strata – including high government officials, corporate bureaucrats and technocrats, and ministers – avail themselves of medical facilities from such private institutions.

The services offered by public government hospitals have generally failed to equal those of many private health care institutions, with public hospitals facing difficulties in areas such as cleanliness, queue management, logistics, timeliness, and avoiding a level of confusion that might bewilder foreign visitors. Given the perhaps more organised care offered by many private institutions, large numbers of people who are in employment and whose health care costs are thus covered by their employer and/or insurance company are voting with their feet and using private health care services; this is particularly true of people living in cities. However, it is important to bear in mind that whilst this includes millions of people, as a proportion of the total population of India the number of people turning to private health care is still small.

The effective deployment of information technology (IT) in health care service processes could potentially serve as a tool to counter cost-related pressures and offer an acceptable means of monitoring analysis and intervention, which would keep universal health care goals in reach for all. Health care auditors, consultants, the government, and insurance companies are indeed able to use IT data analysis tools to keep tabs on increasing health care billing by monitoring spending through the mining of data from billing records. The analysed data can be used to audit spending and thus control frivolous cost increases. In the same way as significant financial savings have been made in business through processes of internal control, or in energy through the use of IT-based energy monitoring and control, health care processes can be streamlined by the use of IT, reducing costs. Such a system would integrate preventative measures such as screening and the enforcement of regular health check-ups into wider health processes, preventing future health care costs to insurance companies, the government, and individual households that pay for health care.

Harnessing the power of IT for health care service processes

IT has been heavily utilised for core business processes for some time now, and the Indian workforce in the technology sector has supported this global trend in the role of a major outsourcing centre. In terms of countering the pressure of cost increases in health care in India, an important means for health care coverage providers – such as insurance companies and the government – is tools that extract and analyse data from health care systems; such tools may also provide mechanisms through which auditors and care providers can improve efficiency and effectiveness in health care service processes.

If they are to achieve quality, value for money, and effectiveness, health care providers and auditors will need to make use of information technology and specialised analytical packages to achieve a greater depth and breadth of coverage regarding medical and health care facilities and services. In particular, in rolling out universal coverage, continuous and automated monitoring and course corrections will be essential to prevent waste and fraud. The power of IT also has the potential to open up new opportunities and give rise to new industry. Health care providers, such as nursing homes, that are at present disparate and operated by numerous NGOs and the voluntary sector – often to an extremely high standard – could be connected to other institutions, such as the insurance reimbursement system or the saving schemes of financial institutions, through the increased connectivity made possible by database technology.

Recently, a news story broke that attracted worldwide attention. It concerned two companies: Apollo Hospitals – a renowned chain of health care facilities in India, which increasingly serves the market for medical tourism from industrial countries – and HealthNet Global, an IT company. Through a microfinance company, Equitus, Apollo and HealthNet Global have started to offer telemedicine services to the poor for only $1, in a scheme that has reached 8 million poor people. This example effectively illustrates the potential of the private sector to extend coverage to the poor and how the power of IT can facilitate this through the formation of strategic alliances between able and willing participants. In harnessing the power of IT, a great deal of value is created for the following segments:

1 The monitoring and management of chronic disease
2 A mix of the traditional Indian system and modern medicine – a unique niche in India

3 Rural health care challenges – personnel monitoring and enforcement
4 The distribution of tablet PCs in rural areas

Chronic non-communicable diseases

By 2020, India will be among the countries with the largest incidence and prevalence of non-communicable diseases (NCDs). Many chronic non-communicable diseases are caused by lifestyle; one problem particularly pertinent to the Indian case is smoking, which has been endemic for generations, and the ill effects of which are clearly visible throughout the country. Another such problem is propensity to truncal obesity, which, combined with a diet that is high in sugar and fat, has led to diabetes being among the commonest ailments in people over 40 years of age.

In response to the global problem of NCDs, the United Nations General Assembly held a special session on the topic in September 2010, and to tackle the problem in India, the government launched the National Programme for Prevention and Control of Cancer, Diabetes, Cardiovascular Diseases and Stroke (NPCDCS), and the National Programme for Health Care of the Elderly. The programme is currently in the pilot stage, with projects being trialled in 100 of the most remote and backward districts in the country, spread over 21 states and reaching 100–150 million people; the cost of this is approximately $245 million.

India is organised into 29 states and 7 union territories; these states and union territories are further subdivided into 640 administrative districts, which were covered by the 2011 Census of India. The average population of Indian districts is in the millions, but there are districts, especially in the north-east, with populations of fewer than 50,000 people. At present, the NCD programme is being implemented in 100 districts through the introduction of 100 district hospitals and 700 community health centres for the diagnosis and management of cardiovascular diseases, diabetes, and stroke. The district hospitals are also to become a hub for chemotherapy and the early detection of cancer. Further, in view of the impending explosion in cases of diabetes, metabolic syndrome, and hypertension, the scheme is to provide screening for diabetes and hypertension for everyone over 30 years of age (as well as pregnant women of all ages) at 20,000 subcentres in the 100 districts. Covering 100–150 million people as it does, the government programme to combat NCDs is the largest of its kind attempted anywhere in the world.[5] Given the vast number of patients, combined with the fact that they require long-term chronic care management, cost control is essential, as is making savings wherever possible. This means that the scheme is an ideal target for the streamlining of health care service processes through the use of IT.

A paradox: hunger and undernutrition existing among skyrocketing chronic diseases

The National Food Security Bill passed in 2013 is to provide for food security to 75 per cent of the rural and 50 per cent of the urban population with a focus on the nutritional needs of children and pregnant and lactating women. It entails providing subsidised food grains to approximately two thirds of India's 1.2 billion people. Eligible beneficiaries are to be able to purchase 5 kilograms per person per month of cereals at the following prices:

>Rice at 3 India rupees (INR) (5 yen or 5 US cents) per kg
>Wheat at INR 2 (3.3 yen or 3.3 US cents) per kg
>Coarse grains (millet) at INR 1 (1.6 yen or 1.6 US cents) per kg.

Further, pregnant women, lactating mothers, and certain categories of children are eligible for daily free meals.

Proponents of the bill see it as being able to largely end hunger and undernutrition, while opponents point to the problems in the public distribution system and alleged 'fiscal irresponsibility'. Nevertheless, the debates highlight the paradox of old threats such as malnutrition coexisting with a rising tide of chronic NCDs, thus doubling the challenge to public health.

A unique niche in India: mixing the traditional Indian system and modern medicine

The wellness market in India is estimated to be worth more than $2 billion and has a projected growth rate of around 33 per cent. Worldwide, the health and wellness movement is drawing on components of traditional Indian medicines such as ayurveda, siddha, and yoga, and the domestic and export potential of these medicines could be boosted further by efficacy studies. However, a dearth of resources for those studies has made it difficult to scientifically document and analyse the impact of these traditional medicines, meaning that the proof of their value remains in the realm of assertions, dependent on anecdotal evidence accumulated over centuries. This type of evidence is in itself powerful but is not necessarily sufficient to secure entry into pharmacopoeia or diagnostically related groups, or to be covered by insurance reimbursement schemes.

This situation makes India an ideal subject for the creation of a unique health care system that offers a rich mix of traditional and modern medicine. Such a system is only possible where there is modern technology for monitoring, data mining, and the analysis of various health parameters,[6] as well as hardware devices that can be used to collect clinical data in a systematic way in order to present acceptable scientific evidence to health care providers, patients, contributors, regulators, and policy makers.[7] For India, tradition is a strong asset – of both the country and its people – and in light of this, it is essential that the emerging new health care system utilises this ancient wisdom in providing quality health care that is accessible to all.

Rural health care challenges: personnel monitoring and enforcement

There have been debates concerning the issue of medical doctors, nurses, and other personnel not wanting to stay in isolated regions: despite having been posted in a remote location and continuing to be paid a government salary, medical personnel often migrate back to cities for personal, family, and financial reasons. In some rural districts and low-income states, it is estimated that up to 50 per cent of staff are on leave at any given time. To counter the effect of this absenteeism, proposals have been floated to train people as health workers with the capacity to diagnose and treat 'common ailments'. Getting a professional consensus on this idea will not be easy, as it is very controversial among the medical and nursing professions, with many doctors and nurses questioning some of the components of the scheme on professional grounds, while the government attempts to cater to the felt needs of communities that, at present, are not receiving adequate care provision. To avoid the difficulties raised by this proposal whilst still tackling the problem of absent staff, an alternative solution could be sought in IT-based controls. Such controls could be put in place to track the non-attendance in the workplace of salaried personnel, thus creating incentives to actually turn up to work.

Enhancing patient care based on protocol and data evidence

Further to the issues raised above, there are signs that there may be some loss of faith in public hospitals, even amongst the poor, because of concerns regarding quality. In light of this, it is clear that a mere increase in spending will not be enough to bring back widespread trust in the system; rather a whole host of complementary steps are required to boost the quality of care provided. Yet, in spite of this apparent lack of faith amongst the poor, there is evidence that some government hospitals do indeed offer primary- and secondary-level treatment to those who cannot afford it elsewhere. Thus we can see that it is not only the history of medical care that has to be dealt with, but its reality and perception too.

One means of improving patient care could be to set up protocol-based care and ensure that treatment is supervised by at least two medical doctors; emphasis should be placed upon accurate diagnosis, cost-effective management, and the availability of a range of treatment choices that can be calibrated against a patient's ability to pay. Quality of patient care could also be enhanced by implementing institutional standards of facilities and care, audits, and improvements to professional attitudes in private hospitals; the unempathetic attitude of professionals in medical institutions – including the often harsh attitude of non-medical staff towards poor patients – is a problem in public and private hospitals alike. Further, decision making in hospitals should be based on the quality of work and not return on equity, especially in those institutions that claim non-profit and tax-exempt status. Similarly, licensing and licence renewal for hospitals should also be carried out on this basis.

Insurance programmes: a step towards universal coverage

Various attempts have been made to encourage more people to obtain health insurance, but so far to little effect. For the very poorest among the population, various groups and organisations offer coverage. The Self–Employed Women's Association (SEWA) – founded by Indira Gandhi Prize winner Ela Bhatt – provides

Table 5.3 Net earned premium in health insurance, 2008–9

New India Assurance	$244 million
United	$162 million
National	$161 million
ICICI Lombard	$157 million
Star Health	$72 million

Other providers include, amongst others, Bajaj Allianz, IFFCO-TOKIO, Royal Sundaram, Reliance, Cholamandalam, and Tata AIG.

Source: Health Insurance in India: A Review. *The Insurance Times*, 2009

inexpensive life, hospitalisation, and asset insurance to the 1.3 million working women who are its membership. Similarly, the Confederation of NGOs of Rural India (CNRI) and the Life Insurance Corporation of India (LIC) have teamed up to offer affordable life and health insurance. Another means of obtaining medical coverage is to open a fixed deposit with the SEWA Bank – the interest is then used to pay the premium. However, the benefit from such coverage is extremely limited, at just Rs 2,000 (around $33) per person per year. The sectors of society that are the target clientele of such schemes are precisely those sectors that would benefit were government institutions to step up coverage and service, as they are poor or abjectly poor. Indeed this is the justification for the fact that a steep increase in government spending is being seriously considered despite rising concerns regarding the fiscal deficit, which currently stands at around 5 per cent of GDP. For those who are employed in salaried positions or who have substantial incomes and thus do not fall into the category of poor, a range of medical care options are available, with at least 15 major insurance companies competing for business.

From historical experience to the emerging subject of public health in India

With a level of foresight far ahead of its time, in British India the Bhore Committee,[8] headed by Sir Joseph Bhore, recommended the integration of preventive and curative services throughout the health services. It advocated an intersectoral approach, the provision of training in preventive and social medicine for all medical students, primary health centres with beds, and fixed ratios of beds per 10,000 population, none of which has ever been implemented; indeed, concepts such as the creation of a village health committee to decentralise and demystify care were first advanced through the Bhore Committee. Later, a series of subsequent committees advised the government on topics such as health institutions, prevention, and care development, and included the Mudaliar Committee, Jungalwalla Committee, Kartar Singh Committee, and Shrivastav Committee. In 1978, the community-based care movement received a big boost from the Alma Ata Declaration of 'Health for all by the year 2000', which was championed by the then director general of the World Health Organization, Dr Halfdan Mahler. At the turn of the century, the declaration was neatly changed to 'Health for all in the 21st century'.

In contrast to these historical proposals, recently there has been some consideration that it may be necessary to split the responsibilities and roles of public health and clinical medicine. This has come about through recognition of the fact that doctors in clinical medicine are already overburdened with clinical practice and have little time, inclination, or, indeed, expertise to take on additional roles as health managers, programme implementors, and supervisors of field workers. Thus the High Level Committee appointed by the Planning Commission (prior to its abolition in 2014) urged the hiring of additional personnel to take care of public health needs and preventative and promotive parts of health. The responsibilities covered by these fields include school health programmes, adolescent health and development, preventive health management, and community-level screening, particularly for the emerging non-communicable diseases. Recently, the government has included preventive care among themes that can be funded through corporate social responsibility as per the new Companies Act of 2013.

Naturally, the operational mode of health and medicine in India will continue to evolve using the available technological infrastructures such as robust smartphones, affordable tablet PCs, more dynamic databases, and data-transmitting electronic hardware in various forms. New technology always becomes affordable eventually, and the new goal is to find its cross-sectoral applications, such as a tool to make universal coverage possible in order to achieve human security, or as a means to strengthen new professionalism and discipline to meet emerging health care needs.

Human security: India and Japan

As has been graphically illustrated by the huge earthquakes and tsunami witnessed in Japan and India (which will be discussed in greater detail below), one emerging subject in public health is how to deal with an unanticipated disaster situation that requires large-scale intervention and lifeline infrastructure. In such situations, partnerships with other countries are critical to saving as many lives as possible, and such partnerships serve to open up further collaboration and knowledge-sharing that is useful not only for disaster preparedness, but also for social development; these things are also the building blocks of social security. Interestingly, rural development in India and disaster management in Japan share common challenges and goals for the future: lifelines such as power, water, communication, and infrastructure become public health issues in situations where millions of human lives are at risk. In light of this, this section draws comparisons between disaster management in Japan and rural development in India (with a focus on coastal communities) with regard to the public health concerns arising in these situations and the ways in which IT may be used to alleviate these problems.

The horrific sequence of events that followed from the earthquake and tsunami that hit Japan in March 2011, resulting in a nuclear crisis and the relocation of thousands of survivors from the affected Tohoku region, has come to serve as a poignant example of a severe human security crisis. An estimated 30,000 people lost their lives in the disaster. The problems were compounded by the magnitude of the earthquake (it measured 9.0 on the Richter scale), as well as the proximity of the nuclear plant to the ocean, meaning that the plant suffered damage from both the earthquake itself and the seawater from the ensuing tsunami. India was quick to send a team from the National Disaster Response Force, led by Commandant Alok Avasthy, to take an active role in the emergency rescue and recovery operations that followed the catastrophe. It also sent blankets and other relief goods. The Tohoku prefectural public health team at the time was coordinated by Dr Naruo Uehara, Professor of Medicine and Public Health at Tohoku University. India had faced its own human security crisis following a natural disaster when, in December 2004, the Indian Ocean tsunami killed an estimated 18,000 people, including foreign tourists, and displaced about 700,000 in India alone.

In terms of lifeline infrastructure, there are stark parallels to be drawn between the aftermath of the catastrophic events in Tohoku and what happens every day in millions of rural hamlets and villages in India. In Tohoku, hundreds of thousands of people are having to manage without functioning lifeline infrastructures in terms of phone connections, the supply of electricity and water, poor housing, a weak supply chain for essential goods, and lost or drastically reduced livelihoods. These problems are all faced routinely in significant swathes of rural India.

Special challenges faced by coastal communities

Families living on the 7,517 km of India's coast generally survive through the precarious business of individual fishing, often in overfished waters. These fishermen go out on rickety canoes in the early hours of the morning; their catch is unpredictable and often declining. Thus, coastal villages are often desperately poor and suffer from very weak infrastructures. If they have an electricity supply at all, they are without power for large parts of the day and night, there is little potable water, and housing is unstable and easily washed away. In some areas an opportunity to diversify is afforded by tourism, but the vast majority of those living in coastal villages continue to earn their living through fishing. Women in the community often work as the retail salespeople of the fishing business and also engage in very basic processing operations, such as drying part of the catch for later use or sale. This author served on the coast of Kerala State as a then-young medical doctor, including once in the midst of a cyclone.

For such communities, in the event of dangerous sea conditions there is a need for early warning all along the affected coastline, whether the waves are the result of an undersea earthquake or of strong winds. At the very least, families living on the coast should be able to expect modern warning systems to alert them of such conditions. The growth in the use of mobile phones and social media presents new avenues for crisis management and public communication during public health emergencies and is useful for information-sharing, monitoring, surveillance, and public engagement; such tools would be of great benefit in warning those living in coastal regions of dangerous conditions. However, human security remains elusive for many coastal communities in India.

Electricity, communication infrastructure, and IT for public health

As experienced in Japan following the Tohoku earthquake, and routinely in many parts of India, the loss of electricity paralyses all basic needs, including vital communication infrastructure that is powered by electricity. At such times, decentralised power solutions such as solar-powered chargers for mobile phones and other devices and their base stations become essential. Dependence on a single vast electrical grid is too risky when it comes to managing a disaster situation in Japan, let alone in villages scattered around India, whose land mass is 10 times greater than that of Japan.

In any disaster situation, there are short-, medium-, and long-term humanitarian needs that have to be met. Immediate, short-term needs include fresh water, chlorine tablets for the decontamination of water, water purification equipment, and rehydration solution, all of which are required to combat the threat posed by outbreaks of diarrhoeal diseases following the incident. Similarly, antibiotics and analgesics, rice and other foodstuffs, tents, and clothing are all standard requirements that, time and time again, make up a common denominator of need in countless disasters across the globe. Despite being amidst so much seawater, there is surprisingly little coastal desalination in India, especially that powered by renewable energy, which would provide a reliable water supply in times of crisis. Further, information and communication technology also has a role to play in meeting various needs in the relief effort following a disaster situation. Such technology can assist medical professionals in accessing medical data stored in remote locations, advanced IT-enabled logistics could minimise delays in obtaining the correct supplies, and two-way Internet communications and a telemedicine system can help to make more robust estimates in the overall management of the situation. These are just some of the many ways in which the latest technology can be used to deliver public health interventions in disaster situations, as well as in overcoming existing challenges in rural health development.

Partly in response to the 2004 tsunami, India created the National Disaster Management Authority (NDMA) and a National Disaster Response Force (NDRF) with a 10,000-strong staff. As IT is one of India's core competencies and also an essential component of disaster management, there is an opportunity for such tragedies to lead to a safer future for coastal villages (given the similarities in problems faced by coastal communities and those arising from natural disasters), as well as for greater security in lifelines and infrastructure to arise in India, Japan, and across Asia.

Disaster management involves linking up and drawing on the expertise of

- Medical and public health sciences
- Social sciences

- Engineering
- Electronics and IT networking
- Basic science
- Law
- Laboratory support
- Military or paramilitary support (e.g. NDRF)

Beyond the immediate security issues inherent in the management of natural disasters, human security can be an all-encompassing theme under which to deal with issues such as the infrastructure of lifelines (power, communication, and water), poverty, malnutrition, and ill-health. It is capable of uniting countries, companies, foundations, civil society, and governments. Indeed, the Japanese government has already begun to advocate pan-Asian financial frameworks, and human security is a key point in Japan's official foreign policy.[9] Thus, it is clear that lifeline infrastructure and public health can provide vital bases for further cooperation between India and Japan, leading to increased human security.

Conclusion

Access to health care is a key aspect of attaining human security. In India, attempts are being made to remedy years of neglect of the public health system through tremendous boosts in spending aimed at achieving universal health care coverage. However, an increase in spending alone will not be enough to achieve this goal – it is only one of a range of necessary measures. IT-based tools also have a part to play: they can be used for monitoring and surveillance and to ensure accountability and transparency in the medical system, thus augmenting the outreach of health care coverage to greater numbers of people. The availability of decentralised lifeline infrastructure technologies means that for public health, lifeline infrastructure of electricity, water supply, and communications needs to be considered and these decentralised technologies utilised to ensure human security. Only then will the government's bold dream of universal health coverage become a sustained reality. To this end, the government of India has sought broad involvement, and it is incumbent upon all of us who wish India well, in the spirit of celebrating nearly seven decades of its independence, to join hands in this noble endeavour.

Notes

1 *Faster, Sustainable, and More Inclusive Growth: An Approach to the Twelfth Five Year Plan*. New Delhi: Planning Commission of India, October 2011.
2 *High Level Expert Group Report on Universal Coverage* (K. Srinath Reddy committee). New Delhi: Planning Commission of India, November 2011.
3 Indian Health Statistics Report 2012, in Nassir Ul Haq Wani, Kanchan Taneha, & Nidhi Adlakha, 'Health System in India: Opportunities and Challenges for Enhancements'. *IOSR Journal of Business and Management* 9(2): 74–82.

4 Azad, Ghulam Nabi, Minister of India, Speech at the Pravasi Bharatiya Divas, Jaipur, January 2012.
5 Ibid.
6 Chacko, Sunil & Michael Proschan (January 2009) 'Innovations for Phase IV Clinical Trials for Change in Health Care', *Huffington Post*.
7 Chacko, Sunil (2002) 'Developments in Private Sector Knowledge-Based Entrepreneurship in the South', in S. Fukuda-Parr, C. Lopes, & K. Malik (eds.) *Capacity for Development: New Solutions to Old Problems*. United Nations Development Programme; London: Earthscan.
8 Bhore, Sir Joseph (1946) *Health Survey & Development Committee* (Bhore Committee), Government of (British) India.
9 Ministry of Foreign Affairs of Japan, 2012, personal communication.

6 Being Muslim in India today

Mushirul Hasan

The expression 'Muslim identity' has been in vogue in the Indian subcontinent for well over a century. It was used by Syed Ahmad Khan, the founder of the Muslim University at Aligarh, to lend weight to his educational and reformist mission. Muslim organisations like the All-India Muslim League (founded in December 1906), which in its early years represented just a handful of government servants and landlords, invoked the 'separate' and 'distinct' identity of their co-religionists to stake their claim in the imperial system. Several reformers, publicists, writers, and poets took up the same theme to devise communitarian strategies, advance religious rights and political representation, and promote the vision of a unified, pan-Indian Muslim community. Thus the poet Mohammad Iqbal argued that Hindus and Muslims were in fact aiming at different and, more often than not, conflicting concepts of the future, the 'Muslim demand for the creation of a Muslim India within India, was therefore justified.' Iqbal added, 'I would like to see the Punjab, North Western Frontier, Sind and Baluchistan amalgamated into a single state.' This, he said, appeared to be the ultimate destiny of the Muslims. In March 1940, Mohammad Ali Jinnah, the 'Ambassador of Hindu-Muslim unity', changed course to emphasise the separate and distinct civilisational identity of the Muslims. This was the cornerstone of his 'two-nation' theory and the central plank of the Muslim League's demand for a Muslim nation.

What is clearly discernible in the writings and pronouncements of these individuals and groups is their self-image of being part of a community themselves – a monolithic *umma* – that remained, or was normatively expected to remain, the same across divisions in space and time. This theme was often powerfully expressed across a number of elite scholastic factions, especially of Sunni Islam, for whom Sufi and Shia beliefs in general were just deviations from the norm. Time and again the theme of eternal and unmitigated Hindu-Muslim hostility was echoed; so too was the view that 'internal' differences among groups of Hindus and/or Muslims were secondary and irrelevant to the more fundamental religious cleavage.

The colonial perception of Indian Islam and its followers was remarkably similar. For most British travellers, missionaries, administrators, and ethnographers, Islam was part of the 'great tradition' – codified, rigid, unchanging, and closed to external influences. They cast its followers, whether converted or not, in a specifically Muslim/Islamic mould and defined their identity, regardless of economic status, caste, language, or region, in strictly doctrinaire terms. In the constitutional plans, which broadly reflected colonial assumptions about Indian society, the British government showed no sensitivity to the wide-ranging differences that separated the followers of Islam from one another; though familiar with the great strength of intercommunity networks and syncretic practices, officials were wary of translating their knowledge and understanding into constitutional decrees.

In this context, separate electorates, along with reservation and weightages, gave birth to a sense of Muslims being a religio-political entity in the colonial imagination – of being unified, cohesive, and segregated from Hindus. They were homogenised like 'castes' and 'tribes' and suitably accommodated within political schemes and bureaucratic designs. In consequence, self-styled leaders – mostly drawn from *ashraf* (honourable) families and without any tangible links with the Muslim masses of *ajlaf* (ignoble) – were emboldened to represent an 'objectively' defined community and contend with others for patronage, employment, and political assignments. In this way, separate electorates created space for reinforcing religious identities, a process which was, in both conception and articulation, profoundly divisive. In effect, the act of 1909 (the Morley-Minto Reforms) ingeniously challenged those assumptions, which guided many nationalists to cultivate a pan-Indian identity, and undermined, through a judicious mixture of concessions and guarantees, the broadly secular underpinnings of Indian nationalism. The ideological contours of the future Pakistan were thus delineated by British opinion and policy makers long before Jinnah burst upon the political scene with his insistence on a Muslim nation.

This writer's most recent book, *Moderate or Militant: Images of Muslims*, offers a bird's-eye view of the many different traditions within the broad sweep of Islam across the length and breadth of South Asia: from pan-Islamism to socialism, from an appeal to nationalism to an equally rousing call for Unitarian Islam, and from sectarianism to Sufism, giving a picture of the many Islams. But those who thought in terms of communitarianism or political representation did not understand the people of whom they wrote, and because they did not understand them they falsified them with trappings of the make-believe. They misled Muslims into believing that they had been 'rulers', and that the resurgence of Islam would answer their dilemmas and predicaments.

In his play *You Can Never Tell* (1898), Bernard Shaw heralded the new age through Mrs Clandon. One can say the same about Syed Ahmad Khan, but not about Mohammad Ali Jinnah's arrogant and heartless determination to achieve Pakistan. Similarly, Iqbal's whimsical world was a place of imaginative personal refuge. Some of his poems pass into the realm of fantasy and betray his great emotional immaturity. Possibly he lacked both Syed Ahmad's intellectual strength as a critic of contemporary Muslim inhibitions and Maulana Azad's verve and buoyancy of spirit.

> *Nakarda gunahon ki bhi hasrat ki mile dad*
> *Ya rab agar in karda gunahon ki saza hai*
> [If we are to be punished for the sins we have committed, at least we should be praised for not yearning for the sins we have not committed.]

I

In an important study published in 1989, Farzana Shaikh underlined 'the profound sense of the distinctiveness of being Muslim'. There was, according to her findings, 'an unmistakable awareness of the ideal of Muslim brotherhood, a belief in the superiority of Muslim culture and a recognition of the belief that Muslims ought to live under Muslim governments' (Shaikh, 1989: 230). The elements of Muslim culture that sustained the politics of Muslim representation were also grounded deep in tradition, the sources of which were believed to lie in divine revelation. 'It is this tradition', she concludes, 'that imparted to Muslims in India the body of assumptions concerning the pivotal role of the religious community, its exclusive claim to individual allegiance, the nature of political consensus and the organisation of power in society' (ibid.: 233).

Farzana does not pretend to provide an all-explaining interpretation of the evolution of either 'Muslim identity' or Muslim nationalism. She claims only that 'Muslimness' is an elementary condition of legitimate political power and has constituted for Muslims the ultimate test of representative status and political legitimacy. She discusses the conditions under which Muslims have demanded special consideration in excess of that commonly granted to political minorities. In the process, she challenges old orthodoxies and generates active controversies. This writer does not believe that Muslim communities acquired any special leverage to bargain for a special political status; all was well in the Muslim-majority provinces before the politics of 'separatism' wrecked the cross-communal political networks.

Which elements of Farzana's generalisations are valid and which questionable? It seems that until Farzana's claims are verified through regional and local studies, their accuracy will remain unknown. As one who does not see the world through the prism of my faith and commitment, I approach identity, history, belief, culture, and social mores from a secularised, if not 'secular', position and stress that Muslim identity should not be reduced to a mere rationalisation of normative Islamic discourse. In *Legacy of a Divided Nation: India's Muslims since Independence* (1997) I argued that being a Muslim is just one of several competing identities for any individual; that there has never been a homogeneous 'Muslim India', whether in doctrine, custom, language, or political loyalty; and that to make the most of their potential, Muslims should hold firmly to the idea of a society committed to social justice and freedom.

It is all very well to trace the roots of communal (this term is not used here in a pejorative sense) consciousness, but it is equally important not to lose sight of the significant variations in its articulation, mode of expression, and manifestation. Besides, there were vital differences in the consciousness of the *ashraf* and the *ajlaf*, a fact conveniently ignored by proponents of the two-nation theory. The existence of these categories itself suggests the great social and cultural divide – note the recent demand of Dalit Muslims for reservations. Incidentally, this divide could not be bridged by the poets Altaf Husain Hali or Mohammad Iqbal.

Ayesha Jalal, on the other hand, points out that a decidedly elitist discourse should not be seen as reflective of Indian Muslims or their so-called communal consciousness; nor can the politics of Muslim identity in the subcontinent be reduced to a mere rationalisation of normative Islamic discourse. There is, according to her, 'much variation even within this elitist discourse, not all of which focused on the knotty issue of electoral representation, and still greater evidence of Muslim willingness to differ from rather than defer to the consensus of the community, however construed, in the rough and tumble of practical politics'. Indeed, the problem of 'identity in South Asia has been more complex and nuanced than permitted by the protagonists of the "two-nation" theory of the practitioners of a historiography based on a binary opposition between secular nationalism and religious communalism'.

Notwithstanding the proliferation of scholarly literature in Muslim communities in South Asia, there is still much resistance to the fact that Islam in India, past and present, unfolds a bewildering diversity of Muslim communities and that there is much variety in their social habits, cultural traits, and occupational patterns. Given the fact that 'communal' solidarities are forged at different levels of society for self-defence or self-assertion, much of the discussion in the subcontinent tends to centre around imaginary and invented notions of Muslim cultural homogeneity and continuity.

A simple fact that eludes the grasp of scholars and generalists alike is that Islam came to the subcontinent not in a single time span, but in stages, divided unevenly in different periods; consequently, its diffusion took place in a variety of forms from class to class and from one area to another. The difference in the phases in which people 'experienced' Islam brought with it variations in the nature of the challenges facing its followers in different regions. In its local and regional specificity, therefore, the 'essential' core of Islam, so to speak, was not immune to changes through historical influences. Ordinary Muslims were not, as one is often led to believe, members of a monolithic community sitting sullenly apart, but were active participants in regional cultures whose perspective they shared (Mayer, 1981; Bayly, 1986; Roy, 2006).[1] They took their commitment to Islam not only as one among other values, but also as something which was itself differentiated internally into a number of detailed commitments.[2]

In the terms of a typical Orientalist cliche, 'Islam' is still seen not just as a religion but as a total way of life. It provides, as such, a complete identity, explanation, and moral code for the actions of Muslims. The mere fact of people being Muslim in some general sense is conflated with that of their adherence to beliefs and policies that are described as 'Islamist' or 'fundamentalist'. What these approaches share is the analytic primacy of culture and ideology and the privileged place assigned to Islam. It is thus commonly assumed, both in India and elsewhere, that Islamic religions are essentially distinctive and thus inherently incompatible with Western ideals of democracy and secularism.[3] Islam as a religion is considered to be essentially different from all others in that the concepts of belief and political rule are fused through the unity of *din wa dawla*, the Prophet having both revealed a religion and founded a state. Predicated on this statement is an assumed resistance to secularism.

In reality, the commitment of some Muslim groups to specifically Islamic ideas and symbols does not indicate a unified structure of consciousness or a community acting in unison. What should not be assumed is a monolithic conception of Islamic ideology and practice, a teleology dictating the actions of Muslims, or a general acquiescence in the actions of a few. Instead of considering what political ideas a particular group of Muslims holds, and the relations between these and their social conditions and practice, the reification of Islam in the realm of political ideas leads to essentially circular suggestions that both practice and ideas conform to the 'Quranic political culture' (Mayer, 1981: 496). Scores of local and regional studies reveal how large segments of the Indian population have been integrated with other communities, how their views and responses are more diverse and complex than the statements found within the corpus of received opinion on the subject. These studies illustrate, moreover, the disjunction between the formal ideology of Islam as constituted by certain political groups and the actual day-to-day beliefs and practices of Muslims, and point to those regional and local traditions and cultural features of Indian Islam that were components of, and contributed to, what the liberal and secular nationalities meant by the concept of a composite culture.

The debates on such themes are also exclusively based on writers and publicists who are known to stress the elements of discord and separation, while explanations boldly constructed around secular and pluralist conceptions and counterpoised to the essentialist view of Indian Islam remain neglected in the discourse. For a balanced, objective, and rounded view, it is necessary to explore the terrain of those scholars, artists, and creative writers who contest the definition of Muslim identity in purely religious terms and refute the popular belief that Islamic values and symbols provide a key to understanding the 'Muslim world-view'. It may well be discovered that they, more than anybody else, discovered elements of unity, cohesion, and integration in India's past, sensed the bitter consequences of political identity being built on religious ties, and questioned the conviction (or myth) in certain Muslim circles that the future of Islam was endangered by Hindu nationalism. Their notable contribution in providing historical legitimacy to multiculturalism and religious plurality should not go unnoticed, and their sane and sober voices should not be stifled by the weight of Muslim orthodoxy, Hindu revivalism, and Orientalist discourse.

Who, then, is a Muslim? What, if any, specific identity is associated with Muslims generally and with India's Muslims in particular? Is it divinely ordained or related to features that have always been characteristic of Islamic governments and societies? How important is the Muslim self-image? Is it the outcome of colonial images and 'nationalist' constructions, of treating Muslims as an undifferentiated religious category? To what extent has the post-colonial state also viewed Muslims as an undifferentiated religious entity who are also presumed to represent a separate political entity?

When the first all-India census was tabulated and analysed in 1881, the enumerators found that Muslims numbered only 19.7 per cent of the population. They included a geographically dispersed aggregate of Muslims forming neither a collectivity nor a distinct society for any purpose – political, economic, or social. Out of a total population of about 50 million, Muslims in Bengal spoke Bengali and those in Punjab used largely Punjabi as their language.[4] Those living in Tamil Nadu spoke Tamil; those settled on the Malabar coast – mostly Mapillas – spoke Malayalam. They found Muslims whose religious rituals had a very strong tinge of Hinduism and who retained caste and observed Hindu festivals and ceremonies. In Bengal, where the second largest population (after Indonesia) of rural Muslims in the Islamic world developed between the fifteenth and eighteenth centuries, many Muslim cultural mediators, writing in Bengali, expressed Islam in the local cultural medium as an idiom greatly enriched in the same period by translations of the great Hindu epics, the *Ramayana* and the *Mahabharata,* into Bengali, and the expression of Nath and Vaishnava teachings. In fact, the entry of Muslims into South Asia through so many and such separate doorways then spread over the subcontinent by so many different routes, and the diffusion of Islam in different forms from one area to the other ensured that this religion would present itself in those different forms. Neither to its own adherents nor to non-Muslims did Islam seem monochromatic, monolithic, or indeed mono-anything (Hardy, 1988: 39–40).

This claim is borne out by a report compiled by Justice Mohammad Munir in 1953, following the anti-Ahmadiya (Qadiani) riots in Pakistan. The committee he headed asked the *ulama* to define a Muslim. No two learned divines agreed. The committee's own dilemma was summed up succinctly: 'If we attempt our own definition as such learned divine has done and that definition differs from that given by all others, we unanimously go out of the fold of Islam. And if we adopt the definition given by any one of the *ulama*, we remain Muslims according to the view of that *alim* but *kafirs* according to the definition of everyone else.' In face the enquiry was 'anything but satisfactory'. The report concluded on a wary note: 'If considerable opinion exists in the minds of our *ulama* on such a simple matter, one can easily imagine what the difference on more complicated matters will be' (Hasan, 1997: 12).

The variety of meanings and perceptions in defining a Muslim suggest that boundaries are multiple and that at no time is one boundary the sole definer of an identity. Yet at different times and for different reasons there is a 'relevant boundary' that gains prominence and defines the us/them divide. It tends to reject the 'other' and frequently reinforces itself by defining the 'us' not by any specific positive attributes of its members but by the elements in opposition to the 'other'. This mode stresses the negative, expands elements of separation, and sometimes makes it harder to identify the broader groupings that always exist, albeit in weaker forms (Serageldin, 1994).

II

The us/them divide, created by the institutional and bureaucratic structures introduced by the colonial government towards the end of the nineteenth century, eventually led to the partition of India along religious lines. The following decade was a period of trial and soul-searching for the Muslim communities, especially those that had hitched their fortune to the Muslim League bandwagon but stayed put in their country of birth. How did such people respond to their situation after partition?

The first point that needs to be underlined is that the political and intellectual currents reflected the mixed and diverse aspirations of the highly segmented and stratified Muslim communities. Second, Islamic issues were not the sole concern of educated Muslims; in fact, many were inspired by and wedded to a broadly secularised view of politics and society. The religious and political leadership, too, was anxious to come to terms with the socio-economic consequences of partition, assess the losses and gains, and work out arrangements – in the form of a social contract – with other social and political entities. The secular and democratic regime rather than the Islamic dimension provided the overarching framework to forge new alliances and electoral coalitions. In effect, those holding the reins of leadership had to locate problems and find answers to contemporary dilemmas within the democratic and secular paradigms and seek adjustments not as Muslims per se but as members of a larger Indian fraternity. They had to accept state laws enacted by parliament and not insist on the 'application' of the Islamic law, except with regard to marriage, divorce, and inheritance. After the departure of their British benefactors, who had created their separate political identity and patronised them in order to counter nationalist forces, the remnants of a highly dispirited Muslim leadership had to tread carefully in a world that was fashioned differently.

The Muslim divines themselves, many of whom had steadfastly resisted the movement for a Muslim homeland, realised that Islam was a living and vital religion, appealing to the hearts, minds, and consciences of millions, and setting them a standard by which to live honest, sober, and God-fearing lives (see Hasan, 1997; Troll, 1995: 245–262). Although they nursed many grievances, they did not find much evidence of an organised or concerted attempt to undermine their interests as a 'community'. If anything, Jawaharlal Nehru tried his best, despite stiff resistance from the Hindu right in the Congress Party, to draw Muslims into political and economic structures.

Undoubtedly, the choices and casts within the emerging national theatre were manifold. Muslims could draw on their Indian Islamic inheritance and the secular legacy of the nationalist movement or combine elements from a variety of cultural and political entitlements. In other words, if they were to move forward in their quest for a better life, their representative organisations had to be guided by fresh responses to the challenges facing the nation and not just the community. They had to come to terms with an untested and unexplored social and political reality, for which they were accountable to the nation at large, a point emphasised by Maulana Abul Kalam Azad and the leading *alim*, Husain Ahmad Madani of the seminary at Deoband's Dar al ulum. They had to demonstrate a new political imagination for rewriting their agenda within the ground rules being laid out on the Indian turf. Indeed, the critical issue before them was to strengthen, for their own survival and progress, the existing cross-community networks and to discover new meanings to their existence not in isolation from, but through close interaction with other social and economic entities. They had to find new forms of expression within a secularised idiom and explore fresh avenues to articulate their aspirations, anxieties, and misgivings.

What does one make of 'Muslim identity', an expression widely in vogue but without any clear intellectual underpinnings? It is doubtless true that economic discontent, coupled with escalating violence, lends weight to notions of identity and acts as a catalyst to community-based strategies. Yet Muslim scholars and activists, both before and after independence, have taken recourse to a definition that has rested uneasily on the Islamic concept of a unified *millat* (community). Such a definition will always be problematic – so too its projection in the political arena, more so after 50 years of independence, when the political landscape has changed drastically and new social groups have come to the fore with higher levels of consciousness and greater stakes in the power structures. Community-based politics, which is so often backed and sustained by political parties for electoral reasons, may yield short-term gains, but in the long run is not likely to produce any tangible benefits to the majority of poor, backward, and impoverished Muslims,[5] hence the importance of drawing a sharp distinction between political polemics and the actual realities on the ground.

For Muslim communities, in particular, it is important to reiterate secular positions, oppose the mixing of religion with politics, revive internal discussions on reforms and innovation, and ignore the rhetoric behind pronouncements on 'Muslim identity'. The nature and outcome of a meaningful dialogue along these lines will surely determine the direction of change and progress amongst them in the next millennium. A creative process of reform, initiated by Syed Ahmad Khan and some of his illustrious colleagues exactly a century ago in the small town of Aligarh, can no longer be postponed. For the contemporary Muslim leaders, many of whom are burdened by the past and preoccupied with inconsequential issues, the challenge is not to create 'communal' solidarities but to equip their constituency to compete in the wider world and fashion their lives in the 'Indian environment' as co-citizens in a society where most people conform to democratic and secular values. The turf is tricky, but also negotiable.

Notes

1 See Roy (2006) pp. 45–78 for an incisive conceptual and historical revaluation of Islamisation in Bengal.
2 Akeel Bilgrami, 'What Is a Muslim? Fundamental Commitment and Cultural Identity', *Economic and Political Weekly*, 16–23 May 1992.
3 See, for example, the entry for 'Islam' by Charles F. Gallagher, in *International Encyclopaedia of the Social Sciences*, Vol. 7 (New York, 1972, rpt), especially pp. 215–216.
4 Wikeley (1991): this was written as a handbook for the instruction of 'young officers' on 'the history, customs, etc., of men with whom they are serving'.
5 This is especially true of the recent demand for Muslim reservations in the civil service and education. I agree with Theodore P. Wright, Jr., that it would be more fruitful for the Muslim leadership to 'forgo the hopeless and politically counterproductive campaign for quotas in the civil service and to concentrate on literacy, technical education, and, if need be, FEPC (New York State Fair Employment Practices Commission in the 1950s) to open up the private sector to Muslim employment' (Wright, 1997: 858). 'A New Demand for Muslim Reservations in India', *Asian Survey*, Vol. 37, No. 9 (September 1997), p. 858. See also D. L. Sheth, 'Muslim Reservations: No Provision for Communal Quotas', *Times of India*, 20 September 1997.

Bibliography

Bayly, Susan (1986) 'Islam in Southern India: "Purist" or "Syncretic"', in C. A. Bayly & D.H.A. Kolff (eds.) *Two Colonial Empires*. Dordrecht: Martinus Nijhoff Publishers.

Hardy, Peter (1988) 'Islam and Muslims in Asia', in Raphael Israeli (ed.) *The Crescent in the East: Islam in Asia Minor*. London: Curzon Press.

Hasan, M. (1997) *Legacy of a Divided Nation: India's Muslims since Independence*. Boulder, Colo.: Westview Press.

Mayer, Peter B. (1981) 'Tombs and Dark Houses: Ideology, Intellectuals and Proletarians in the Study of Contemporary Indian Islam'. *Journal of Asian Studies* 40(3): 481–502.

Roy, Asim (2006) *Islam in South Asia*. Oxford: Oxford University Press.

Serageldin, Ismail (1994) 'Mirrors and Windows: Redefining the Boundaries of the Mind'. *American Journal of Islamic Social Sciences* 2(1): 79–107.

Shaikh, Farzana (1989) *Community and Consensus in Islam: Muslim Representation in Colonial India, 1860–1947*. Cambridge: Cambridge University Press.

Troll, Christian W. (1995) 'Sharing Islamically in the Pluralistic Nation-state of India: The Views of Some Contemporary Indian Muslim Leaders and Thinkers', in Y. Y. Haddad (ed.) *Christian-Muslim Encounters*. Gainesville: University Press of Florida.

Wikeley, J. M. (1991, 1st edn, 1915) *Punjabi Musalmans*. New Delhi: Manohar Publications.

Wright, Theodore P. (1997) 'A New Demand for Muslim Reservations in India'. *Asian Survey* 37(9): 852–858.

7 Democracy and violence in India
The example of Bihar

Kazuya Nakamizo

The question

How can we understand violent conflicts in stable democracy? India, the motherland of non-violence movements, has experienced numerous violent conflicts since independence – starting from the tremendous violence at the time of partition to religious riots occurring well into the twenty-first century. The memory of the riots that took place in Gujarat in 2002 is still fresh; they constituted the largest-scale riots seen in the country since independence.

Aside from religious riots, India experiences various kinds of violent conflicts, such as those relating to caste and class. For example, caste riots occurred briefly following the implementation of the Mandal Commission report in 1990 – the extent of violence was relatively small; however, the confrontation between governments and Maoists has recently started to intensify. The 'Naxalite problem' is one of the most serious on the agenda of present governments. On the other hand, India is one of the rare examples among developing countries which have maintained democratic institutions. According to Dahl (1971: 248), India was listed with 25 other countries as 'fully inclusive polyarchies' in 1969. Following Dahl's framework, up to the present among the developing countries there are only four that have not experienced authoritarian rule. Those are Costa Rica, Jamaica, Trinidad and Tobago, and India (except during the brief emergency period). It is understandable then that India takes pride in being 'the world's largest democracy'.

How, then, can we interpret the above-mentioned violent conflicts in Indian democracy? One of the important functions of democracy is to solve conflict within the framework of institutions, without violence. Considering numerous violent conflicts in India, it seems that Indian democracy has failed to meet the requirement of a democracy, despite its proclaimed title of 'the world's largest democracy'. At the same time, attention must be paid to the effects of violence. In India, violent conflicts have not occurred continuously. For example, after the Gujarat riots in 2002, there were no major religious riots for 13 years. The Bharatiya Janata Party (BJP), which bears the responsibility for not containing the Gujarat riots, was defeated twice, in the 2004 and 2009 Lok Sabha elections. It is too simple to say that the Gujarat riots had a decisive influence on the defeat of the BJP; however, it seems to be quite difficult for the government to instigate riots like those seen in Gujarat at this present moment. How can such on-off violent conflicts in Indian democracy be understood?

To consider these difficult questions, this essay uses as a case study the state of Bihar. Bihar is known as one of the so-called *bimaru* ('ill') states of India, and is especially infamous for violence. Before independence, in a chain of communal holocausts starting from Calcutta in 1946, Bihar was one of the scenes of terrible communal riots which resulted in at least 7,000 deaths. Noting that most of the victims were Muslims, Nehru reported as follows, 'The real picture that I now find is quite as bad, and even worse than anything that they (the League leaders) had suggested' (in Sarkar, 1983: 433–434). After independence, large-scale religious riots occurred up to 1990 – for example, the Ranch riots of 1967, the Jamshedpur riots of 1979, and the Bhagalpur riots of 1989–90.

In addition to religious riots, Bihar has experienced caste- and class-related violent conflicts. For example, Bihar was one of the centres of the 'Mandal riots' which followed the announcement of the implementation of the Mandal Commission report in 1990. Regarding class conflicts, left-wing extremists have been very active in Bihar, and as a reaction to this, landlords' private armies have massacred many low-caste and poor peasants since the 1970s. The most brutal private army of upper-caste landlords, Ranvir Sena, emerged in 1994 and killed 300 low-caste, poor peasants in the period until 2005 (Kumar, 2008: 188). Observing the activities of private armies in the 1980s, Kohli wrote as follows: 'If Bihar were an independent country, such conditions of breakdown would by now have precipitated a military coup or external intervention, or some combination of the two' (Kohli, 1992: 225). The activities of private armies in the 1990s were much worse than those of the 1980s.

Interestingly, Ranvir Sena did not commit any major massacres after 2000. Caste riots were a temporary phenomenon in 1990, and since 1990 major religious riots have been successfully contained in Bihar. Although critiques of the then-state government emphasise 'law and order problems' in Bihar, the extent of violence has decreased. Why has this change occurred? What is the most important factor in explaining this change? Examining the extreme case of Bihar, this chapter will consider the relationship between democracy and violence in India. The next section analyses the political process of violent conflicts.

Process of violent conflicts

This section will examine three types of violent conflict: religious riots, left-wing extremist movements (Naxalite movements), and massacres by private armies. These types of conflict are not specific to Bihar alone, but can also be observed throughout India. These kinds of violence are suitable cases for use in considering the relationship between democracy and violence in India. Religious riots will be examined first.

Religious riots

Bhagalpur riots

As mentioned above, Bihar has experienced numerous religious riots since independence. However, there has been no occurrence of major religious riots since 1990. The watershed was the 1989–90 Bhagalpur riots, in which more than 1,000 Muslims were massacred. The Bhagalpur riots were the largest-scale religious riots in the history of Bihar since independence. Why did the Bhagalpur riots occur in 1989–90 and why did they become a watershed? Let us examine the process of the Bhagalpur riots. There are many causes of religious riots and the Bhagalpur riots are no exception. Various factors – including political, economic, and social factors – are generally hopelessly intermingled; however, in the case of the Bhagalpur riots, it is clear that political factors played the decisive role in the process of the riots. Let us briefly expand upon this point. The Bhagalpur riots were triggered by the Ram Shila procession organised by Sangh Parivar, the combined group of Hindu nationalists, in the middle of the 1989 Lok Sabha election campaign.[1] It was the election campaign of the BJP, despite their denial of a connection between the Ram Shila procession and the 1989 election.

Why did the BJP accelerate Ayodhya mobilisation before the 1989 election? To understand the strategy of the BJP, we must follow the development of the BJP (Jaffrelot, 1996). The BJP was formed in 1980 as a successor of Bharatiya Jan Sangh (BJS), which was formed in 1951. Both BJS and BJP are the political wing of Rashtriya Swayamsevak Sangh (RSS), which aims to build 'Hindu Rashtra'. After a long period of being seen as 'untouchable' in Indian politics following the assassination of Mahatma Gandhi by an RSS member, in 1977 the BJS joined the national government for the first time as a constituent of the Janata Party. Although the Janata Party government collapsed following the Jamshedpur riots in 1979, in which the RSS played a decisive role, the former BJS fought in the 1980 Lok Sabha election as the self-proclaimed successor of the Janata Party. After defeat in the 1980 election, the former BJS formed a new party – the BJP.

The experiment of joining the central government made clear the collision between two strategies within the BJP. On one side is a liberal strategy, which was the initiative of moderates represented by Atal Bihari Vajpayee. Aiming to construct another catch-all party like the Indian National Congress (Congress Party), these moderates insisted that the BJP should downplay the Hindu nationalist cause and pay more attention to socio-economic problems in order to gain wider support (Jaffrelot, 1996: 314–320). On the other side is the hardline strategy which insists that the BJP should pursue the Hindu nationalist cause more vigorously to consolidate and expand its support base (Jaffrelot, 1996: 338–368). Initially, the moderates had the upper hand in the BJP; however, the 'liberal approach' lost credibility after the very serious defeat of the party in the 1984 Lok Sabha election. The BJP was able to secure only 2 seats out of 543 in that election.

The BJP was on the brink. Replacing the moderates, hard liners, represented by L. K. Advani, took the initiative in the BJP after 1985 to enable its survival in Indian politics. Sang Parivar accelerated religious mobilisation by highlighting the Ayodhya dispute. The Ram Shila procession, in which Vishwa Hindu Parishad (VHP) activists collected bricks inscribed with the name of Ram (Ram Shila) from villages all over India and carried them to Ayodhya for construction of the Ram temple, was an important ceremony of Ayodhya mobilisation. The Bhagalpur riots were instigated by this Ram Shila procession on 24 October 1989, just a month before the 1989 Lok Sabha election (Jaffrelot, 1996: 369–403).

This essay is not going to go into the detailed proceedings of the Bhagalpur riots, but it will emphasise one important point. The Bhagalpur riots were not only a creation of the BJP's Ayodhya mobilisation, but also a product of the then Congress government's appeasement policy. Let us develop this point. First, the role of the BJP must be clarified. One of the characteristics of the Bhagalpur riots is that they were not confined just to the city area; they spread beyond the city into the vast surrounding rural areas. Without VHP's Ram Shila procession, the Bhagalpur riots would not have happened on such a large scale. As already mentioned, the Ram Shila procession mobilised the rural area in a substantial way and stimulated communal feelings by offering puja and collecting 'sacred bricks'. Second, the Congress governments, especially the Rajiv Gandhi-led federal government, hesitated to stop the Ram Shila procession, fearing the loss of the 'Hindu vote' in the upcoming 1989 election. Even after the outbreak of the Bhagalpur riots, Rajiv Gandhi refused to prohibit the procession.[2] It was not until one week after Rajiv's decision that the Bihar Congress government decided to prohibit it, an action forced by the deteriorating situation.[3] The Congress government's hesitant and half-hearted response uncovered its appeasement policy, which betrayed its long cherished tradition of secularism.

Lastly, Rajiv Gandhi's 'Himalayan blunder' had a decisive impact on the development of the riot. The S. N. Sinha-led Bihar Congress government had replaced the then superintendent of police (SP), who was responsible for the outbreak of the riot.[4] But the then SP and his men were strongly offended by this decision. When Rajiv Gandhi visited Bhagalpur to take stock of the situation, they made a strong demand to repeal the state government's decision, masquerading as an ordinary citizen's petition. Surprisingly, Gandhi accepted their demand and cancelled the replacement of the then SP, who had not paid enough attention to the serious need to contain the riot.[5] It is said that this decision by the prime minister had the effect of instigating the police vandalism. The Logain massacre and the Chanderi massacre, which had the largest and second largest number of victims respectively, both happened after the Rajiv Gandhi visit, with the active involvement of the local police force.[6] One local Muslim said, 'Rajiv Gandhi gave the order to kill Muslims.'[7] At least in the perception of Muslims, Rajiv's decision to cancel the transfer of the problematic SP is directly connected with these massive massacres. This perception has played a decisive role in alienating Muslim voters from the Congress party in the 1989 election.

114 *Kazuya Nakamizo*

Impacts of Bhagalpur riots

The impact of the Bhagalpur riots was grave. Until the 1990 state assembly election, the Congress Party had been the dominant party in Bihar since independence, except for the periods 1967–72 and 1977–80. After the 1990 election, however, Congress lost the dominant position completely. In the present assembly, Congress has only 4 seats out of a total of 243 members. Why has the Congress Party declined so drastically in Bihar? What impact did the decline of Congress have on the development of politics in Bihar after Congress?

Though there are many reasons for the decline of Congress, the response of the government to the riots has had a decisive influence on the political change in Bihar.[8] The Congress Party lost credibility among Muslims, who had traditionally been an important support base of Congress, by failing to contain the Bhagalpur riots, leading to its decline. This section will seek to prove this hypothesis by using data. It is said that the Bhagalpur riots had a substantial influence all over North India, beyond Bihar.[9] In the case of Bihar, an opinion poll conducted by *India Today* reveals that Muslim support for the Congress Party dropped by 12 per cent, and the impact of the Bhagalpur riots is supposed to be behind this.[10] Let us examine the behaviour of Muslim voters by using proportional relationship analysis. Table 7.1 shows the proportional relationship between the percentage of Muslims in each constituency and the percentage of the vote won by the various parties in Bihar.

Congress will be examined first. Regarding the change of mean party vote between the 1984 election and the 1989 election, the proportion constituted by the Muslim population is in direct proportion to the gap between the results of two elections, except in the two constituencies where the Muslim population is over 30 per cent. Concerning the number and percentage of seats won and the valid vote percentage, the proportion of the Muslim population is in inverse proportion to them, as these two constituencies can be classified as deviation cases.[11] The data shows that Muslims had a tendency to feel alienated from Congress, which ultimately caused its defeat. For the Janata Dal (JD), the proportion of Muslims in the population is in direct proportion to the percentage of the valid vote and seats

Table 7.1 Number and percentage of seats won and valid vote percentage by party by Muslim population proportion (1989 parliamentary election in Bihar)[12]

Muslim Population Proportion	INC: 89–84	INC	JD+	BJP
0–9% (13 constituencies)	−22.1	2 (28.6/15.4)	8 (43.6/61.5)	1 (20.9/14.3)
10–19% (32)	−24.5	1 (28.2/3.1)	23 (54.0/74.2)	7 (32.4/46.7)
20–29% (7)	−28.8	0 (24.8/0)	7 (59.2/100)	0 (22.0/0)
30% (2)	−11.8	1 (35.3/50.0)	1 (40.1/50.0)	–
Total number and mean %	−24.0	4 (28.1)	39 (51.7)	8 (28.2)

INC = Indian National Congress; JD + = JD (Janata Dal) + CPI (Communist Party of India) + CPM (Communist Party of India [Marxist]) + JMM (Soren) (Jharkhand Mukti Morcha); BJP = Bharatiya Janata Party.

won, except in two exceptional constituencies (over 30 per cent). This shows that Muslims had a tendency to support the JD, which contributed to the victory of the JD coalition.

This shows that the issue of 'how to respond to the riots' had the strongest impact on the Muslim vote. If 'how to respond to the riots' is interpreted in a broad sense, the Janata Dal made a lot of effort to win the confidence of Muslims. For example, V. P. Singh started his election campaign from Bhagalpur,[13] which was in sharp contrast to Rajiv Gandhi, who started his campaign from Faizabad, close to Ayodhya. V. P. Singh clearly opposed the founding-stone ceremony of the Ram temple in Ayodhya and rejected the campaign with the BJP candidate, although the National Front had seat adjustment with BJP. This attitude is quite different from that of Rajiv Gandhi, who permitted the holding of the ceremony. Shahi Imam of Jama Masjid of Delhi declared his support for the JD, and called for the backing of the JD or secular forces in light of the JD's sincere effort to protect secularism.[14] The majority of Muslims shifted their support from Congress to Janata Dal in the 1989 Lok Sabha election in Bihar. At the state level too, many Muslims supported Janata Dal in the 1990 Bihar state assembly election, which led to the formation of the Laloo Prasad Yadav-led Janata Dal government. It was the Laloo government that consolidated Muslim support by preventing and containing the religious riots. This is expanded upon below.

Bihar after the Bhagalpur riots

Contrary to the previous Congress governments, the Laloo government took firm actions against religious riots. Immediately after the formation of the government, Laloo rushed to the sites of the riots and took firm actions to contain them at their source. He made it clear that the district magistrate (DM) and SP were responsible for the riots, and when the riots happened, he immediately transferred the DM and SP of that district. Laloo never allowed religious processions in an area where riots were likely to happen, in contrast to the previous decision of the Rajiv-led Congress government.[15] As a result, the riots were prevented from spreading, which made clear the contrast of its response with that of the Congress government, which had hesitated to prohibit the procession, ultimately leading to the large-scale riots (Bharti, 1990: 1373). It was the arrest of the BJP chief L. K. Advani in 1990 that made Laloo famous nationwide as the guardian of secularism. Though riots happened in many other states after the arrest of Advani, Laloo succeeded in containing the riots in Bihar.[16] In his 15 years of rule from 1990 to 2005, the Sitamarhi riots posed the most serious threat to Laloo's credentials as a custodian of secularism.[17]

The Sitamarhi riots were triggered by a traditional Hindu festival in October 1992, just two months before the demolition of the Babri Masjit in Ayodhya (People's Union For Civil Liberties, 1992; Engineer, 1992). There are two important points to note in regard to this riot. Firstly, Hindus perceived that the government had a bias against Hindus, not Muslims. In the clash between Hindus and Muslims before the outbreak of the riot, more Hindus were arrested than Muslims, which contributed to such a perception. Additionally, the Laloo government's firm commitment to secularism may have affected this perception. This is contrary to the case of the Bhagalpur riots, in which the local police, especially the SP, were considered as anti-Muslim.

Second, the Laloo government tried its best to contain the riot. Although the number of victims of this riot was around 50, the worst under the 15 years of the Laloo regime, Laloo succeeded in keeping the loss of confidence to a minimum. When Laloo rushed to Sitamarhi to contain the riot, he slapped a police officer who seemed to be non-committal and he himself took the lead in suppressing the riot (Wilkinson, 2004: 202). This act was a real contrast to that of Rajiv Gandhi, who did not ask to take on the responsibility of the problematic SP. In this Sitamarhi riot, Laloo's stern action contributed to keeping the Muslim vote intact for his party. And when nationwide riots occurred after the Sang Parivar demolished the Babri Masjit in December 1992, the Laloo government also succeeded in containing religious riots that followed in their wake, which thus further consolidated the firm support base for his government and enabled it to rule for 15 years despite the nationwide trend of anti-incumbency rule.

In the election of November 2005, the Laloo-led Rashtriya Janata Dal government was defeated by the Janata Dal (United)–BJP coalition. The new government, led by Nitish Kumar, is very careful not to invite religious riots, although BJP is a coalition partner. For example, Kumar declined the offer of the Gujarat chief minister Narendra Modi to attend the oath ceremony. This shows consideration for Muslim votes and his archrival Laloo Prasad Yadav, who never allowed the VHP leader Togadiya to land in Bihar. Although the BJP had been in power as an important constituent, it has become quite difficult to allow religious riots to break out in present-day Bihar.

Left-wing extremism (Naxalite)

The development of the Naxalite movement

Bihar has been a centre of left extremism. At present, Maoists are very active in Bihar and Jharkhand, which separated from Bihar in 2000. The Naxalite movement, which is named after the place where it started – Naxalbari in West Bengal, spread to Bihar in around 1970. Many revolutionaries have devoted their lives to the cause of socio-economic liberation between then and the present.

Considering the relationship between democracy and violence, it is very interesting to examine the development of the Communist Party of India (Marxist-Leninist) Liberation (ML). They initially denied parliamentary democracy totally and believed in armed revolution leading to the 'annihilation of class enemies'. However, after experiencing JP movements and emergency, they changed their tactics gradually to participate in parliamentary democracy. Finally, they succeeded in winning one seat from Bihar in the 1989 Lok Sabha election. Why did ML change its strategy? In order to gain a better understanding of these dynamics, let us examine the party documents since the formation of ML.[18]

According to the Resolution ('Resolution on Elections') adopted in 1968 by the All India Coordination Committee of Communist Revolutionaries (AICCCR), which was the predecessor organisation of ML, they denied parliamentary democracy as a 'positive impediment to the advance of revolutions in general and to revolutions in semi-feudal, semi-colonial countries like India, in particular, which is feudal and not bourgeois' (Ghosh, 1992: 33). Following this sentence, the resolution says:

> The experiences of the last twenty years have taught the Indian people the bitter truth that the parliamentary path as an alternative to the Chinese path of armed struggle chalked out by Chairman Mao perpetuates their shackles of slavery and impoverishes them still further. . . . So, Comrades, our call is 'Down with Elections!' We call upon all revolutionaries and the revolutionary people to come forward and frustrate this sinister counter-revolutionary manoeuvre of reactionary ruling classes and their lackeys, the Dange clique and the neo-revisionists, by raising the slogan, 'Boycott these Elections'.
> (Ghosh, 1992: 33–34)

In this resolution, it is very clear that the basic strategy is to deny parliamentary democracy and vigorously pursue armed revolution. However, the ML changed strategies drastically after the death of Charu Majumdar, who led the 'annihilation of class enemies' strategy. Vinod Mishra, who became the new general secretary in 1975, initiated a new strategy. In 1982 he formed the Indian People's Front as a mass organisation to gain wider support and prepare for participation in parliamentary elections. It was in the Third All India Congress of 1982 that ML formally changed its party strategy. In the Political Organization Report, which was adopted at the Third Party Congress, ML admitted the failure of the 'annihilation of class enemies' strategy and declared to abandon it.

> . . . In many areas annihilation was conducted as a campaign, with a lot of indiscriminate and unnecessary killings, and it got isolated from peasants' class struggle so that no resistance could be built up against police repression, and our struggling areas were smashed. . . . In this context, the declaration in our first Party Congress (in May 1970) – 'Class struggle, i.e. annihilation, will solve all our problems' was definitely wrong.
> (Mishra, 1999: 274)

Adding to this, ML continued its self-criticism, discussing the opportunity it missed to lead the anti-Congress struggle in 1974 as follows.

> . . . Over this entire period of 1974–76, our main drawbacks consisted, firstly, in our failure to link up with the anti-Congress upsurge of students, youth, and all sections of people of Bihar (the leadership of this upsurge was later captured by JP and it degenerated into impotency) and secondly, in our failure, when the movement collapsed with the arrest of leaders and repression on the masses, to provide a new guideline to organize the remnant forces. Although we maintained the political line of building an anti-Congress united

front and upheld our areas as models of the same, we could not link this with the actual anti-Congress mass upsurge.

(Mishra, 1999: 279–280)

What should have been ML's plan of action for the future? Mishra analyses the situation of 1982 and highlights two points (Mishra, 1999: 309). First, 'where red terror is exercised over the class enemies', peasant movements either 'perished or suffered setbacks and are in the process of reorganization'. Second, 'there is a trend of democratic movements of vast sections of the Indian people, movements coordinating various sections of the people and even of nationwide character'. However, 'now there are opposition parties, revisionists, and selfish people who will try to divert these movements' (Mishra, 1999: 309). That's why 'there must come up an all-India people's front basing on the areas of resistance struggle'. It goes without saying that 'all-India people's front' indicates the Indian People's Front.

Although ML set up a mass organisation, its attitude towards election was ambiguous:

> The election question at a certain time may be linked up with insurrection and then you will be forcing elections on the government. In other times, when there are no prospects of slogans for a constituent assembly and provisional revolutionary government getting popular for a long time, you may think of utilizing elections, while in other prospects you should not.
>
> (Mishra, 1999: 310)

After this formal decision, ML candidates participated in the 1985 Bihar state assembly election as independents.

ML changed its attitude towards elections at the fourth All-India Party Congress in 1988. Reflecting on the experience of participating in elections for the past few years, it admitted the utility of elections, saying, 'True, the system of elections itself imposes many a fetter on us; but nonetheless election results are sensitive indicators of our influence over the masses and of the state of our organization' (CPI[ML]/Praveen K. Chaudhry, 1988: 1.7.1). ML then harshly criticised the opponents of electoral participation as follows.

> If we cannot build an organization capable of winning even a few parliamentary seats, how could we ever accomplish the revolution which is a thousand times more difficult? . . . Advocating boycott on the basis of the very nature of the Indian parliament, on the plea of its being more reactionary than European parliaments is simply ridiculous.
>
> (CPI[ML]/Praveen K. Chaudhry, 1988: 1.7.1)

Following this criticism, the party declared the necessity of participating in elections as follows.

> The Party desperately needs a group of resolute and capable representatives in the parliament as well as in State assemblies, because the combination of

mass action outside the reactionary parliament and assemblies with an opposition directly supporting it within these institutions will provide a veritable boost to the revolutionary struggles. The whole party must earnestly strive to make this combination a reality.

(CPI[ML]/Praveen K. Chaudhry, 1988: 1.7.2)

After this resolution, ML fought in the 1989 Lok Sabha election under the banner of Indian People's Front for the first time, and succeeded in winning one seat from Arrah constituency in Bihar. Since 1989, ML had occupied a certain position in the state assembly until they lost seats in the 2010 election. For example, the election of November 2005, ML got 5 seats – 4 fewer than the Congress party.

'Democratisation' of Bihar politics

Why did ML change its attitude toward parliamentary democracy? As Mishra admitted, 'democratisation' has been gradually advanced in Bihar by democratic institutions, especially the institution of elections. Here 'democratisation' does not mean the ordinary usage in comparative politics, that is, the change from a totalitarian/authoritarian regime to a democratic regime. 'Democratisation' here means the change of political and social power structure, in which the centre of power shifts from the upper strata of society to the lower strata, that is, on this occasion, from upper castes to backward castes.

As mentioned above, the Congress Party dominated politics in Bihar up to 1990. The rule of the Congress had the character of being based on upper-caste landlord dominance in Bihar, as the Congress Party relied upon the socio-economic influence of the dominant landed castes (Frankel, 1990b: 502–504). In spite of the small percentage accounted for by the upper castes in terms of the total population (almost 13 per cent), their representation in the legislature and cabinet was overwhelming during the time of the Congress regime (Blair 1980: 68; Srikant, 1995: 25–26; Chaudhary & Srikant, 2001: 325–326). The backward castes expressed their discontent against this dominance of the upper castes. Despite the strength of their numbers (51.3 per cent of the total population), the backward castes were carefully excluded from the centre of power. They thus started to support socialist parties which claimed to support 'social justice', that is, the fulfilment of the reservation policy for the backward castes. The JP movement and the success of the 1977 Lok Sabha and state assembly elections were a second turning point for the rise of the backward castes after the 1967 elections (Frankel, 1990a: 81–106).

In the 1977 state assembly elections, the Janata party defeated Congress, and Karpoori Thakur, who was the leader of the backward castes, became chief minister. As a strong advocate of 'social justice', he succeeded in introducing the reservation system for backward castes in state government institutions, in spite of severe opposition from BJS (Frankel 1990a: 106–111).

The realisation of 'social justice' attracted the backward castes. In Bihar it has become clear, through an analysis of the proportional relationship between the backward castes' share of the population and the share of the votes for socialist parties, that there has been a tendency for the backward castes to support the

Table 7.2 Percentage of valid vote by socialist parties by OBCs population proportion (state assembly election in Bihar: 1977–95)[19]

Percent of OBCs	1977	1980	1985	1990	1995
Below 39% (100)	41.98	17.4	14.84	20.99	23.29
40–49% (44)	48.55	25.79	19.43	25.46	37.95
50–59% (166)	44.43	27.46	25.79	32.54	39.98
Above 60% (14)	47.88	37.87	44.33	47.72	39.60
Average (324)	44.44	24.85	22.70	28.80	34.54

The figures show the vote percentage of socialist parties as follows: in the 1977 election, Janata Party; 1980, Janata Party + Janata Party (Secular: Charan Singh) + Janata Party (Secular: Raj Narain); 1985, Lok Dal + Janata Party. In the 1990 election, the figures show the vote percentage of the Janata Dal (JD). The 1995 figures show the JD alliance: JD + CPI + CPM + JMM (Mardi) + Marxist Coordination Committee.

socialist parties since the 1980 state assembly election (Table 7.2). The proportion of the population made up by Other Backward Classes (OBCs) is in direct proportion to the percentage of the socialist parties' valid vote from the 1980 parliamentary election onwards.

Vinod Mishra and members of ML would have carefully observed this political change. If a parliamentary party can uplift backward castes and get their support, the next target logically would be scheduled castes. If they were to expand their support base to scheduled castes, ML would definitely lose its core support base. In fact, this concern came true after 1990 under the Laloo-led Janata Dal government.[20]

Initially, ML rejected parliamentary democracy as bourgeois and impotent in terms of bringing about socio-economic liberation. 'Bourgeois democracy', however, is slowly changing 'feudal society', and the lower strata have begun to raise their voices under the institutional framework of parliamentary democracy. The self-criticism of ML and its change of strategy can be understood in this context. The 'democratisation' of Bihar politics urged ML to abandon its 'annihilation of class enemies' strategy and participate in elections, the core institution of parliamentary democracy. In short, democratic practice in Bihar has the potential to absorb violent conflicts and solve them under the framework of democratic institutions.

Private armies

The formation of Ranvir Sena

Relating to Naxalite movements, private landlord armies have been active in Bihar since 1970s. Private armies were formed by landlords mainly from the upper and upper backward castes to cope with Naxalite movements. In particular, they feel they need to combat the risk posed by the 'annihilation of class enemies' tactics of Naxalite movements. In the history of private armies in Bihar, the most brutal organisation has been Ranvir Sena, which massacred 300 low-caste, poor peasants between its formation in 1994 and 2005, as mentioned above. This section focuses on Ranvir Sena to consider the relationship between democracy and violence.

Why was Ranvir Sena formed in 1994? Analysing the sequence of events that unfolded in the Belaur village, which was the birthplace of Ranvir Sena, it becomes clear that politics is the most important factor in explaining the emergence of Ranvir Sena.[21] In Bihar, 'democratisation' processes slowly progressed and finally, after the 1990 election, the dominance of upper castes in the state assembly was overthrown (Table 7.3).

The first year in which the number of backward-caste members of Legislative Assembly (MLAs) overtook that of upper-caste MLAs was 1990. In the 1995 election, the gap between upper castes and backward castes was more than 100 seats in a 324-member assembly. The removal of power from upper castes by backward castes constituted an irreversible change in Bihar politics.

At government level, Laloo Prasad Yadav, who is from a backward caste, led Bihar Janata Dal and consolidated his power. As the son of a poor peasant, Laloo was proclaimed the Messiah of the poor. Regarding Naxalite movements, Laloo announced a government policy not to intervene in agricultural conflicts, announcing that 'if the agricultural labourers and landless grab land, police will not fire at them' (Louis, 2002: 139). This was totally contrary to the policy of the previous Congress governments. During the Congress regime, the government harshly suppressed Naxalites with fully armed police forces in order to protect the interest of landlords. Recognising the shortage of police forces, the Congress government urged landlords to arm themselves by giving them gun licences and even set up a shooting training centre for landlords (Das, 1983: 253; Kumar, 2008: 97). In terms of actual operations to smash Naxalites, police forces and private armies cooperated to kill poor peasants who were suspected of being Naxalite.[22]

The situation changed after the collapse of the Congress government. According to the DM of Bhojpur district, in which Belaur village is located, the Laloo government regarded the 'Naxalite problem' more as a socio-economic problem than as a 'law and order problem'.[23] That is not to say that the Laloo government did not suppress Naxalite movements, but the extent of suppression was less than in the former Congress regime. This change of policy was revealed in concrete police actions in the incidents that occurred in Belaur in 1994.

In Belaur village, ML started activities from 1990 onwards and succeeded in organising mainly scheduled-caste agricultural labourers to fight against the

Table 7.3 Caste composition of Bihar state assembly (1967–2005)[24]

Caste	1967	1969	1972	1977	1980	1985	1990	1995	2000	2005
Upper castes	133	122	136	124	120	118	105	56	56	68
Backward castes	82	93	77	92	96	89	117	160	121	112
Number in total	318	318	318	324	324	324	324	324	324	243

oppression of the upper-caste Bhumihar landlords. The decisive incident happened in 1994. The events will not be described in detail here, but the important point is that the police were unable to save the Bhumihar landlords. One Bhumihar landlord was killed accidentally or incidentally by the ML side in a chain of numerous incidents, although ML denied the charge. The police did not take 'effective' measures to prevent the killing, which would have been inconceivable under the Congress regime.

The Bhumihar landlords of Belaur village certainly felt political isolation after 1990. At state level, the government was grabbed by backward castes; at parliamentary constituency level, ML candidate Rameshwar Prasad won in the 1989 election from its own constituency as a Naxalite candidate for the first time in India; at state assembly constituency level, Janata Dal candidate Sonadhari Singh (Yadav caste) won for the second time.[25] Most importantly, ML started activity in 1990, as mentioned above.

It was the ineffectiveness of police in the Belaur incidents of 1994 that led to the materialisation of the upper castes' apprehension. If a government does not have the political will to protect the life and security of an upper-caste landlord, landlords must defend themselves. The commander of Ranvir Sena, Brahmeshwar Singh, explained the reason for the formation of Ranvir Sena as follows: 'Government becomes our enemy. Government doesn't protect life and property of peasants, that's why Ranvir Sena was formed. Peasants have to protect themselves by their own force.'[26] Considering the development of Bihar politics and the detailed process of the formation of Ranvir Sena, it becomes clear that upper castes' perception of insecurity came from the 'democratisation' of Bihar.

Disintegration of Ranvir Sena

It is said that Ranvir Sena initially got support not only from the Bhumihar caste but also from the other upper castes.[27] However, after the Lakshmanpur Bathe massacre in 1997, in which 61 low-caste, poor peasants were massacred by Ranvir Sena, they gradually lost upper-caste support, including Bhumihar support. Since the Mianpur massacre in 2000, in which 35 poor peasants – including Yadavs – were killed, Ranvir Sena have not committed any further major massacres. In 2002, the commander Brahmeshwar Singh was arrested; he allegedly surrendered because of internal conflict within Ranvir Sena. Ranvir Sena has become dormant, and Brahmeshwar Singh was assasinated in 2012.

The disintegration of Ranvir Sena does not mean the end of upper-caste opposition to the Laloo government. They continue to show their will not through violence, but in the ballot boxes. After the 1995 state assembly election in which Laloo consolidated his power base, the upper castes shifted their support decisively from Congress to the BJP alliance (Table 7.4).

The Laloo government was finally defeated in the election of November 2005 and the Janata Dal (United)–BJP alliance formed a new government. It could be said that upper castes have regained their political and social power to a certain extent, though backward castes continue to dominate the power centre (Kumar, 2008: 88–89).

Table 7.4 Voting behaviour of upper castes in Bihar (1995–98), %[28]

	1995 State Assembly	1996 Lok Sabha	1998 Lok Sabha
Indian National Congress	39.1	10.1	8.7
BJP alliance	16.5	59.5	77.6
Janata Dal alliance	20.9	29.1	11.6
Rashtriya Janata Dal alliance	NA	NA	Negligible

The phenomenon of Ranvir Sena is an extreme expression of the 'democratisation' of Bihar. Their violence was terrible, but their activities did not continue for long. Some upper castes, mainly Bhumihar, supported their activities, but that did not last long either. On the other hand, their opposition to the Laloo government has been repeatedly expressed in elections. Even Brahmeshwar Singh ran in the 2004 Lok Sabha election from jail and gained third position. The difference between Singh and the ML candidate Ram Naresh Ram was just 706 votes. Considering the rise and fall of Ranvir Sena, it is possible to say that democratic institutions have the power to absorb violent conflicts.

Conclusion

This essay examined three types of violent conflict, that is, religious riots, Naxalite movements, and massacres by the private armies of landlords. The requirements of democratic politics played an important role in inviting these conflicts. In the case of the Bhagalpur riots, the 1989 election itself was a decisive factor. Ayodhya mobilisation by the BJP and the appeasement policy used by Congress to win the election together led to the Bhagalpur riots. In the case of Naxalite movements, the dysfunction of democracy was the major cause. Indian democracy failed to solve poverty and inequality in the 20 years following independence, which led to the spread of the Naxalite movements. Lastly, regarding the emergence of Ranvir Sena, the 'democratisation' of Bihar had a deep impact. The phenomenon of Ranvir Sena is an extreme manifestation of the discontent of upper castes who felt isolated under the Laloo regime. Examining these three cases, it is undeniable that democracy has some role in invoking violence. It may then be asked, does democracy or 'democratisation' just contribute to the wilds of violence? As observed in the three cases examined in this chapter, the violent conflicts did not last for a long time. In Bihar, politicians and political parties recognised that religious riots could severely damage their political future. Though BJP is in power, the present Nitish Kumar government puts a great deal of effort into not inciting religious riots; the situation is different from the time of the Janata Party government in 1979.

Similarly, ML may not return to its 'annihilation of class enemies' strategy, as general secretary Dipankar Bhattacharya criticised Maoists who presently adhere to the armed struggle line (Bhattacharya, 2006). Reflecting on the failure of the annihilation strategy, ML now thinks that it can expand the support base for its movement by participating in parliamentary democracy. Lastly, the leaders of Ranvir Sena have ambitions to become politicians. As in the typical case of

Brahmeshwar Singh, many of them do not want to finish their lives as mere murderers. In Bihar, many criminals or those who have a criminal background become politicians ('criminalisation of politics'), and the leaders of these private armies are no exception.[29] The 'criminalisation of politics' is usually condemned as a crisis of democracy; however, from a different point of view, it also can be said that democracy has the power to absorb violent elements and violent conflicts.

This essay has focused on the case of Bihar and examined only three types of violent conflict. In this sense, its argument has a natural limitation in commenting on the relationship between democracy and violence in India. However, these violent conflicts are not specific to Bihar only, but can be observed all over India, and it is helpful to table an extreme case such as Bihar. Democracy has the potential to absorb and solve violent conflicts even in one of the most violent states in India. An experiment of Bihar indicates that Indian democracy has the possibility to overcome violence in future.

Notes

I am very grateful to Prof Imtiaz Ahmad of Jawaharlal Nehru University, Prof Kamal Mitra Chenoy of JNU, and Prof Achin Vanaik of Delhi University for their thoughtful guidance and great help. In the Bihar survey, the Asian Development Research Institute, especially Dr Prabhat P. Ghosh and Dr Shaibal Gupta, provided me with a great deal of insightful guidance and very kind help. Without their support, I would not have been able to conduct my work. Of course, *I take full responsibility for any errors*, factual or those of interpretation, in the content of this article.

1 To understand the Bhagalpur riots, the following reports and articles informed this study, adding to the fieldwork that was conducted in 2004. See: People's Union for Democratic Rights (1990), People's Union for Civil Unity (n.d.), Bhagalpur Riot Inquiry Commission (1995), Bharti (1989), Dogra (1990), Engineer (1990, 1995), Jha (1991). I have published a detailed analysis of the Bhagalpur riots in Nakamizo (2012: 159–203) and a summary of it in Nakamizo (2013: 79–91). The analysis of the Bhagalour riots in this essay is based on these works.
2 *The Hindustan Times*, 27 October 1989, p. 1.
3 *The Hindustan Times*, 4 November 1989, p. 1.
4 *The Hindustan Times*, 25 October 1989, p. 1; *India Today*, 15 November 1989, p. 77; Bhagalpur Riot Inquiry Commission (1995: 94).
5 Many reports and news reports mention this incident: People's Union for Democratic Rights (1990); Engineer (1990: 306); *Frontline*, 11–24 November 1989, pp. 25–26. I also confirmed this through interviews with Mr Ali Anwar (a famous journalist, presently a member of Rajya Sabha from Janata Dal(U): 15 August 2004); a resident of Parbatti (17 September 2004); and a Muslim professor (22 August 2004). Buta Singh, the then home minister, however, denied this incident (*The Hindustan Times*, 28 October 1989, p. 24).
6 People's Union for Democratic Rights (1990: 59–60, 63–65); Engineer (1995: 1731); *India Today*, 15 March 1990, p. 63. I confirmed this through interviews with the Muslim survivors of the Logain (9 September 2004; 20 September 2004) and Chanderi massacres (20 August 2004; 17 September 2004).
7 Interview with local villagers near Logain village (20 September 2004).
8 I develop this hypothesis in detail in Nakamizo (2012: 205–232).

9 Interview with Dr Ram Jatan Sinha (the then president of Bihar Pradesh Congress Committee: 6 and 9 March 2005). Dr Sinha told me that it was the Bhagalpur riots that alienated Muslims from Congress in North India.
10 The percentage of Muslim support for the Congress is actually unclear, since this varied greatly in previous elections. It thus averaged at least 58.3 per cent in 1984 compared with 22.6 per cent in 1989, suggesting a far sharper decline. See, 'The Rajiv Whirlwind', India Today, 31 December 1984, pp. 26–29; 'The Voters' Profile', India Today, 15 December 1989, pp. 52–53.
11 The two deviant constituencies are Kishanganj and Khatihar. In Kishanganj, the most powerful candidate, Syed Shahabuddin, could not file nomination papers due to a procedural error. In the constituency of Khatihar the Congress candidate was Taliq Anwar: a rising Muslim leader. In the 1989 election, his high vote percentage can be attributed to his own personal popularity, not that of his party. The Hindustan Times, New Delhi, 1 November 1989, p. 1; 11 November 1989, p. 7; 11 November 1989, p. 12; India Today, 15 November 1989, p. 21; Election Commission of India (1977–1999).
12 Data calculated by the author based on the Election Commission Report and Singh (1998: 60–88). The first column, 'INC: 89–84', shows the figure after subtracting the mean vote of Congress in 1984 from the mean vote of Congress in 1989. The remaining columns show the number of seats won, the valid vote percentage, and the percentage of seats won (from left to right) of the various parties.
13 *India Today*, 30 November 1989, p. 12.
14 *The Hindustan Times*, 12 November 1989, p. 1.
15 Regarding the Nawada riots, *The Hindustan Times* (17 March 1990, p. 13) praises the Laloo government's rapid action.
16 *Frontline*, 10–23 November 1990, pp. 26–27; *India Today*, 30 November 1990, p. 62; Bharti (1991: 91–92).
17 Regarding the Sitamarhi Riots, see People's Union For Civil Liberties (1992); Engineer (1992). I have published a detailed analysis of the Sitamarhi riots in Nakamizo (2012: 283–289) and a summary of it in Nakamizo (2013: 95–96). The analysis of the Sitamarhi riots in this essay is based on these works.
18 I consider this question in detail by comparing Bihar with Andhra Pradesh (Nakamizo, 2009).
19 Data compiled by the author from Election Commission of India reports (1977–1995). For detail, see Backward Classes Commission (1980). Figures in parentheses in 'Percentage of OBCs' shows the number of constituencies.
20 According to Pradeep Jha, a member of Central Working Department of ML, ML was deprived of the support of scheduled castes by Laloo, but it was a temporary phenomenon. Scheduled castes soon realised that Laloo's promise was just lip service, and they returned to ML (interview with Mr Pradeep Jha [Central Working Class Department], 24 October, 2002).
21 See Nakamizo (2010) for an examination of the detailed process of the formation of Ranvir Sena.
22 Patnaik (1990) reports the cooperation between police and landlords in the Danwar-Bihta massacre in which 23 ML supporters were killed by local landlords. The victims were just going to a polling booth to cast their votes in the 1989 Lok Sabha election.
23 Interview with Mr Sanjay Kumar, District Magistrate, Bhojpur District (7 September 2003).
24 Sources: data up to and including the 2000 election, Srikant (2005: 37). Data for the 2005 election supplied by the Asian Development Research Institute, Patna (unpublished).
25 When Sonadhari Singh visited Belaur village after the 1990 election, he was slapped by Bhumihar landlords using a chappal. According to Bhumihar landlords, he was slapped because he belonged to a different caste (Yadav caste) and different party (Janata Dal).

This episode shows the strong hostility of the Bhumihar caste to the 'democratisation' of Bihar. Interview with Bhumihar landlord in Belaur village, 25 August 2003.
26 Interview with Brahmeshwar Singh, November 2002.
27 Interview with Mr Sanjay Singh, *Hindustan Times*, 29 October 2002.
28 Data from V. B. Singh, 'Class Action', *Frontline*, 2 June 1995, p. 101; and Kumar (1999: 2477).
29 Kalayan Chaudhri, 'Bloodied Bara Naxalite Revenge in Bihar Village', *Frontline*, 13 March 1992, pp. 25–26.

References

Reports/party documents

Backward Classes Commission (1980) *Reservations for Backward Classes. Mandal Commission Report of the Backward Classes Commission*. Delhi: Akalank Publications.
Bhagalpur Riot Inquiry Commission (1995) *Report of Bhagalpur Riot Inquiry Commission 1989 (Honourable Chairman's Report)*. Bihar, Patna: The Superintendent Secretariat Press.
CPI(ML)/Praveen K. Chaudhry (1988) *Documents of the Communist Party of India (Marxist-Leninist) as Adopted by the Fourth All India Party Congress*. Delhi: 1–5 January.
Election Commission of India (1977–1999) *Statistical Report on General Election to the Legislative Assembly of Bihar*. New Delhi: Election Commission of India.
Patnaik, B. N. (1990) *Harijan's Franchize – An Alibi of Class Conflict (A Case Study of Dhanwar-Bihta Massacre)*. Patna, Harijan Study Centre: A. N. Sinha Institute of Social Studies.
People's Union For Civil Liberties (1992) *Sitamarhi Riots: The Truth*. Patna.
People's Union for Civil Unity (n.d.) *The Statement of Fact, Opinion, Suggestions* (Bhagalpur riot). Bihar: State Unit.
People's Union for Democratic Rights (1990) *Bhagalpur Riots*. Delhi: April.

Secondary Sources

Bharti, Indu (1989) 'Bhagalpur Riot and Bihar Government'. *Economic and Political Weekly [EPW]* 2 December: 2643–2644.
Bharti, Indu (1990) 'Bihar: New Government, New Hope'. *EPW* 30 June: 1373–1374.
Bharti, Indu (1991) 'Survival against Heavy Odds'. *EPW* 19 January: 91–93.
Bhattacharya, Dipankar (2006) 'Trail Blazed by Naxalbari Uprising'. *EPW* 16 December: 5191–5194.
Blair, Harry Wallace (1980) 'Rising Kulaks and Backward Classes in Bihar – Social Change in the Late 1970s'. *EPW* 12 January, 15(2): 64–74.
Choudry, P. K. & Srikant (2001) *Bihar mem samajik pari-vartan ke kuch a-yam (1912–1990)* [Some Aspects of Social Change in Bihar]. Patna: Vani Prakashan.
Dahl, Robert A. (1971) *Polyarchy: Participation and Opposition*. New Haven, CT.: Yale University Press.
Das, Arvind N. (1983) *Agrarian Unrest and Socio-economic Change in Bihar, 1900–1980*. New Delhi: Manohar Publications.
Dogra, Bharat (1990) 'Bhagalpur: Communal Violence Spreads to Villages'. *EPW* 20 January: 145.
Engineer, Asghar Ali (1990) 'Grim Tragedy of Bhagalpur Riots: Role of Police-Criminal Nexus'. *EPW* 10 February: 305–307.
Engineer, Asghar Ali (1992) 'Sitamarhi on Fire'. *EPW* 14 November: 2462–2464.

Engineer, Asghar Ali (1995) 'Bhagalpur Riot Inquiry Commission Report'. *EPW* 15 July: 1729–1731.
Frankel, Francine R. (1990a) 'Caste, Land and Dominance in Bihar – Breakdown of the Brahmanical Social Order', in Francine R. Frankel & M.S.A. Rao (eds.) *Dominance and State Power in Modern India: Decline of a Social Order,* Vol. I. Delhi: Oxford University Press.
Frankel, Francine R. (1990b) 'Conclusion: Decline of a Social Order', in Francine R. Frankel & M.S.A. Rao (eds.) *Dominance and State Power in Modern India: Decline of a Social Order*, Vol. II. Delhi: Oxford University Press.
Ghosh, Suniti Kumar (1992) *The Historic Turning-Point: A Liberation Anthology*, Vol. I. Calcutta: S. K. Ghosh.
Jaffrelot, Christophe (1996) *The Hindu Nationalist Movement and Indian Politics, 1925 to 1990s: Strategies of Identity-Building, Implantation and Mobilisation (with special reference to Central India)*. New Delhi: Viking.
Jha, Alok Kumar (1991) 'After the Carnage – Relief and Rehabilitation in Bhagalpur'. *EPW* 5–12 January: 19–21.
Kohli, Atul (1992) *Democracy and Discontent – India's Growing Crisis of Governability*. New Delhi: Foundation Books (Indian edn).
Kumar, Ashwani (2008) *Community Warriors: State, Peasants and Caste Armies in Bihar*. New Delhi: Anthem Press.
Kumar, Sanjay (1999) 'New Phase in Backward Caste Politics in Bihar: Janata Dal on the Decline'. *EPW* 21–28 August: 2472–2480.
Louis, Prakash (2002) *People Power: The Naxalite Movement in Central Bihar*. Delhi: Wordsmiths.
Mishra, Vinod (1999) *Vinod Mishra Selected Works*. New Delhi: A CPI(ML) Publication.
Nakamizo, Kazuya (2009) 'Bouryoku kakumei to Gikai Seiji-Indo ni okeru Naxalite undo no tenkai' [Violent Revolution and Parliamentary Democracy: Naxalite Movements in India], in Kondo Norio (ed.) *Indo minshushugi taisei no yukue* [Prospects of Indian Democracy: Challenge and Adaptation]. Chiba: The Institute of Developing Economies, JETRO.
Nakamizo, Kazuya (2010), 'Jinushi to Gyakusatu-Indo Bihar shuu ni okeru siheishuudan no kessei to seijihendo' [Landlords and Massacre – the Formation of Private Armies and Political Change in Bihar, India]. *Asian and African Area Studies* 9(2): 180–222.
Nakamizo, Kazuya (2012) *Indo Bouryoku to Minshushugi – Ittouyuuishihai no houkai to Identity no Seiji* [Violence and Democracy in India: The Collapse of One-Party Dominant Rule and Identity Politics]. Tokyo: University of Tokyo Press.
Nakamizo, Kazuya (2013) 'Political Change in the Bihar: Riots and the emergence of the "Democratic Revolution"', in Lal, Sunita and Shaibal Gupta (eds.) *Resurrection of the State: A Saga of Bihar — Essays in Memory of Papiya Ghosh*. New Delhi: Manak Publications, pp. 69–108.
Sarkar, Sumit (1983) *Modern India: 1985–1947*. New Delhi: Macmillan India.
Singh, H. D. (1998) *543 Faces of India: Guide to Parliamentary Constituencies*. New Delhi: Newsmen Publishers.
Srikant (1995) *Bihar Main Chunav – Jaati, buth, loot aur hinsa* [Election in Bihar: Caste, Booth, Loot and Violence]. Patna: Sikha Prakashan.
Srikant (2005) *Bihar Main Chunav – Jaati, hinsa aur booth loot* [Election in Bihar: Caste, Violence and Booth Loot]. New Delhi: Vani Prakashan.
Wilkinson, Steven I. (2004) *Vote and Violence: Electoral Competition and Ethnic Riots in India*. Cambridge: Cambridge University Press.

8 Microfinance and gender
The *Magalir Thittam* in Tamil Nadu

Antonysamy Sagayaraj

While the concept of human security that emerged during the post–Cold War years was limited to efforts to protect the state from external military threats in order to preserve one's national integrity, this essay explores the notion of human security from a wider, more anthropological perspective. That is to say that here human security is explored from the point of view of not only protecting people from violence, but more importantly, empowering them to fight for themselves, with the goal of giving them the necessary tools to emancipate themselves from socio-economic bondage.[1] This latter meaning of human security, then, reaches the more fundamental issue of providing economic and social security to human persons in their efforts to live a good life, an issue that is more pronounced in suburban communities, which are mostly composed of lower-middle-class families.[2] These families do whatever they can, with limited resources and opportunities, to prevent themselves from falling into dire poverty.

The question of human security, then, that this essay will try to address is intertwined with the human person's effort to achieve and maintain a good quality of life. The living standard that is expected by families in fast developing countries like India should, at least, go beyond the issues of a person's basic needs such as shelter, food, clothing, etc. – an expectation that is sadly not met by the government and other agencies concerned.[3] Suburban communities in India and other developing countries remain below the middle-class line, which inevitably causes a sense of insecurity among members of the same class, thereby impeding any possibility for them to participate in the development of their country. The main preoccupation in these communities is still to provide for families' daily sustenance, not only for male members, but also for women in the community. Women in suburban communities are now expected to play an active role in the effort to maintain the financial stability of their respective families. The social set-up, therefore, of countries like India that are basically male-oriented and patriarchal, is now undergoing massive change precisely because of the growing demands of rapid modernisation.

The issue of a decent standard of living remains unresolved despite the joint efforts of husbands and wives in suburban communities; and while the cost of basic commodities is barely covered because of the low income of these families, events that are equally important would only further tighten these families' already tight belts. On the one hand, the poor need to spend to meet their daily needs, such as food, medicine, clothing, livestock, small business, ceremonies, and so on; but these are not the only expenses that human beings, rich or poor, should worry about. So, on the other hand, events like weddings and matriculations, hospitalisation and funerals, which obviously require large sums of money being acquired and handed over, have to be taken into consideration too.

These events would, of course, not become problematic if the families had savings put aside to cover them, but this is an unaffordable luxury for such suburban families. Lending agencies, whether formal or informal, institutional or non-institutional, thus become the final resort for these people. Lending institutions play an important role in meeting the needs of suburban communities for financial aid.[4] However, the services of conventional financial institutions are unaffordable for the poor because of their precarious economic situation. From the point of view of a conventional bank, the poor usually do not have enough assets to show as collateral and cannot access conventional financial systems (Getubig, Johari, & Kuga Thas, 1993). Additionally, a traditional bank would rather deal with someone with money than someone who is poor. Also the potential profit from microfinance lending is small. Furthermore, there is nobody who will act as a guarantor for the poor when they need financial support.

What must be noticed is that the financial pattern – income, savings, and loans – of the poor is not stable. In terms of an income pattern, their income is sometimes in surplus and sometimes in deficit due to work conditions, i.e. being in temporary work or jobless. Although the poor understand that they need to save cash, livestock, and jewellery in their houses in case of an emergency, sometimes unexpected situations occur, such as robbery, sudden disasters, and calls for help from relatives. In such cases, the poor have no option but to depend on moneylenders, who charge high interest rates on loans, or rely on their relatives for a smaller amount. But as with all human transactions, these useful (and supposedly helpful) agencies can inflict more harm than good, and they can be agents of exploitation rather than emancipation. Another related problem is that the majority of the poor are uneducated, so they might not be aware of the interest rates set by moneylenders.

Two connected problems can immediately be discerned from these initial analyses. On the one hand, poor families in suburban communities would have great difficulty accessing formal or institutional credit agencies such as banks precisely because of these institutions' strict policies in terms of lending and payment. And precisely because some of these institutional lending agencies are inaccessible for many of these needy families, they are forced to rely on the help of other agencies, some of them malicious and inhuman enough to abuse the urgency of the needs of these people.

The second problem, which is closely linked to the first and is most prevalent in patriarchal societies like India, is that wealth is a monopoly of men, precisely because in patriarchal societies it is men who have control of the family properties that are used as collateral. In these cases, excesses are not impossible occurrences. The poor reputation of male creditors, who borrow money but do not use all of it for the purpose for which it was borrowed, and the low repayment rate that becomes its immediate consequence cause further problems for families, putting them in more debt and in more detrimental positions. Some of the repercussions of irresponsible borrowing and abusive lending include loss of property and credit privileges, and sometimes even being forced into bonded labour. Deeper problems that are domestic in nature can also be pointed out: mental stress among members of the family – including the children, fighting between husbands and wives, and domestic violence, which are an inevitable result of an insecure household. It is precisely because these homes lack the peace that is supposedly the first characteristic of a home or a sanctuary that the children are led elsewhere, which leads to juvenile delinquency.

In view of all these problems, the question has to be asked: How can the poor manage their money? One way is through a village-level savings club, an informal financial system, called Rotating Savings and Credit Associations (ROSCAs). According to the analysis of Adams and Fitchett (1992), ROSCAs are local, informal financial groups that pool savings and tie loans to deposits by the members. The main features of ROSCAs are the regularity of contributions and the rotation of the funds. In addition, ROSCAs involve the social connectedness of members; their interactions are face-to-face (Gugerty, 2003). This means that members of ROSCAs have mutual confidence in each other. This case shows that the poor can participate in the financial system; even if it is in an informal way, it is still local and within reach. However, it is likely that ROSCAs are not sufficient as a financial system for responding to the needs of the poor. Their financial scale is small compared with an ordinary financial market, and their functionality is restricted to a limited area, community, and people. This means that diverse financial systems for the poor must be considered because the poor have diverse demands for financial services in different situations at different times.

What kind of financial services do the poor need? Conversely, what improvements can be made in the financial situation of individuals? The answer is microfinance.[5] In recent years, governmental and non-governmental organisations (NGOs) in South Asia have introduced microfinance programmes offering financial services to low-income households, and targeting women specifically.[6] It is based on the premise that women in poor households are more likely to be credit constrained, and hence less able to undertake income-earning activities. Access to credit has received even greater attention in the context of poverty reduction and objectives linked to the empowerment of women. In India, in the early 1990s, the National Bank for Agriculture and Rural Development (NABARD), a financial institution of the government of India, started a new nationwide microfinance initiative linking banks, NGOs, and informal local groups (self-help groups, or SHGs).

> A[n] SHG is a group of about 20 people from a homogeneous class, who come together for addressing their common problems. They are encouraged to make voluntary thrift on a regular basis. They use this pooled resource to make small interest bearing loans to their members. The process helps them imbibe the essentials of financial intermediation including prioritization of needs, setting terms and conditions and accounts keeping. This gradually builds financial

discipline and credit history for themselves, as the money involved in the lending operations is their own hard earned money saved over time with great difficulty. This is 'warm money'. They also learn to handle resources of a size that is beyond their individual capacities. The SHG members begin to appreciate that resources are limited and have a cost. Once the groups show this mature financial behavior, banks are encouraged to make loans to the SHG in certain multiples of the accumulated savings of the SHG. The bank loans are given without any collateral and at market interest rates. Banks find it easier to lend money to the groups as the members have developed a credit history. 'Cold (outside) money' gets added to the own 'warm money' in the hands of the groups, which have become structures, which are able to enforce credit discipline among the members. The members have experienced the benefits of credit discipline by being able to decide the terms of loans to their own members. The peer pressure ensures timely repayments and replaces the 'collateral' for the bank loans.

(Harper, 2002)

The main aim of the programme is to improve the potential of an SHG to bring banking services to poorer communities. It was upgraded to a regular banking programme in 1996 and allows SHGs to get loans from commercial, rural, and cooperative banks. These banks lend money to SHGs and allow NABARD to refinance the loans at a subsidised interest rate. The cumulative number of SHGs has grown almost ten-fold and achieved an outreach of about 31 million families through women's membership in about 2.2 million SHGs by 2006.

This SHG bank linkage programme initiated by NABARD, an Indian version of the Grameen Bank founded by Mohammad Yunus, in Bangladesh, has been running effectively in all states under various names. In Tamil Nadu, it is known as 'Magalir Thittam' (Women Scheme). This essay presents experiences from Magalir Thittam, one of the largest microcredit programmes for women, designed and initiated by the Tamil Nadu government to address the problem of poverty and women's empowerment. Conceived as a poverty alleviation programme, Magalir Thittam was introduced to bring about social development for people living under the poverty line through the provision of access to institutional loans for self-employment and income generation. The main focus of Magalir Thittam was on mobilising the poor and the disadvantaged to seek institutional credit so as to engage in profitable activity to meet basic needs. The basic approach to implementation was that of welfare distribution, and it was seen as an innovative step towards women's empowerment (Sagayaraj, 2010: 196–199). Since then SHGs have proliferated with varied activities, even as state government employees, as in the case of *Amma Unavagam* (Amma Canteens) in Tamil Nadu.

Self-help groups: a tool for women's empowerment

This essay discusses SHG outcomes from the perspectives of the poverty alleviation paradigm and the empowerment paradigm. In this respect, it both departs from and intersects with other perspectives. The SHG movement in India is engaged in microcredit activities and is often examined within an economic framework. Within this there is a vigorous debate regarding whether a focus on women and income generation benefits women in development or has any impact on women's poverty.[7] Some scholars argue that microcredit does not fulfil its claims of economic empowerment (Poster & Salime, 2002). However, this perspective is criticised on the ground of taking too narrow a view of poverty. While poverty is concerned with a lack of money, others take a more encompassing view (Sen, 1999), distinguishing between income poverty and capability poverty. The former refers to income level and deprivation; the latter concerns inadequacies in capabilities and a paucity of opportunities to expand one's ability. Sen (1999) introduces the concepts of human capital (skills) and social capital (community networks and strength of supports) as important factors in alleviating capability poverty. The two types of poverty are inextricably linked; however, relieving income poverty without addressing capability poverty will not lead to the effective alleviation of female poverty. It is evident from Sen's description of capability poverty and the nature of those approaches that place importance on participation that community development can be instrumental in contributing to the alleviation of capability poverty.

In relation to women and development, gender issues tend to be ignored in prevailing trends in development literature and work. The focus has shifted from women to the relationship between women and men, unequal power relations at all levels (household to global), and the need for development to become a process that is more gender equitable (United Nations, 1999). Hunt (2004) argues that this entails not only changes in legislation and policy, but complementary bottom-up community development approaches and processes that understand and challenge oppressive gender relations and create change that is geared towards greater power equality. Moser's (1993) view on such processes argues that they need to meet the strategic rather than the practical needs of women. Practical needs are those that perpetuate women's existing positions, whereas strategic needs, including the need to participate in decision making, would challenge existing structures and contribute to change and transformation.

Some may argue that such local-level initiatives do no more than ameliorate discontent and have little broader impact. However, there is a growing support for the view that local activity can extend its reach to other similar activities and can also influence policy at higher levels. This is what Robertson (1995) refers to as 'glocalization' and is based on the assumption that globalisation is not only a one-way, economic process, but the local can also influence broader levels of activity. It is certainly reasonable to argue that no matter what opportunities may be created for participation, poverty still means a lack of income and finance.

Three types of empowerment[8]

Economic empowerment

In this paradigm, women's access to savings and credit gives them a greater economic role in decision making through their decisions about savings and credit.

When women control decisions regarding credit and savings, they can take better care of their own welfare and that of their household. The investment in women's activities will improve employment opportunities for women and thus have a 'trickle down and out' effect. The financial sustainability and feminist empowerment paradigms emphasise women's own income-generating activities. In this development paradigm, the emphasis is more on increasing incomes at the household level and the use of loans for consumption. In the feminist empowerment paradigm, individual economic empowerment is seen as dependent on social and political empowerment.

Increased well-being

Access to savings and credit facilities and women's decisions about what to do with savings and credit strengthen the say women have in the economic decisions of the household. This enables women to increase expenditure on the well-being of themselves and their children; this is the main concern in the poverty alleviation paradigm. Women's control over decision making is also seen as benefiting men through preventing the leakage of household income through unproductive and harmful activities. Financial security in the household results in less anxiety about the future and the improved emotional well-being of women. In the financial sustainability and feminist empowerment paradigms, improved well-being is an assumed outcome of increasing women's economic activities and incomes.

Social and political empowerment

This is the combination of the increased economic activity and control over income that women experience as a result of access to microfinance and the improvement of improved women's skills, mobility, and access to knowledge and support networks. The status of women within the family and the community is also enhanced. These changes are reinforced by group formation, leading to wider movements for social and political change. Both the financial self-sustainability paradigm and the poverty alleviation paradigm assume that social and political empowerment will occur without specific interventions to change gender relations at the household, community, or macro levels. In contrast, the feminist empowerment paradigm advocates explicit strategies for supporting the ability of women to protect their individual and collective gender interests at all these levels.

Empowerment is a process of socio-economic change by which individuals or groups gain economic power and the ability to organise their livelihood. It involves increased well-being, access to resources, increased participation in decision making, and control over the use of resources. In other words, empowerment is a process that challenges the traditional power equations and access to economic resources. Microfinance facilitates the organisation of poor women into groups and rotates funds among the members, which builds up economic capacities. The deepening and widening of institutional credit among the poor is achieved to a greater extent through microfinance channels. Loans at very high interest rates from moneylenders and informal sources also significantly decline as a result of substantial financial interventions. Microfinance is not used only for the economic activities of SHG members but also sometimes for essential family needs. Consumption loans as well as financial assistance for economic activities facilitate the social empowerment of SHG members. A gradual change in the values and attitudes of the members of SHGs results in socio-economic empowerment, leading to social change.

Social networks

Creating a network of group support and forming alliances with professional groups or like-minded organisations provides strength and enhances the ability of women to make demands for shares of assets and resources. NGOs provide support systems and strengthen local initiative and capacity, working from the perspective of the people, and provide intermediary or bridging links between bureaucracy and SHGs. Institutional bureaucracies, be they government or financial institutions, provide services and mobilise the poor.

Until the 1980s, the root mechanism for the government to reach the majority of the poor was by creating the necessary preconditions and infrastructure to ensure access to development opportunities through the public sector-driven development model; it was thought that private sector could not be held accountable to the poor, or for their social and human development. From the early 1980s, the role of NGOs in social development has become prominent, and they are globally recognised as leading players in various development sectors. From the 1990s onwards, building partnership between the government, NGOs, banks, and communities has become essential. This partnership entails the partners having a stake in development for sustainability and accountability.

Sharma Nagar SHG: a case study in urban women's empowerment

Sharma Nagar was first planned and built by the Housing Board and Buckingham and Carnatic Mills (B & C Mill) in the 1960s. This housing was built with basic amenities for the low-rung labourers of B & C Mill for a fixed rent of Rs. 20 a month. Precisely because this housing was meant for labourers, the community that was created in it was made up of a mixture of different people from all kinds of religions and castes. Initially Sharma Nagar comprised 450 plots (760 sq ft each) that housed a total population of 2,600. Established in 1877 by an English businessman, the spinning mill that was the reason for the establishment of Sharma Nagar finally declared bankruptcy in 1996.

North Chennai – which is constituted by localities from Kasimedu to Park Town, Vyasarpadi, and Perambur, and municipalities including Manali, Tiruvottiyur, and Madhavaram – is home to lakhs of blue-collar workers. Tiny industries, including lathes, stainless steel polishing units, soap manufacturers, and those making electrical fittings, are sandwiched among residences on the narrow streets. An area that has always been a trading hub for merchants and residents from across the city and neighbouring districts, it has lost its sheen following the development of other commercial localities such as T. Nagar and Purasaiwalkam. Sharma Nagar, in the Viyasarpadi block, is an integral part of North Chennai and is also a unique site as it is the location of the former living quarters of workers from the defunct B & C Mill. Sharma Nagar (Figure 8.1) was a planned residential area, with sewage facilities, and it has 12 streets with 450 houses. The workers were class-based rather than caste- or religion-based. In spite of the government intervention, the spinning mill was closed down in 1996 due to bankruptcy. In 1997, as a negotiated settlement, the government agreed to donate the land and the houses to the workers at a minimum payment of Rs. 9,600, under the condition that it should not be sold for the next 10 years. Real estate prices shot up from Rs. 50,000 in 1990 to Rs. 22 lakhs (1 lakh = 100,000) in 2007 and doubled to 44 lakhs in 2014. While present-day buyers are lower-middle-class people, the original owners, namely the B & C Mill workers, moved to the outskirts. The egalitarian set-up of the area means that 'outsiders' find it easy to move in.

At present, visible changes can already be seen in Sharma Nagar, with the arrival of lower-middle-class 'outsiders' who buy the land and build three to four floors and rent them. Thus, high-rise buildings are already present (Figure 8.2) and other important establishments have been renovated. The school building, for instance, has been remodelled, but more importantly the standard of the school is being raised with the introduction of English as the medium of instruction. Reconstruction and renovations of the temples have also been made possible; and the renovation of parks and the construction of a weight training centre have become some of the most important improvements that can now be seen in Sharma Nagar. And with the intervention of enterprises that are initiated by microfinance agencies, the quality of life of the people who live in this once-depressed community has improved tremendously.

In Sharma Nagar, SHGs are constituted by women belonging to various castes and religions in heterogeneous groups of 20, who guarantee one another's debts and meet every two weeks to make their payments and discuss family or social issues. The meetings are held in an open public place, under a tree (Figure 8.3), creating a 'women's space' where they freely discuss their concerns. In the local cultural milieu, women are not supposed to leave the house without the permission of their husband, but husbands tolerate this act of insubordination because it is profitable. Typically, the women start small, but after they have repaid the first loan in full they may borrow again – this time a larger amount. This encourages attendance at the meetings and the ongoing exchange of ideas, and it builds up the habit of dealing with money and paying debts promptly. An overwhelming 90 per cent of women responded that the SHG has made a significant difference in their emotional lives as they had fewer fights with their husbands over money and less anxiety about the future. Of the six SHGs interviewed, 49 per cent said that their husbands respected them more, and 70 per cent said that the SHG has also transformed the educational prospects of their children.

The NGO SEED[9] took between 6 months and one year to form the groups. The process of evolving the SHG was voluntary. Source of funds to the SHG were initially savings and contributions from the NGO; bank credit came later. Activities financed by the SHGs were need-based, and the SHGs were flexible in their approach. The interest on loans was 20 per cent, with longer repayment periods. Conducting regular weekly meetings was one of the hallmarks of the functioning of the groups. Savings by members serve as the main bond for being together in the group, and the pattern of savings differs from one group to another, mainly on the basis of the income-generating activities of the members. The recovery of the loans by banks is excellent, without any default. Members of the SHGs were not very aware of the NABARD scheme of linking the groups with banks but refer to the 'Mahalir Thittam' of the state government.

The NGO has played a pivotal role in ensuring the proper training and coordination of groups and putting them on a scientific approach. Before the sanction of loans to the NGO for lending to the groups, bank branch managers visited the groups and participated in meetings to satisfy themselves of their functioning. Satisfied by the excellent recovery under the programme, the banks have shown an interest in extending loans through the NGO; bankers felt that direct lending to groups could be done once they attained maturity. The NGO provided training in bookkeeping at the SHG level either at its training centre or through federation members.

The groups usually create a common fund by contributing their small savings on a regular basis. Most of the groups evolve flexible systems of working and manage their pooled resources in a democratic way, with the participation of every member in decision making. Requests for loans are considered by the group in their periodic meetings, and competing claims on limited resources are settled by consensus. The amounts loaned are small, frequent, and for a short duration. The periodic meetings of members also serve as a forum for collecting dues from members. Defaults are rare mainly due to group pressure and intimate knowledge of the end use of credit.

Findings

Empirical evidence and experience reveal mixed blessings for women and the poor in general. On the one hand, outreach to women through SHGs has given them access to income, savings, and community development activities and brought them together in groups for economic empowerment. As it targets women, Magalir Thittam has been supported and subsidised by the government. On the other hand, Magalir Thittam is still viewed and handled as one of the state government's welfare measures. The welfare approach allows political parties in Tamil Nadu to call upon the services of members of self-help groups for electioneering; they become the foot-soldiers for electioneering. The political character of these SHGs was evident during the 2006 and 2011 assembly election campaign and 2009 and 2014 Lok Sabha (House of the People) election campaign. Members of SHGs, directly or indirectly associated with the parties, formed the core of their campaign. For instance, the DMK and the ADMK already have a strong presence in the government-sponsored Magalir Thittam poverty eradication programme, which aims at empowering women. Political party cadres dominate the 'Suya Udhavi Kuzhus' (Self-help Groups) that have been set up under the programme. Political parties started taking an active interest in sponsoring SHGs only after caste- and faith-based organisations made their presence felt in the microfinancing sector. Politically, these organisations are potential threats to mainstream parties because of their transformation into veritable vote banks.

As mentioned earlier, Magalir Thittam is actually the SHG bank linkage programme initiated by NABARD, a financial institution of the government of India, running effectively under a different name. After an extensive transformation it has been politically appropriated as a pseudo-welfare movement, and as a vote bank for party political purposes. Here again, the unintended positive outcome is that the SHG members gain an opportunity to become actively involved in political discourse, which further opens up the possibility for contesting and winning local elections. Thus, political empowerment is ensured.

Women are still viewed as the keepers of the home and supporting agents of men's efforts. The primary focus of the programmes has been to administer cycles of loans and loan repayment, as repayment has been the main criterion of success of the programme. It can be argued that, for example, the pressure exerted on women to repay their loans entrenches rather than challenges existing social hierarchies along lines of caste, class, ethnicity, and gender. On the contrary, the very fact that women from various castes and creeds could come together once a week not only for the purpose of microfinance but also for solving family or community problems and having meals together during celebrations brings about a new set of social networks. Notably, the children who accompany the mothers for the meetings and gatherings become friends and freely mingle with each other. This unintended effect opens up the possibility of a casteless society or at least a route to the eradication of caste- or creed-based discrimination. Thus the intended objectives of the central and state governments together with the NGOs to alleviate poverty and empower women have resulted in the achievement of new social networks and political participation.[10]

Some critical notes

To avoid painting an overly rosy picture and in the process distorting the entire truth of a reality that one wants to portray honestly, it is necessary to stop and view the subject matter with a certain amount of objectivity and not be blinded by some of its successes. While microfinance, specifically through SHGs in the case of Shamar Nagar, has been a huge success in Indian suburban communities, one should not be misled into thinking that the women who are members of SHG enterprises are all entirely emancipated. No matter how desirable this outcome, some complications and new sets of challenges are bound to arise whenever new efforts are exerted to alleviate the suffering of a human community. And the communities that this essay has tried to discuss are not exempted from this reality.

First, while one might expect that the women involved in the SHG programmes in their community are already freed from stress, this is far from the truth. It is true that most of these women members have fewer worries about domestic fights or that some of them are able to fulfil some demands that are already beyond the basic necessities, such as ceremonies of rites of passage, matriculation, or emergency hospitalisation, but precisely because these women are able to provide the money for these expenses, there is a great tendency for their husbands and other male members of the family who are supposed to be working as well to relax and thus leave the women to do all the work alone. In this respect, these women experience an increased workload that was not the case before: aside from their domestic responsibilities, they have to attend to their economic activities, which, of course, will take its toll on them in the long run. And while the responsibilities of these women are increasing, men become freer to do whatever they want and spend their money on their own pleasures.

Second, as with all activities that involve money – quite a large sum of money in the case of some of these communities – emergencies are bound to happen that are beyond one's control. In such cases, one could only conclude that while these enterprises free women at some level, they also tie them up, and most of the time, rather more tightly. For example, the treasurer of a particular SHG group got into trouble when the money that she was supposed to deposit in the bank was stolen by her adolescent son. Of course, considering that these communities are tightly knit, escaping from the responsibility was not a realistic option. And so, the money had to be given back. In this particular case, as in other cases, the husband wanted nothing to do with the incident, and so asking for his help was no longer a possible course of action. The only thing that the woman could do was to ask for help from the group, which meant borrowing money from another group just so she could pay the amount that she was supposed to surrender. This particular case illustrates that some contingencies that are beyond one's control could be an agent of bondage, rather than emancipation.

Third, and this is closely connected with the first, since microfinance operates on the understanding that the debtors are really poor and most of the time would borrow money without the backup of any collateral, the only way to force them to pay their debts is through peer pressure. As in the case mentioned above, the other members are there not only to help, but to see to it – by any means necessary – that all the other members of the group are on time in their payments. While this kind of pressure is, of course, very good, the question has to be asked, 'What kind of life can these people really lead if their peers keep on tailing them just to keep them up-to-date with their responsibilities?' This question is not only about the unnecessary pressure that these women have to face; it has more to do with the concept of emancipation that should actually be connected with all the efforts that are exerted by microfinance through the SHG. In the end, when women are being chased by their peers, and most of the time they have to resort to further borrowing just so they are able to pay their initial debts, the most important question to ask is: 'Are these women really emancipated and empowered?'[11]

Fourth, and to some degree more importantly, while the SHG and its enterprises are initially designed for the poor, this ideal in some cases was not really translated into reality. Since SHGs are basically for women, any woman can borrow; this provision becomes the very loophole that some rich women in the community use to take advantage of what would otherwise be a good opportunity for the poor. Some of these women would borrow from the pool of SHG groups to create their own lending businesses, and of course, some of them, if not most, would be lending this money to their poorer neighbours at higher interest rates, thereby creating more problems for the poorer members of the community. In some cases, these women are, as a matter of fact, used by their husbands to borrow money from SHGs, thus making them an extension of their husbands' businesses. In such cases, men become more empowered, yet again, than women, which is not supposed to be the case.

Finally, the SHGs can be a good opportunity for abusive politicians to gather more votes for themselves. SHGs, then, become the medium for political interference where party members become SHG leaders and vice versa. In this particular case, the actual purpose of the SHG is being trampled by the greedy ambitions of some who are only after the popularity that membership of the SHG could give.

The empowerment of women and the emancipation of the poor cannot then be expected to happen magically just because new programmes like microfinance and the SHG have brought a little comfort to the poorest members of the community. Both emancipation and empowerment are movements that are in process, and so each one still has a responsibility to keep a vigilant watch against abusive agents and members of the community. The negative points that are noted here are not supposed to be taken as a signal to stop the efforts that are initiated by microfinance through the SHG. On the contrary, it is an invitation for each member of the community to take up the challenge of furthering the successes of the enterprises started by the SHG and to try to change the anomalous parts of the system. One has to keep working for emancipation and empowerment, and any success that comes from one's effort should not stop one from trying to do more.

Epilogue

The arrival of microfinance has been a shining shaft of light that promises to dispel the darkness of poverty that has long been cast on poor suburban communities. Also known as 'self-help groups' in India, microfinance initiatives do just that – that is, they provide small loans that are to be repaid within a short time period for low-income individuals and households who have limited assets to use as collateral. Microfinance, then, becomes a low-risk alternative for creditors that promises empowerment and gradual social change. It has to be noted that the success of microfinance can be attributed to women, who are the ones who manage the borrowed money and see that it is repaid. Through the help of the group that these women are involved in, the amount borrowed is paid precisely because of the presence of peer encouragement and pressure. Women, then, who have always been in the background in all transactions that are led by men in a male-oriented

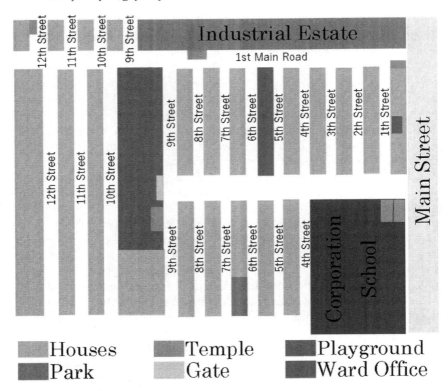

Figure 8.1 Sharma Nagar layout

society, now come to the fore, for they are the ones who are greatly involved in microfinance; and because of this, social transformation which is initiated from the very roots of society becomes ever more pronounced and promising. The social landscape of patriarchal societies will inevitably have to change now that women are equipped to fend for themselves.

Microfinance is the most palpable source of human security for these suburban communities, providing them with more reasons to hope for better social and economic participation. Macroeconomics has always given more importance to the overall income and economic status of the state, and has therefore inevitably neglected the people who are on the margins, which in India's case is still 70 per cent of the population; 'Shining India' is still a distant reality for most of the people in this fast-developing country. Human security has yet to be provided, and this will not happen unless all the people are secure enough to actively participate in this national effort. In a male-oriented society such as India's, the mere participation of women – especially despite their poverty – in the effort to create for themselves a more secure social and economic standing in their community, and thereby create a better life for themselves and their families, could be a beautiful picture of empowerment and emancipation.

Figure 8.2 High-rise buildings in Street No. 3

Figure 8.3 SHG meeting held under a tree in front of an original house in Street No. 7

The success of microfinance in India through the SHG is a good indication that a new kind of social network is arising and preparing to supplant the old system that divides people based on caste and religion, making it impossible for them to cooperate with each other. The new community that microfinance is able to create empowers the people who were formerly marginalised because of their status, giving them a new-found confidence and esteem that allows them to participate more actively in the social and economic activities of their community. Now more than ever these poor communities can hope for a society that is above class, caste, religion, and language; a society that is genuinely concerned for human security and humanity. And while all other efforts are so far failing, microfinance promises something better: the birth of a new social security for the entire Indian community.

Notes

1 The simplest definition of security is the 'absence of insecurity and threats'. This definition, then, gives a good starting point for understanding why the concept of human security should be understood not only as the absence of external military threats, but also as the provision of a better quality of life for the people in the state. The state is not only threatened from without, it can be threatened from within. Tadjbakhsh explains this succinctly: 'To be secure is to be free from both fear (of physical, sexual or psychological abuse, violence, persecution, or death) and from want (of gainful employment, food, and health). Human security therefore deals with the capacity to identify threats, to avoid them when possible, and to mitigate their effects when they do occur. It means helping victims cope with the consequences of the widespread insecurity resulting from armed conflict, human rights violations, and massive underdevelopment. This broadened use of the word 'security' encompasses two ideas: one is the notion of 'safety' that goes beyond the concept of mere physical security in the traditional sense, and the other the idea that people's livelihoods should be guaranteed through '"social security" against sudden disruptions' (Tadjbakhsh, 2005).
2 Tadjbakhsh discusses the shift of meaning of human security from a strictly militaristic perspective to a people-centred perspective. He says the following: 'It sought to find answers to questions such as "security from what?", "whose security?", and "security by what means?" And to find answers to such questions in terms of people's experience. "Security" for a farmer growing poppies in Badakhshan or Helmand was the livelihood he gained from selling his crops to a middleman, but this form of security was very different from the "security" interests of recipient states concerned about their drug addicts and about the terror-crime-drug-mafia networks. For a school teacher in Jalalabad security was the fact that he could properly clothe and educate his children and invest in the construction of his house, confident that the little he had today would not be taken away from him tomorrow. His security was quite a different matter from that of the coalition troops in Paktika, fearful of a suicide attack or a renewal of insurgency by the Taliban or Al Qaeda' (Tadjbakhsh, 2005: 4). Understanding human security in this manner allows for one to focus on human beings and not just the state. This time around, the threats are no longer expected from the outside but from within: 'Primary threats were seen as internal: economic failure, violation of human rights, political discrimination. Hence, the guarantee of national security no longer lay in military power, but in favorable social, political and economic conditions, the promotion of human development, and the protection of human rights' (Tadjbakhsh, 2005: 4–5).
3 Poverty does not just mean scarcity and want; it also means rights denied, opportunities curtailed, and voices silenced. Women all over the world suffer from the latter meaning of poverty (CARE International, c. 2005: 1).

4 As Fernando explains, the majority of poor families are often ignored by the formal-sector financial institutions. And precisely because these families are ignored by the formal sector, the existence of the informal is inevitably legitimised; their existence now becomes a permanent condition in the economy. This is more so for the communities that can be found in rural settlements (Fernando, 2006: 17).

5 Microfinance today stands for financial assistance to the poor not only at reasonable rates of interest but also at sustainable quantum. Microfinance lending includes bank assistance to a broader range of services, i.e. credit facility, insurance coverage, marketing of products, government subsidy, etc. Financial institutions address the poor and very poor categories of the population who lack access to formal financial assistance to take up a small business venture. Microfinance interventions are well recognised the world over as an effective tool for the alleviation of poverty and improving the socio-economic conditions of the weaker sections of society. Microfinance is also considered to be a 'humanising capitalism'. As Fernando explains, '[It] means providing opportunities for the poor to unleash their hidden entrepreneur potential and enabling them to actively participate in capitalist development, and benefit from it. The identity of the poor in development was configured as "new entrepreneurs". The explicit message is: we need to bring capitalism to the homes of the poor!'

6 A majority of microfinance programmes target women with the explicit goal of empowering them. However, their underlying premises are different. Some argue that women are amongst the poorest and the most vulnerable of the underprivileged. Others believe in investing in women's capabilities and that some of the most wretched suffering is caused not just by low incomes, but also by unwise spending by men. Several studies suggest that when women gain control over spending, less family money is devoted to instant gratification and more for education and family needs. As Fernando says, 'Microcredit as a social movement attempts to redefine the trajectory of development by privileging the empowerment of women in it, which entails the enactment of cultural politics of empowerment, which . . . can help shed light on the economic, cultural, and political consequences of microcredit not only of women, but also for other social struggles over social change' (Fernando, 2006: 11).

7 As an article of CARE states: 'Women work two-thirds of the world's working hours, according to the United Nations Millennium Campaign to halve world poverty by the year 2015. The overwhelming majority of the labour that sustains life – growing food, cooking, raising children, caring for the elderly, maintaining a house, hauling water – is done by women, and universally this work is accorded low status and no pay. The ceaseless cycle of labour rarely shows up in economic analyses of a society's production and value. . . . Women earn only 10 percent of the world's income. Where women work for money, they may be limited to a set of jobs deemed suitable for women – invariably low-pay, low-status positions. . . . Women own less than 1 percent of the world's property. Where laws or customs prevent women from owning land or other productive assets, from getting loans or credit, or from having the right to inheritance or to own their home, they have no assets to leverage for economic stability and cannot invest in their own or their children's futures. . . . Women make up two-thirds of the estimated 876 million adults worldwide who cannot read or write; and girls make up 60 percent of the 77 million children not attending primary school' (CARE International, c. 2005: 1).

8 According to Cheston and Kuhn (2002), there is a good reason to believe that women who participate actively in the enterprises put up by microfinance and SHGs are more empowered than those who do not. According to them, these women are more confident in terms of decision making at home. This self-confidence that is developed by attaining a certain level of independence from the male members of the household allows for improved gender relations at home, and this reduces, in most cases, instances of domestic violence. This ultimately improves the status of women in the community, as they and their efforts become more visible. As Cheston and Kuhn state, 'Several

microfinance and microenterprise support programs have observed improvements in women's status in their communities. Contributing financial resources to the family or community confers greater legitimacy and value to women's views and gives them more entitlements than they would otherwise have. Studies of microfinance clients from various institutions around the world show that the women themselves very often perceive that they receive more respect from their families and their communities – particularly from the male members – than they did before joining a microfinance program' (Cheston & Kuhn, 2002: 25).

9 SEED (Socio Economic and Education Development trust) is an NGO funded mainly by Hand in Hand, Sweden, whose main purpose is to spread the word about the work of SEED in the field, shape public opinion in favour of its self-help development model, and seek funding.

10 One can find a parallel of this kind in the Noon Meals scheme of the 1980s in Tamil Nadu. The scheme was introduced by Kamaraj to improve enrolment in schools and arrest the drop-out rate. M. G. Ramachandran appropriated it by expanding it with some nutritious content and took the credit. MGR was criticised for politicising the scheme for his own popularity. Later the demographers found that Tamil Nadu was doing better in the human index score over the next two decades and found the answer in the Noon Meals scheme. The girls who benefited from the scheme grew to be empowered women, equipped with and utilising the knowledge of government programmes for health and welfare. This is the unintended result.

11 This implicitly indicates that despite the successes of SHG in giving women self-confidence and self-esteem, the problem remains: fundamentally speaking they are still bound to their husbands and their social status. As CARE beautifully states, 'Until women are accepted by men as equally human, attempts to help women change their lives will necessarily always result in achievements that are limited in scope and longevity. Women alone cannot empower themselves, nor should we expect them to bear that burden. Men too – especially in their status as power holders in the family, community and formal government – must act' (CARE International, c. 2005: 4).

References

Adams, Dale W. & Delbert A. Fitchett (1992) *Informal Finance in Low-Income Countries*. Boulder, CO: Westview Press.

CARE International (c. 2005) *Women's Empowerment*. CARE International. www.idpwa.org.ge/upload/21019Women%20and%20Empowerment.pdf [last accessed 7/2/15].

Cheston S. & Lisa Kuhn (2002) 'Empowering Women through Microfinance'. Paper presented at the Microcredit Summit +5, New York, November 2002.

Fernando, J. (2006) 'Microcredit and Empowerment of Women: Blurring the Boundary between Development and Capitalism', in J. Fernando (ed.) *Microfinance: Perils and Prospects*. New York: Routledge.

Getubig, I. P., M. Yaakub Johari, & Angela M. Kuga Thas (1993) *Overcoming Poverty through Credit: The Asian Experience in Replicating the Grameen Bank Approach*. Kuala Lumpur: Asian and Pacific Development Centre.

Gugerty, Mary Kay (2003) 'You Can't Save Alone: Testing Theories of Rotating Saving and Credit Associations in Kenya'. Mimeograph, University of Washington.

Harper, Malcolm (2002), 'Promotion of Self Help Groups under the SHG Bank Linkage Programme in India'. Paper presented at the Seminar on SHG-Bank Linkage Programme at New Delhi, 25 and 26 November.

Hunt, J. (2004) 'Gender and Development', in D. Kingsbury, J. Remenyi, J. McKay, & J. Hunt (eds.) *Key Issues in Development*. Basingstoke: Palgrave Macmillan.

Moser, C. (1993) *Gender Planning and Development: Theory, Practice and Training.* London: Routledge.
Poster, W. & Z. Salime (2002) 'The Limits of Microcredit: Transnational Feminism and USAID Activities in the United States and Morocco', in N. Naples & M. Desai (eds.) *Women's Activism and Globalization: Linking Local Struggles and Transnational Politics.* New York: Routledge.
Robertson, R. (1995) 'Glocalization: Time-Space and Homogeneity-Heterogeneity', in M. Featherstone, S. Lash, & R. Robertson (eds.) *Global Modernities.* London: Sage.
Sagayaraj, A. (2010) 'Democracy and Development in India: A Focus on Self Help Groups of Tamil Nadu', in Asian Cultures Research Institute (eds.) *Acculturation and Development in Asian Societies.* Tokyo: Tokyo University Asian Cultures Research Institute.
Sen, A. (1999) *Development as Freedom.* Oxford: Oxford University Press.
Tadjbakhsh, S. (2005) *Human Security: Concepts and Implications with an Application to Post-Intervention Challenges in Afghanistan.* Centre d'études et de Recherches Internationales Sciences Po, No. 117–118: September. www.sciencespo.fr/ceri/sites/sciencespo.fr.ceri/files/etude117_118.pdf [last accessed 7/2/15].
United Nations (1999) *World Survey on the Role of Women in Development.* New York: United Nations.

9 Rural lives and livelihoods

Perceptions of security in a Rajasthan village

Ann Grodzins Gold

Tremendous changes have continuously affected India's rural spaces since independence. These include the agrarian revolutions of the 1960s and the communications revolutions of the present. Such changes permeate every aspect of everyday existence, from crops planted to foods eaten; from entertainment choices to employment opportunities; from social and gender hierarchies to political formations. Government development projects as well as a multitude of non-governmental organisations concerned with improving agricultural productivity, primary education, adult literacy, health care, gender equity, and environmental sustainability – to mention only a few major foci of ongoing interventions – are persistently at work contributing to rural India's modernisation. All such efforts would broadly serve to enhance human security in a variety of ways – some measurable, others less easily specified.

Regional variations of change in rural India are enormous, and this chapter will not attempt to outline comprehensively any concrete, quantifiable elements of these ongoing transformations.[1] Rather, my contribution to this volume draws on qualitative ethnographic research and speaks of security at the micro level. While I shall of course note concrete evidence of material developments, I pay most attention to subjective perceptions and assessments of change as articulated by people experiencing and reflecting on it. Thus I highlight both my own independent, casual observations, and the ways that residents of one small region in central Rajasthan have described to me transformations in the conditions of life which they understand to be both material and moral. In focusing on the experiential, I not only consider livelihoods and corporal existence, but internal dispositions and interpersonal relationships.

I proceed as follows: In the first section, 'Ghatiyali longitudinally', I briefly describe both my fieldwork site and research methods. Next, in 'Observed changes' I list some striking, visible elements of rural development I have noticed between 1979 and 2009. The largest segment of this essay, 'Experienced changes', examines in greater detail three specific areas that Rajasthanis emphasised to me in interviews – all of which are connected with human security in the broadest understanding of the term. These are: environmental change and practices of food production; domestic change including household labour, gender roles, and education; intangible change: community, morality, aspiration. To conclude, I summarise these findings in terms of *security and insecurity*. While the former has increased significantly along several dimensions, I note some emergent forms of insecurity, both physical and psychological.

Ghatiyali longitudinally

I have personally witnessed, at intervals, almost 30 years of change in Ghatiyali, a large village in the southeast corner of Ajmer district, Rajasthan. Ghatiyali is located in a geophysical region known, after its major river, as the Banas Basin. In the years preceding India's independence and Rajasthan's slightly later incorporation into the new Indian republic, Ghatiyali was part of a 27-village kingdom named after its capital, Sawar. While Sawar had at one time been attached to the preeminent princely state of Mewar, by the early twentieth century it had come under direct British rule from Ajmer. People here still retain acute memories of the double rule and double taxation of local kings and remote colonisers, and thus by and large express heartfelt appreciation for present-day regimes (Gold & Gujar, 2002).

The Banas Basin supports a mixed agricultural-pastoral economy. Ghatiyali is a large and diverse village with over 25 *jatis* or caste communities, spanning the Hindu social hierarchy and including Muslims and Jains. Farming, gardening, and herding are primary occupations for the majority of village residents. Stone quarrying and stonecarving together make up another historically significant local industry – one that has both mechanised and expanded rapidly in recent years. Although subject to periodic drought followed by bursts of temporary outmigration (as is all Rajasthan), in good monsoon years Ghatiyali is a relatively prosperous place. The gradual transformation of its houses from mud to stone amply testifies to this, as does a consistent trend of shrine improvement and construction – evidence not only of enduring religiosity but of surplus wealth.

I arrived in Ghatiyali for the first time in September 1979, and my most recent visit was in August of 2008. While I have returned at more frequent intervals for a day or two to visit dear friends, my actual fieldwork periods – ranging in length from as little as six weeks to as long as 21 months for my doctoral research – took place in 1979–81, 1987, 1993, 1997, and 2003. I was able to visit for a few weeks at a time during three recent consecutive summers: 2006, 2007, and 2008. My research in 1993 and 1997 was specifically concerned with oral histories of environmental change reaching back as far as living memories would go, and thus at least a decade or more before independence. In 2003 I focused on more recent developments in agricultural technologies.

The broadest chronological scope of my research in this one location thus spans the 60 years under consideration in this volume. Moreover, I have often explicitly solicited residents' views on the differences between past and present. Throughout my career, my methods have remained on the far side of qualitative. They usually included traditional participant observation combined with extensive, open-ended, tape-recorded interviews and the gathering, transcription, and translation of expressive traditions.

Observed changes: an outsider's notes

In this section I summarise a few of my own direct observations – things striking to me during comings and goings over the past 30-odd years. The section that follows will elaborate in greater detail on areas of transformation that captivate the critical imaginations of rural Rajasthanis. Some things have changed less than I might have anticipated. For example, grain is still traded for vegetables, and, as in the past, little fruit is available for purchase in the village (although much improved transportation provides far more opportunities for people to bring it from nearby markets). The vast majority of Ghatiyalians continue to cook meals on traditional cooking hearths (*chula*s), requiring a constant supply of firewood – of which there is no shortage thanks to the mixed blessing of imported, fast-growing mesquite trees. Many well-to-do homes possess gas or kerosene stoves but use them sparingly due to fuel rationing and cost. Stoves are most often used to prepare tea for visitors; rarely to prepare meals. Health care available in the village remains minimal: a resident nurse, and a few private 'compounders' (purveyors of medicines). However, many more people are quick to take sick family members to clinics and hospitals in surrounding towns, a practice made possible by multiple daily buses, improved roads, and more private motor vehicles – which brings me to the first enormous plus for security I would like to highlight.

Year-round transportation

I arrived for the first time in Ghatiyali during the late monsoon season of 1979. It was not raining and the roads were not muddy. Nonetheless, there was no public transportation available to this populous village at either of the two nearest bus hubs (Kekari and Devli). At that time, during eight months of the year, at least four buses a day plied between Ghatiyali and these hubs. But, for the entire four months of the rainy season – more or less from mid-June to mid-September – all bus service officially shut down. The stated cause was the condition of the roads – none were paved, and the Devli route then required driving right through the Banas river bed (a fine new bridge has since been constructed). Rather than face occasional disruptions should there happen to be heavy rains, bus managers found it expedient to shut down the route altogether and hire their buses out during the rainy season for chartered purposes such as pilgrimages and other excursions. Thus, to go and come from the village, one had to hire a jeep; cajole one of the few owners of motor vehicles (countable at that time on the fingers of one hand); or bike; or walk.

Less than 15 years later, by the early 1990s, all of this had changed radically. Multiple buses were available year-round and several spent the night in Ghatiyali; private vehicles had also multiplied. People took for granted the ability to get where they needed to go. To be thus stably linked to networks (health, business, education, shopping, and extended family, just to name a few that leap to mind) made an enormous difference in peoples' lives. Yet, oddly to me, when asked to summarise contrasts between past and present, no one I interviewed ever emphasised transportation. I might speculate the reason for this omission is that people view the regular bus service as an unmitigated good, while many of the changes they single out for commentary are ambivalently construed.

Schools and schooling expand

There was one school near the bus stand when I first worked in Ghatiyali – today known as the 'Big School'. Two additional schools were constructed to serve particular neighbourhoods and another for girls only. Although girls can and do attend any of the village schools, the option of gender-segregated education is one that many families, nervous about their daughters, appreciate; other parents complained that this school focused too much on domesticity and the arts, to the detriment of its academic curriculum. There are also several private schools for the primary grades, charging tuition; one of these promises English-language education from an early age. No school in Ghatiyali goes beyond grade 10, but the Sawar bus carries Ghatiyali students back and forth daily from this nearest town, allowing them to complete their pre-collegiate education.

While universal enrollment in primary education has not yet been achieved, it has increased enormously, even for girls. Those farming communities considered resistant to development efforts, the Malis and Lodhas in particular, are gradually sending more children, who are staying in school longer. While pursuing research focused on education in the late 1990s, I saw clearly how children's important work tending livestock was the major impediment to their schooling. Although the government offered a night school for working children, most of them were far too tired to take advantage of it. During fieldwork in 1993 and 1997 I spent considerable time with the then numerous herding children. They tended their animals, played complicated games, and denied any interest in acquiring education (Gold, 2002; Gujar & Gold, 2007). Ten years later, I observed, and friends confirmed, more elderly people out with animals. Why was this? So that children could go to school. As in other states, the 'midday meal' initiative has provided an effective incentive for families to send children to school, and has especially helped to reduce gender disparity (Afridi, 2007).

Building boom

In 1980 the majority of houses in Ghatiyali were still *kachcha*, that is, made of mud and organic materials, requiring yearly replastering. Now, a great many more are *pakka*, made of stone. The building boom has not only improved housing comfort and durability but disrupted traditional jati-based residency in neighbourhoods. To give just one of numerous examples, my friend Shambhu Nath, who had formerly lived in a kachcha house in the neighbourhood inhabited exclusively by his Nath community, built his new pakka home close to the centre of the village, where many of his neighbours are Brahmans, but there are also gardeners, Rajputs, and others. I should also note one counterexample: the leatherworkers' spacious new colony built with government assistance on the outskirts of the village. As a side effect to uplift efforts on behalf of a formerly oppressed community, caste segregation has been reinforced. This colony has its own school and is considered enviably well equipped with hand-pumps and electricity.

The building boom has transformed not only private homes but many deities' places. For example, the Dev Narayan shrine called Puvali ka Devji on the outskirts of the village has been tiled, walled, and improved in multiple ways since I first visited it in 1979. In Ghatiyali proper, an ancient platform shrine on a hill by the water reservoir, also for the worship of Dev Narayan, was rebuilt and elaborately rededicated in 2007. The Gujar community associated with Dev Narayan took the lead in these two cases, although devotees from other groups contributed and participated. Similarly, the Nath community undertook renovations of the shrine of Jaipalji hereditarily tended by Naths, while Minas improved the goddess temple in their neighbourhood. A great many more local temples and shrines have been upgraded by devotees.

Waste

When I first lived in Ghatiyali it seemed that there was virtually no garbage that was not eaten by livestock, or composted, or recycled. Every tin can had its multiple uses; my magazines were in huge demand for shelf liners; old clothes cycled down through the caste system and finally became multipurpose rags; every food scrap was consumed by buffalos or carried carefully to the compost pile. (Traditional prenuptial rituals include a 'worship of the compost pile'.) Any packaging was of paper or cardboard, most often already recycled, and biodegradable or burnable. Now, the era of plastic bags and other manufactured packing materials has caused garbage to be visible; because there is no system of dealing with debris, it is just placed beside particular pathways on the edge of the village.

Sanitation remains imperfectly realised. Many better-off homes have installed flush latrines built over privately constructed septic tanks, but public facilities are inadequate and continue to be avoided by many who prefer a cleaner open-air environment. Pigs (and the sweeper or *harijan* community that keeps them) remain important ecological actors in rural sanitation.

Communication and migration

More people today are working outside the village, linking it directly not only with global economies but global consumer cultures. These links are forged both by wealthier, higher-caste persons and by labourers. Ghatiyalians stick together at the Anurag filling station in Rajasthan's capital and increasingly cosmopolitan metropolis, Jaipur. Owned by a successful, entrepreneurial member of Ghatiyali's Mali community, this petrol pump has employed persons from the proprietor's home village for decades. He has prospered, acquiring several shops and cars for hire, and he continues to employ his fellow villagers. Some Ghatiyalians, either landless or with monsoon-dependent agricultural land, spend periods of time – especially in drought years – labouring in the booming Gurgaon area on the outskirts of Delhi. A number of young men are working in the gulf. One Brahman went to Pennsylvania to serve as a priest at a Hindu temple there, but when his contract was up he returned with little good to say about life in the USA.

Access to news and entertainment via television of course links those who do not travel far with images and messages from a much wider world. Yet, perhaps due to the frequent and prolonged power cuts which work against getting too engrossed in any show, it does not seem to me that TV has effected major changes in family or social life. The mobile phone has been there for a much shorter time period, but I would say that it has been genuinely revolutionary. Service arrived sometime between 2003 and 2006; towers shot up everywhere; the low price and the huge convenience attracted persons at every level of society. Phones of course enhance security in really basic ways. For one anecdotal example: my friend Bhoju's wife and mother no longer had to endure prolonged anxiety when, as frequently happened, he was later to arrive than expected. Mobile phones also bring new social anxieties and perils, particularly (for parents) in the realm of teenage romance. As far as I know, no one in Ghatiyali has Internet service yet.

Experienced changes: cultural critique from the inside

I turn now from my own casual observations to three areas of change that have been research foci and on which I can provide commentary from village residents.[2]

Environment and production

In my earlier research, during extensive interviews often conducted in collaboration with Bhoju Ram Gujar, I recorded a remarkably consistent and powerful discourse on environmental, agricultural, social, and moral change. Descriptions of interlinked and interlocked transformations are ecological in their systemic vision, revealing inseparable, circular, and mutually dependent geophysical, biological, sociological, and psychological aspects of a world in flux. Interviewees repeatedly astonished us in the ways their voices echoed one another, and with the ways they linked one factor with others. In the following paragraphs I attempt to summarise very broadly an ecological discourse that emerged from over one hundred interviews conducted in the 1990s with older persons whose memories reach back at least 25 years, and often as much as twice that.

Old growths of indigenous trees are gone. These tall trees that once covered the hills used to create a wind that pulled the clouds to them. Hence, for lack of such trees, rainfall is significantly diminished (Gold, 1998). Wild animals who sheltered in the deep woods are gone. The dominant tree in today's landscape is the 'foreign acacia' (*vilayati bambul; Prosopis juliflora; mesquite*) – often simply called 'foreign'. Thorny and fast-growing, its leaves unappealing to goats, this imported tree is indispensable for firewood. However, it spreads like a weed and is an unwelcome and hard-to-remove coloniser of agricultural land (Gold, 2003).

The destruction of the woods, the cutting, selling, and stockpiling of the old trees is a blatant example of moral degeneration, and the current era is understood as a time when people have grown perniciously selfish (Gold, 2006). The forestry department assigns an agent to protect the trees, but unlike the local landlord's guards of 50 years ago, today's forestry agent wields no respected sanctions. He is both despised as someone out to profit from his government service and accepted as someone who will negotiate with herders – a politically powerful group who require the liberty to violate government restrictions in order to pursue their livelihood.

Agricultural practice changed more gradually than the hillsides but is also substantially altered. Farming is now dominated by the use of tractors to plow, engine-driven pumps to irrigate, and threshing machines to harvest, as well as by the application of chemical fertilisers and by the preponderance of wheat as the favoured food grain and oil-seed cash crops. Coexisting with these forms of modernisation are the continuing if waning practices of plowing, irrigating, and threshing with oxen; winnowing by hand; and cultivating the traditional grain crops of corn, millet, and barley. Food has declined in flavour, as well as nutritional value, according to many (Gold, 2009). Yet, no one here proposes to recover 'heirloom' varieties; no one seeks a way back.

A discourse of tastelessness surrounds new varieties of grains and vegetables, including eggplant. Currently the centre of a stormy controversy over a new genetically modified variety, at the time of my 2003 research, eggplant was already a food symbolic of changing times. As I read about the eggplant protests in December 2009, I developed a retrospective understanding of this humble vegetable's significance – as relished and filling.[3] During my winter 2003 research, talk about modern eggplant's lack of tastiness carried with it a subtle but perceptible moral evaluation.[4] I had many conversations in January 2003 about two species of eggplant, one readily visible and one largely invisible. The latter scarce item is '*deshi*' eggplant, literally 'of the land', implying that it was local and indigenous. Deshi eggplants are whitish in color, and the vine on which they grow has annoying thorns on it, but everyone with whom I spoke asserted this variety to be the most delicious. Yet the widely prevalent species nowadays is called '*disko*': it is small, shapely, perfectly purple, its stem free of unpleasant prickles, but people say it lacks in taste. Disko is not only easier to cultivate, but also sells better.

Barji Mali, a gardener woman, was among several who told us, 'There used to be local eggplant (*deshi bangan*). We used to grow it, but now we have modern (*adhunik*) eggplant, called "disko". Now, disko is available.' Shambhu Nath, an educated villager in his forties who has worked with me on and off over the years, immediately chimed in to emphasise a contrast in flavour: 'The local eggplant was tasty, but it had prickles on it. It was really delicious, but the disko has no flavour. Even today, the local is available in the market but it costs more than disko.' He then gave an elaborate recipe for what he said was the best way to cook deshi – stuffed with spices after roasting. Nostalgia for the tasty past is invested in the white variety which has shifted from staple to luxury, and is now presumably cultivated by a few for sale to the well-to-do in town markets rather than village lanes.

This contrast between the pervasive, modern, shiny, purple, attractive disko and the indigenous variety – white, prickly, flavourful, but no longer consumed – captures much about nostalgia for a past that people do not necessarily strive to reclaim. Pleasures such as the taste of white eggplant, roasted and spiced as Shambhu recalled it, are missed but deemed irretrievable. There is an obvious symbolism in the disko/deshi contrast and the psychology of loss it evokes. Tasteless modernity is perfectly embodied in the shiny purple tasteless eggplant, named after an emblem of urban amorality – disco dancing.

Those who repeatedly lament the cherished tastes of past times seem oddly willing to allow them to vanish from their lives. In this region, awareness of species loss has not translated into any organised protest against the marketing of commercially produced seeds, or even any strong urge to save old plant varieties, as it has elsewhere (Ramprasad, Prasad, & Gopinath, 1999; Shiva, 2001).

In February 2003, Barji Mali spoke about the convenience of commercial seeds in spite of her critique of the flavour of disko eggplant:

> Now we get them all: white radish, spinach, we get them all from the bazaar; small, big, they are all available whether you need a little or a lot. They sell them with a picture on the packet, on each bag; and from that you know what kind of seed it is; we could produce them ourselves if we wanted to, but we don't need to worry because we know we can get them in the bazaar. Whatever we need we can get them and nothing is mixed with them.

As an accomplished and successful produce-gardener, she lauded the modern convenience of commercial seed packets even if, earlier in the same interview, she had expressed preference for the flavour of a local variety. These changes from home-saved to market-purchased seeds have had far-reaching gendered consequences as well as consequences for biodiversity. Women's work is reduced, and Barji appears to appreciate this in spite of some negative ramifications for the evaluation of women's contributions to agriculture and gardening.

Ladu Lodha, a farmer in Ghatiyali famous for his agricultural skills and dedication, along with his political wisdom as a respected member of the village council, described for us clearly in 2003 the implications for gendered work in the change from saved seeds to purchased seeds:

> Women would protect them [seeds]. They would mix them with ashes and store them so bugs could not attack them. That's why they mixed them with ashes. But nowadays the government has sent pills, medicines to use instead....
>
> [In the old days] women did it. When it began to rain [and was time to plant], they would say, 'This is chickpea, this is lentil,' and so they would give advice: 'Put this here and plant this here.' They would have collected all the seeds for one season's crops. But today, direct from the bag, no mixing with ash, no work of women protecting; there is no work left for women.
>
> Cucumber, watermelon, summer squash, green beans, bottle-gourd, white gourd-melon ... all kinds of seeds: now they all come from the store. But in the past women stored all the seeds at home; and before the rainy season, they would gather them all; if they were missing any they would collect them

from their neighbours. Women were the ones who kept seeds, formerly. Now every seed comes in a bag!

The change in seed source from home to market also means less reliance on a community, on helpful neighbours. When I asked, 'So you think the modern way is good?' Ladu immediately responded, 'Yes it is good, there is no difficulty.'

The important role women once played, which involved selecting seeds while crops were still standing; gathering, storing, and protecting those seeds in the home; and bringing them to the fields for planting the next season, has now more or less disappeared without fanfare. Activists deplore such transformations. Vandana Shiva's influential writings, for example, have strongly valorised the time-honoured associations between women and seeds (Shiva et al., 1995). But in Ghatiyali neither men nor women seem bothered by the switch to commercial products.

Domestic change: labour, gender roles, and education

Women are very conscious of evident lived change over generations. Clothing and practices of modesty are often lively topics of conversation. Change in women's dress is indicative not only of changing gender roles but of change in rural political economy and social hierarchy. In the past, the members of each birth-group (caste, jati) had a particular weave to their skirts and pattern to their wraps, all of which were produced by artisans (weavers and cloth-printers) in the local community. Today, however, preferred dress for all but the most senior generation is made of imported, synthetic, town-purchased fabrics, carrying no identity marker. Women also readily articulate gender-specific impacts of development.[5]

A song I recorded in the 1990s, its composition evidently dating back to the 1980s, had the following lines:

> The Chambal broke, the Banas broke, and Udaipur flowed away,
> Indira got down at the station, what did she have to say?
> I've installed elec-tri-city, faucets, street lamps too,
> And installed your sister-in-law's brother [that is, 'your husband'] in a *salaried* job!

This song, a young Mina woman told us, was still popular (then over ten years after Indira Gandhi's assassination) among Mina girls – most of whom at that time spent their childhoods and early adolescence herding.

Women characterise the floods of change in terms of less labourious work for women: electricity means women do not have to grind grain; water taps mean they no longer have to go to the well; streetlights may imply greater freedom of movement. But these are not on a par with wage-earning careers – which the song grants husbands only – presumably literate ones. Other songs, recorded from women and girls, speak of domestic and emotional problems resulting from the skewed education system. Young women come to desire education because the gender gap in schooling leads to marital trouble. Illiterate brides are badly treated, even abandoned, by literate husbands seeking companionship.

Government programmes promoting girls' education do promise jobs along with all kinds of well-being. Anticipating a visit from a district-level officer, Bhoju's fellow teachers in the village of Palasiya decided it was necessary to paint slogans about literacy on every available wall. A pamphlet was their source for slogans, many of them rhymed couplets in the original. Here are a few examples, of which the first seemed to be the most popular in this region.

1   One daughter will be educated, seven generations will be liberated!
2   Every daughter has a right to health, learning, respect, and love.
3   If we educate our daughter, we increase knowledge and honour.
4   Just one vow is to be made: give your daughter an education.
5   Let brothers do the housework too, so girls can go to school!
6   Daughters' education is the family's protection.

Over ten years ago, on Republic Day at the big Government Middle School in Ghatiyali, three primary school girls, dressed in their uniforms, beautifully performed this song:

> Don't get me married when I'm young,
> Let me study, let me study!
> My sister Kajori is unschooled, she has eight children,
> and doesn't know how to raise them, so the lot of them are sick.
> Let their sickness be less!
> Don't get me married when I'm young,
> Let me study, let me study!
> Many literate sisters go to work at jobs, but
> The illiterate sit, their veils pulled down,
> In their homes, darkness and shadow.
> Let me bring the new light!
> Don't get me married when I'm young.
> Let me study, let me study!

One of the schoolgirl singers, from the Gujar community, is now 23. She is still unmarried, and still studying. Moreover, with her parents' full approval she decided to break off an earlier arranged betrothal and to become engaged to a different person. This young woman is training to be a teacher and holds the qualifications of both a BA and B.Ed. She plans to work as a teacher even after marriage. Clearly devoted to her family, she never shows the slightest sign of disrespect to her remarkably intelligent but totally unschooled mother. Her younger sisters follow her courageous, trail-blazing footsteps.

Intangible change: community, morality, aspiration

While old people in Ghatiyali were usually very willing to describe the past, I found none who were not eager to see their children's children advance into an unknown future. As has been documented in many regions of India, the prosperous future imagined for schooled offspring is bound to the vision of salaried jobs. For the young, destined to fulfil their elders' aspirations, the spectre of unemployment dashes not only their own hopes but those of their families and communities (see Jeffrey, Jeffrey, & Jeffrey, 2006, 2008; Morarji, 2010). In and around Ghatiyali, as elsewhere, old and young express conviction that a decline of community spirit and an ascent of selfishness necessarily accompany entrance into the world of education, competition, jobs, and success.

In the 1990s I had a conversation with three village women – Bali Gujar (mid-thirties), Ajodhya Khati (mid-forties), Kesar Gujar (mid-sixties).[6] No men were present, and I opened the conversation by summarising to the women a lot of what I had already heard in previous interviews about the ineffable qualities of change. Ideas unfold here about the ways conceit, technology, the decrease of love, and human dependence on God are interwoven in contexts of radical change. It captures with subtlety why and how love is lost as modern goods spread. Many problems are depicted as existing between persons but at the same time affecting village, nature, and the cosmos.

ANN [ADDRESSING AJODHYA]: I have heard that a lot of change has happened in the village in the last 20 years – like the crops are different and the weather has changed; there used to be lots of rain and now there is less; and people say that there is less love.

AJODHYA: As are the people, so is the rain, and so are the times, and so is production.

ANN: Some other people have said that dharma is less, love is less. . . . Do you also think this?

AJODHYA: Yes, all of it has happened . . . The times are deteriorating, going from bad to worse.

BALI: This is the situation, human beings have become free (*ajād*). [According to Bhoju, she uses 'free' to mean 'lazy'.]

KESAR: Now we have water taps (*nal*) and electricity.

AJODHYA: Yes, and we used to have to grind grain in the hand mill. So, yes, we have water taps, and electric pumps [for irrigating fields] and flour from the power mill . . . and wheat grown with English fertiliser. There is no local (*deshī*) fertiliser [that is, composted manure] left. Where is the local fertiliser?

We used to make our bread from stone-ground grain and drink well water, and there were lots of dairy products. But now? Today there is not even any water in the well.

. . . For this reason we are getting weak.

ANN: Your body is weak, but what about your soul? Is there a difference in your soul, in your heart?

BALI [QUICKLY]: There is no difference in the soul. It is just as before, except that people get puffed up, [thinking] 'Oh I have a water tap connection!' [As Bali and Bhoju have a tap in their home, she may be anticipating criticism of herself here.]

AJODHYA: People [these days] are feeling so proud (*ghamaṇḍ*). People put up fans. If I have a fan in my house, why do I need to go out for the wind? If I feel hot, I will turn on the fan. It is freedom! (*ajād*).

While the motif of jealousy aroused by consumer goods is clear enough, I was generally puzzled by the ways these women used the word 'freedom' in a fashion that seemed simultaneously approving and critical. With the same word they could evoke relished liberation from hard labours brought by new technologies and the resulting laziness, even degeneration of body and spirit and community that seemed to accompany such convenience. I tried to elicit more clarification.

ANN: So, is this good? Is there rest and comfort for women today?
AJODHYA: I had comfort in the past too, but now it has doubled! Now we are really comfortable. It is God who gave us this comfort, what belongs to me? Sometimes we are proud, [thinking] 'Oh, I have this much wealth, this many different kinds of things.' [children, grandchildren] But none of it is ours, it all belongs to God. Nothing is our own . . .
BALI: The people from old times, they were not so proud as they are today.
AJODHYA: . . . It used to be we were not self-inflated (*hambaṛī*) – but today there is too much of it! Like you are talking with me, but I am not talking with you properly, because I feel I am a big person, I feel proud. . . . And if I talk with you happily, but you don't answer, then I'll stop talking. So love (*prem*) has become less.

. . .

ANN: These days, you say there is lots of ease . . . so why is love less? When you're not grinding and you're sitting under the fan, why aren't you happy?
BALI: You sit under the fan and you are happy, but others are not happy with you [because they are jealous]. These others come and they say to themselves, 'Oh they have a fan, the fan is running, maybe they are sleeping,' and they don't come in [to socialise].
ANN: This is jealousy?
BALI: They don't think, 'Oh they have a fan, let's go in and sit down,' but instead they are jealous.

[Bali's explanation shows that the definition of jealousy has divisiveness built into it, based as it is on possession and the division between 'haves' and 'have-nots'.]

AJODHYA: . . . If I get something good, then you go that far away from me; because you are jealous; if you have something, then I will cross from that far away [to avoid you].

KESAR GUJAR: If you have the flour mill at your home you are so proud: 'I have a power mill in my home, me and only me!'

'Me and only me' seems to sum up this discourse.

Interestingly, a decade later young college girls, interviewed on my behalf in the summer of 2007 by Madhu Gujar – herself a 20-year-old college student – also highlighted the ascent of selfishness (see Gold, 2009). For example, when Madhu asked her friend and fellow student Asha Jat, 'So, what do you think the future will be like?' Asha's reply was dramatic:

> Education will increase but love will be finished. Twenty years from now people will say, 'This is not my relative!' People have already become selfish, and the new generation will become even more selfish.

Asha Jat predicts a future of educated selfishness and the rejection of mutual responsibilities among kinfolk. She and other simultaneously worried and ambitious young women with whom Madhu and I spoke also highlighted the insecurities of employment futures for their cohort, both male and female.

Conclusion: security and insecurity

Throughout the preceding pages I have discussed extensively, although far from exhaustively, how change is perceived in many aspects of rural life. In concluding, I briefly summarise these findings, sketching in broad strokes realms of significantly enhanced security as well as areas tinged, or suffused, with insecurity.

First, in Rajasthan with the passing of the time of kings, the role of government has perceptibly diminished. Various government workers play their significant parts in rural life, from teacher to forestry agent to village-level worker who teaches new agricultural techniques. Yet for many reasons, these officials are not in any fashion replications of former authority. This is largely a source of security, but can be at times a factor linked to insecurity, as when people regret that no one takes responsibility for protecting the forest as the king once did. The fort stands empty; the forestry agent whose house is just below the old castle covers his walls with environmental slogans but is nonetheless perceived as ineffectual and indeed 'corrupt'.

There is a common, popular perception of irreversible ecological decline which many people explicitly link to declines in human relationships. Genuine geophysical insecurities do loom over Rajasthan. Some, such as the unforeseen results of tubewell proliferation, might have been regulated but were not; others, such as global climate change, are beyond local control in most ways. The awesome unimaginable abundance of water in the Banas River in 2006 – a river through whose dry bed I had often tramped in earlier decades and where melons and cucumbers were normally cultivated in the hot season – was the result of the Bisalpur Dam, from which many had high hopes of benefiting. By the summer of 2008 the river was once again low in the region near Ghatiyali, and people were complaining that the water from the dam was being channelled elsewhere while their water shortage problems went unheeded. Water was delivered by tanker trucks to supplement reduced supplies from village wells. New agricultural technologies which involve dependence on increased irrigation lead to enormous insecurity in bad monsoon years, when the results of depleted groundwater are exacerbated.

Trevor Birkenholtz's (2009) recent writings describe the ways that new forms of scarcity produce new forms of 'cooperation and adaptation', including 'tubewell partnerships', providing some encouraging news in the generally dismaying picture of Rajasthan's depleted water resources. Birkenholtz's insights may be linked to those of Akio Tanabe, who writes about the ways 'new space' has opened up for previously marginalised groups in Orissa, leading to a kind of social churning generating new visions of community (Tanabe, 2007). Perhaps the tubewell partnerships Birkenholtz describes are evidence of similar processes at work in Rajasthan.

For most of the people with whom I have interacted, enhanced security lies in increased physical and economic well-being, including several kinds of freedom. Soon after independence, people realised their freedom from exploitative taxation and oppressive government. More gradually came other kinds of freedoms, including, for women, from relentless daily labour such as grinding grain by hand and fetching water from the well. Able to retain and allocate the fruits of their agricultural labours, villagers have further improved their lives by investing in land and improved agricultural technology, including means of irrigation; in more comfortable homes; in their children's education.

Yet when people assess the present, it appears that many of the same elements understood as progress may have a negative flip side, one that leads to perceived insecurities. Education, as already noted, is inseparable from aspirations for good jobs that may be disappointed in the highly competitive market. Education is also linked with concerns about a breakdown of tradition in communities, families, and gender roles, thus bringing insecurity right into the home. Yet it seems to me that – as the source of manageable and often emotionally rewarding responsibilities – families remain for most rural Rajasthanis key to care, comfort, and support. Socio-economic insecurities are pervasive, but rather than paralysing, they motivate accelerated effort, and the morality underpinning that effort lies largely in duty, love, and care for families.

As an anthropologist of religion, I will close by gesturing toward an area of life about which I have said little thus far. Deities too contribute to perceptions of security. Devotion to the gods – I might hazard – is an area providing comforting continuity over the past 60 years. By this I certainly do not mean to suggest that there have been no transformations in religion, but only that people – in sustaining their relations with deities, in allocating significant shares of the fruits of economic success to improvements of shrines and temples – tap into another source, another genre of security in uncertain times. Moreover, in donating private wealth to shrine improvement, people work against a threatening vision of rampant egotism (expressed as 'me and only me'), by contributing to a built landscape of visible community, even while responding to invisible presence. Like many human beings the world over, the people of Ghatiyali and its environs are not without worries but not without hope; not without appreciation of the advances they have made; not without realistic humility before the challenges they face.

Notes

1 Two recent panoramic works on changing rural India, squarely focused on development and globalisation respectively, are by Harriss-White and Janakarajan (2004) and Reddy and Bhaskar (2005).
2 What follows here draws selectively and retrospectively on three decades of research. I have found it expedient to incorporate materials from a number of previous publications as well as one that is currently in press; notes will guide readers to the larger works from which I have sometimes extracted whole passages and sometimes condensed, reworded or reframed particular observations.
3 See for just one summary of highly charged and much commented on debates, 'Brinjals at Centre Stage at Rangayana', *Times of India*, 13 December 2009. http://timesofindia.indiatimes.com/city/mysore/Brinjals-at-centre-stage-at-Rangayana/articleshow/5333840.cms [accessed 30/12/09].
4 The following lengthy discussion of eggplant appears in Gold (2012).
5 What follows draws substantially from Gold (2002) but integrates that material with some more recent observations.
6 This conversation is reported in Gold (2006).

Bibliography

Afridi, Farzana (2007) 'The Impact of School Meals on School Participation: Evidence from Rural India'. Working paper. http://74.125.47.132/search?q=cache:qHoIHYcbkWgJ: www.cid.harvard.edu/neudc07/docs/neudc07_s6_p01_afridi.pdf [accessed 30/12/09].

Birkenholtz, Trevor (2009) 'Irrigated Landscapes, Produced Scarcity, and Adaptive Social Institutions in Rajasthan, India'. *Annals of the Association of American Geographers* 99(1): 118–137.

Gold, Ann Grodzins (1998) 'Sin and Rain: Moral Ecology in Rural North India', in Lance Nelson (ed.) *Purifying the Earthly Body of God: Religion and Ecology in Hindu India*. Albany: State University of New York Press.

Gold, Ann Grodzins (2002) 'New Light in the House: Schooling Girls in Rural North India', in Diane P. Mines & Sarah Lamb (eds.) *Everyday Life in South Asia*. Bloomington: Indiana University Press.

Gold, Ann Grodzins (2003) 'Foreign Trees: Lives and Landscapes in Rajasthan', in Paul Greenough & Anna Lowenhaupt Tsing (eds.) *Nature in the Global South: Environmental Projects in South and Southeast Asia*. Durham, NC: Duke University Press.

Gold, Ann Grodzins (2006) 'Love's Cup, Love's Thorn, Love's End: The Language of *Prem* in Ghatiyali', in Francesca Orsini (ed.) *Love in South Asia: A Cultural History*. Cambridge: Cambridge University Press.

Gold, Ann Grodzins (2009) 'Tasteless Profits and Vexed Moralities: Assessments of the Present in Rural Rajasthan'. *Journal of the Royal Anthropological Institute* 15: 365–385.

Gold, Ann Grodzins (2012) 'Scenes of Rural Change', in Vasudha Dalmia & Rashmi Sadana (eds.) *The Cambridge Companion to Modern Indian Culture*. Cambridge: Cambridge University Press.

Gold, Ann Grodzins & Bhoju Ram Gujar (2002) *In the Time of Trees and Sorrows: Nature, Power, and Memory in Rajasthan*. Durham, NC: Duke University Press.
Gujar, Bhoju Ram & Ann Grodzins Gold (2007) 'Contentment and Competence: Rajasthani Children Talk about Work, Play and School', in Karen Malone (ed.) *Childspace: An Anthropological Study of Children's Use of Space*. New Delhi: Concept Publishing Company.
Harriss-White, Barbara & S. Janakarajan (2004) *Rural India Facing the 21st Century: Essays on Long Term Village Change and Recent Development Policy*. London: Anthem Press.
Jeffrey, Craig, Patricia Jeffery, & Roger Jeffery (2006) 'Urbane Geographies: Schooling, Jobs and the Quest for Civility in Rural North India', in Saraswati Raju, M. Satish Kumar, & Stuart Corbridge (eds.) *Colonial and Post-colonial Geographies of India*. New Delhi: Sage Publications.
Jeffrey, Craig, Patricia Jeffery, & Roger Jeffery (2008) *Degrees without Freedom? Education, Masculinities, and Unemployment in North India*. Stanford, CA: Stanford University Press.
Morarji, Karuna (2010) 'Where Does the Rural Educated Person Fit? Development and Social Reproduction in Contemporary India', in Philip McMichael (ed.) *Contesting Development: Critical Struggles for Social Change*. New York: Routledge.
Ramprasad, Vanaja, Krishna Prasad, & Gowri Gopinath (1999) 'The Synergy of Culture and Spirituality Enhances Biodiversity', in B. Haverkort & W. Hiemstra (eds.) *Food for Thought: Ancient Visions and New Experiments of Rural People*. London: Zed Books.
Reddy, A. Vinayak & G. Bhaskar (2005) *Rural Transformation in India: The Impact of Globalisation*. New Delhi: New Century Publications.
Shiva, Vandana (2001) 'Seed Satyagraha: A Movement for Farmers' Rights and Freedoms in a World of Intellectual Property Rights, Globalized Agriculture and Biotechnology', in B. Tokar (ed.) *Redesigning Life: The Worldwide Challenge to Genetic Engineering*. London: Zed Books.
Shiva, Vandana, Vanaja Ramprasad, Pandurang Hegde, Omkar Krishnan, & Radha Holla-Bhar (1995) *The Seed Keepers*. New Delhi: Indraprastha Press.
Tanabe, Akio (2007) 'Toward Vernacular Democracy: Moral Society and Post-postcolonial Transformation in Rural Orissa, India'. *American Ethnologist* 34: 558–574.

10 As hierarchies wane

Explaining intercaste accommodation in rural India

James Manor

Introduction

For a full understanding of human security in India we must consider a fundamentally important social change that has become apparent over the last generation or so in most rural areas – and its implications. The change is a decline in the acceptance of caste hierarchies by members of disadvantaged caste groups. Many people, including some social scientists, are only dimly aware of it – and some refuse to believe that it has happened. But since the mid-1990s, solid evidence of it has emerged from village-level studies conducted in several different regions of India (see for example: Karanth, 1996: 106; Mayer, 1997; Karanth, 1995; Charsley & Karanth, 1998; Gupta, 2004; Jodhka, 2002; Jodhka & Louis, 2003; Manor, 2010). As Dipankar Gupta (2004) has put it, caste is increasingly coming to denote 'difference' more than 'hierarchy'. Investigations by this writer in nine regions of India between 2011 and 2013[1] clearly indicated that this change is – with inevitable variations in its strength and in matters of detail – a widespread reality. The change is of monumental importance because caste hierarchy was long a central element in the rural social order. Indeed, in the view of this writer, this is one of the two most important changes to occur in India since the country gained independence in 1947 – the other being the establishment of a socially rooted democracy.

The old caste hierarchies[2] posed threats to the security and well-being of so-called lower castes. But their increasing – and increasingly open – refusal to accept those hierarchies has generated new and potentially more severe threats, since so-called higher castes may react against the change and seek to enforce the old inequities by force – by violence. This chapter examines processes – accommodations between 'higher' and 'lower' castes – that have eased this danger across much of rural India. Given the limitations on space, it focuses not on accommodations between *all* 'higher' and 'lower' caste groups, but on only the most important set of accommodations – those that have been reached between the formerly dominant landowning castes and Dalits (ex-untouchables).[3]

The discussion below is just one part of a much longer and more complex analysis which requires a book-length treatment. To give readers a sense of the overall picture, a few scene-setting comments follow. The analysis in this essay focuses only on rural areas. It does so partly because that is where roughly two-thirds of Indians still reside, but also because villages have long been the main bastions of traditional caste (and hierarchical) interactions. Although society has undergone less change in rural areas than in towns and cities, quite fundamental changes have now become apparent in rural society.

It is important to note that readers should not conclude from this discussion that caste is becoming weaker. If one meaning of the word 'caste', *jati* – an endogamous group (into which people marry their children) – is considered, then it remains extremely strong. Indeed, jati appears to be the most resilient and durable pre-existing social institution in Asia, Africa, and Latin America. It is not caste (jati) that is in decline, but the acceptance of hierarchies among jatis. Nor should anything in this chapter be taken to imply that Dalits no longer suffer humiliations, abuses, and violence; such outrages persist in strength. This analysis seeks only to show that other important things are also happening. To focus only on outrages is to miss this crucial point. And since our concern here is with interactions between Dalits and others, it is necessary to consider the dilemmas faced by those 'others', and their reactions to them. It is for this reason that this chapter discusses the recent experiences and perceptions of the formerly dominant landowning castes.

India is the most complex and heterogeneous society on earth, so the discovery of variations should not be surprising. The declining acceptance of caste hierarchies has become increasingly evident across most of rural India, but to differing degrees. In some subregions (and even within certain districts within subregions) the old social order has stubbornly resisted change. In such places, challenges to the old order by 'lower' castes are especially dangerous and thus more muted – though not absent. It is also worth stressing that using the presently available evidence, it is impossible to quantify the changes that are noted here. For example, we cannot measure with any precision the degree to which refusals to accept caste hierarchies have increased in different places, or the number and character of violent incidents and other caste-based abuses that have occurred in India overall or in parts of India. However, it is clear from an extensive enquiry by this writer in numerous regions that across most of the country, intercaste accommodations outweigh violence, and to a greater extent than might have been expected, given the momentous nature of the declining acceptance of caste hierarchies.

It is impossible in a single chapter to give adequate attention to the numerous, diverse causes of the waning of the old hierarchies. In brief, they include micro-level economic changes, increasing occupational diversity among Dalits and others, and the spread of education. These and other things have eroded the old *jajmani* system[4] and the material bonds of dependency which once locked 'lower' castes into relationships of subordination. The causes also include changes that flow from the wider political system: reservations for 'lower' castes in educational institutions, government employment and posts in elected bodies; the recognition by political leaders that members of 'lower' castes vote in vast numbers, that they possess immense numerical strength, and that nowadays their support can only be obtained if they are offered real substance and not just empty promises; plus the resulting proliferation of government programmes, some of which address caste and other inequalities. As shall be seen, one response from politicians – the Atrocities Act of 1989 – has facilitated both the increase in open refusals by Dalits to accept caste hierarchies and the emergence of intercaste accommodations when those refusals stoke social tensions. Other changes outside formal state structures that have also had a causal impact are briefly discussed below and include the increasing penetration of rural areas by Dalit organisations, other enlightened civil society organisations, and the media.

The rest of this chapter is divided into three parts. Part II surveys a broad array of actions taken by Dalits in recent years – all of which indicate their refusal to accept the old caste hierarchies. Part III examines the increasing difficulties faced by many members of the formerly dominant landed castes, and their perceptions of these difficulties. The trends discussed in Parts II and III generate intercaste tensions, but Part IV will show that despite this, accommodations between these two sets of castes (Dalits and landed castes) have nonetheless emerged as the predominant trend in rural areas.

Rejecting hierarchies: a repertoire of Dalit actions

Dalits have always harboured doubts and dissenting views about caste hierarchies (Gupta, 2009: chapter 9), but in recent times they have made their increasingly strong rejection of them increasingly apparent. To illustrate how this translates into action – and impinges on intercaste relations – let us consider the diverse repertoire of devices that Dalits have used. In a chapter-length study, there is only room for a tightly compressed survey of these devices, but it will convey a sense of how social interactions have been changing. The actions taken by Dalits fall into two broad categories – those which mainly or entirely entail disengagement from other castes, and those through which they engage with them. Each category is discussed below, proceeding from the least to the most assertive actions.

Modes of disengagement

Dalits in villages sometimes interact – to varying degrees – with Dalit organisations or activists. This may entail merely listening to the activists' ideas or to stories that reinterpret Dalit history by telling of struggles and heroes (Narayan, 2011). Or they may interact with pro-Dalit civil society organisations that are not exclusively Dalit. Such actions usually lead rural Dalits to think and to act more independently and thus to disengage somewhat from interactions with other castes – and from those castes' interpretations of history and their belief in caste hierarchies. At other times, Dalits may take action (and make sacrifices) to ensure that they or their children obtain some level of education because (following the iconic Dalit leader, Dr B. R. Ambedkar) they see that it can make them less dependent upon 'higher' castes. Again, this often enables them to disengage from those castes.[5] They may also take advantage of education, and/or caste reservations to obtain good jobs or to develop small enterprises which provide them with greater material autonomy and enable them to leave behind their traditional (and often degrading) occupations.[6] Further, Dalits may convert to a religion other than Hinduism – usually to Buddhism, as advocated by Ambedkar – in part because this helps them to disengage from the traditional caste hierarchy that is associated with Hinduism.

Dalits sometimes change their lifestyles in ways that emulate those of higher status groups – this process is often referred to as sanskritisation (Srinivas, 1956). They sometimes do this in order to claim higher caste status. Although this does not necessarily entail a disengagement from caste hierarchies, it may serve to enable Dalits to disengage somewhat – in their thinking, and perhaps in their actions – from other castes in a locality.

Individual Dalits increasingly migrate out of villages for extended periods to find work elsewhere, or commute on a daily basis to nearby urban centres for the same reason. This enables them to disengage from other castes in their villages in two ways. Their physical absence removes them from often stultifying local environments and hierarchies; and the wages earned from work elsewhere often reduce or break their dependence upon other castes within their villages, once more by providing them with a degree of material autonomy. Some enterprising Dalits travel back and forth between their villages and government offices at higher levels in the political system in efforts to obtain benefits for their village.[7] Such benefits may be shared only among fellow Dalits or among multiple castes. In the latter case, which of course entails engagement with other castes, they tend to gain esteem in the eyes of members of these castes. In both cases, they break the monopoly that members of the formerly dominant castes once exercised over links to higher levels, enabling Dalits to disengage somewhat from relationships of dependency on other castes.

Modes of engagement

There is abundant evidence from many regions of India to indicate a significant increase in incidences of refusal by Dalits – including some who are quite vulnerable – to accede to the wishes or demands of even powerful members of 'higher' castes.[8] There are marked variations in the precise manner in which people say 'no', and in the degree to which refusals occur. In many places, Dalits are not in a position to say 'no' to every possible demand, but in many others, they routinely refuse to defer to individuals from formerly dominant castes – to the extent that the old 'order' that existed in their villages has substantially or entirely disintegrated (see Karanth, Ramaswamy, & Hogger, 2004).

We have already seen that in many localities Dalits have managed – in a variety of ways – to achieve a significant degree of material autonomy. This tends to embolden them to demonstrate that autonomy more defiantly. For example, there is evidence from Bihar of Dalits earning enough from the Mahatma Gandhi National Rural Employment Guarantee Act to provide them with sufficient autonomy to make possible open acts of defiance of a local landlord, by refusing to work on his lands, even though they remain in the village – something that would have been unthinkable until quite recently.[9] When intercaste disputes and tensions arise, Dalit elders/leaders often negotiate accommodations with their counterparts from 'higher' castes. As this topic is hugely important, it is discussed in detail in Part IV of this chapter.

Dalits occasionally mount boycotts of other castes. Such episodes are rare, but for example, in a village in southern Karnataka, the formerly dominant Lingayats selected as their informal leader a man who behaved offensively towards Dalits. The Dalits were outraged and collectively resolved to impose a total boycott on Lingayats until the leader who had insulted them was replaced. Over several days, the Lingayats realised how dependent they were upon their Dalit neighbours for various things and, remarkably, they agreed to replace their leader with a more agreeable person.[10] (Thus, alongside bonds of dependence which force Dalits into positions of subordination, there are sometimes bonds of interdependence.)[11] Also, on rare occasions, Dalits lash out violently in response to (or in anticipation of) violence from other castes. For example, Dalits in parts of Tamil Nadu who have suffered brutal attacks from 'higher' castes have occasionally hit back violently in return, in order to deter further outrages.[12] Those counter-attacks proved effective enough to persuade other castes to abandon violence for several years.

The dilemmas and perceptions of formerly dominant landed castes

This chapter will now turn to certain key changes experienced by members of the landowning castes who formerly dominated life in India's villages, many of whom have faced increasingly harsh realities in recent years. To understand how intercaste accommodations occur, it is necessary to consider these changes, and landed castes' perceptions of them.[13] For members of such castes, agriculture and the control of land are not the sources of prestige, prosperity, and satisfaction that they once were. Many families have had to divide their landholdings into smaller and smaller plots as they parcel out shares among their children – or at least among male children; these shrunken plots are less economically viable than the larger ones that were the norm a generation or two ago. To this must be added what has often been called India's agricultural 'crisis', which has led 40 per cent of farmers to conclude that they would abandon cultivation if an alternative emerged.[14]

Since the early to mid-1990s, farming has yielded less abundant livelihoods than it had previously. Growth rates for agricultural output have declined, and the availability of credit is a problem for many farmers, in part because of the 'gradual collapse of the cooperative credit system'.[15] Subsidies on some inputs have been cut; government investment in the sector has declined, most damagingly in the key areas of irrigation and infrastructure; and agricultural extension services have been substantially wound down in many states. Further, soils have become less fertile in some areas as a result of the excessive use of fertilisers and pesticides, and cultivators in many areas also face what is sometimes termed a 'water crisis', which often takes the form of chronic shortages of ground water. Some farmers have experienced financial ruin after taking sizeable loans to cultivate risky cash crops that have not met expectations. These issues go a long way to explain the spate of farmer suicides in recent years. The influence of the once formidable 'farmers' lobby' has declined as caste and religious identities (some of which divide farmers) have become more salient in politics at the state and national levels, and as state and national governments have focused more on the manufacturing and service sectors (Reddy & Mishra, 2009; Posani, 2009; Dhas, 2009; Deshpande & Arora, 2011).

The woes of the landed castes do not end there: the attractions of urban centres and the declining prestige of farming have made their children hanker after lives in cities. To make their daughters attractive as potential brides to members of their castes who have good urban jobs, many farmers send them to colleges in cities, where they develop an aversion to returning to the land. (In those colleges, they sometimes develop romantic attachments to young men from other castes – which cause great anxiety among their parents.) Their sons also seek such urban jobs, and many of them who do not obtain enough educational qualifications to gain white-collar employment still move to cities, where they seek low-skilled jobs. Many fail to find work that conforms to their expectations, which are born of caste status, and they return defeated to the villages, where parents often struggle to support them. Yet sons who agree to lives as cultivators often have great problems finding brides, since young women prefer urban living. In Coorg in Karnataka, this problem became so acute that some Brahmin farmers[16] obtained dispensation from a local priest to travel to northern districts to find Lingayat brides, since Lingayats, like Brahmins, are vegetarians. Similar reports have emerged from North India. All of these problems cause intense distress to elders in the once dominant landed castes.

Elders in landed castes also find their former influence within the political/administrative system waning. Their old role as the principal gatekeepers between the village and higher levels in that system has been ended by local political entrepreneurs – *naya netas* or 'fixers' – who travel back and forth between villages and government offices at higher levels to obtain benefits for local residents from a wide array of government programmes (Krishna, 2002; Manor, 2000).[17] These people often come from less exalted castes, and this is also true of leaders and enterprising members of elected local councils (*panchayats*) who also provide links to bureaucrats and elected leaders at higher levels and wield influence within villages. Many senior figures in the landed castes have developed a hearty distaste for involvement in *panchayat* politics, since it exposes them to sometimes searing political contestation and to cross-examination by opponents – both of which they regard as beneath their dignity. Many therefore withdraw from *panchayats*, but this further undermines their political influence.

One further source of exasperation must be mentioned: dismay among the formerly dominant landed castes over increasingly frequent and open refusals by 'lower' castes – especially Dalits – to acknowledge their supposedly superior status and the old caste hierarchies. When that is added to the numerous frustrations described above, the danger arises that members of the landed castes may lash out violently, with Dalits the most likely targets. Such spasms of violence certainly have occurred – although only occasionally – in recent years, and have tended to be more savage than in former times. Thirty years ago, when attacks on Dalits occurred, they were usually calculated and measured – and less than lethal. An individual Dalit who had supposedly violated the informal code of deferential behaviour would be singled out as someone who needed to be 'taught a lesson'. S/he would then be beaten and/or publicly humiliated, as a signal to others not to challenge the hierarchical order. Such violent outrages tended to stop short of murder. In more recent years, however, when intercaste tensions arise, usually after an incident of some kind, it is more common to see violence that is far less measured. The pent-up frustrations felt by the landed castes often lead to sudden, heated (not calculated) attacks of great and often murderous severity. Violent acts tend to be committed by groups, against groups of Dalits, not by or against individuals. They are collective acts in both senses. They are not the result of calculated plans to impart a lesson; instead, they are frenzied outbursts of deep-seated anger at the entire array of troubles faced by the landed castes.

In considering such grotesque atrocities, two things must be borne in mind. First, when such spasms occur, they strongly tend to be confined to a single village – they almost never spread to nearby localities. Visits by this writer to villages close to places where such outbursts have occurred have revealed far more relaxed intercaste relations, and a perception among residents there that the strife-torn village (where tensions usually persist over many years) is eccentric and rather puzzling. Second and far more importantly, such savage outbreaks of lethal violence are far less common than accommodations within villages – even where intercaste tensions clearly exist, and when incidents that might spark violence occur. We must now consider this predominant tendency – towards accommodation – in more detail.

Understanding intercaste accommodations

It is worth re-emphasising that around 30 years ago, acts of violence by the landed castes against Dalits tended to be (i) measured and based on (ii) calculations by (iii) elders or senior leaders within the 'higher' castes. To understand how in recent years, intercaste accommodations have become far more common than spasms of lethal violence, we need to consider all three of these things. When accommodations are forged, senior figures within the landed castes still play key roles, along with Dalit counterparts (although as we shall see below, the authority of both within their castes is sometimes in doubt and under threat). In the majority of recent episodes, decisions by members of the landed castes to opt for negotiations and accommodations – that is, for measured, restrained actions – are based on careful tactical calculations by them. Crucially, those decisions are not inspired by a new-found empathy among 'higher' castes for Dalits – such decisions are the result of a change of mind and not of heart.[18]

What sort of calculations are made? Senior figures within the landed castes know that any violent act, lethal or otherwise, is very likely to become known in the world beyond their village, for several reasons. Dalit organisations are often shot through with factional disputes, but in most parts of India they penetrate at least tenuously into many (and usually most) rural areas. Thus, they tend to get wind of violent incidents, and the result may be a visit to the village by eminent urban Dalits to investigate and publicise the episode. Other (non-Dalit) civil society organisations which are sympathetic to Dalits may also call attention to a violent event. The media now penetrates fairly effectively into rural areas as well and so often reports such incidents. When such reports surface, state governments often respond as well, because most ruling parties cannot afford to alienate Dalit voters through inaction. Judges may also enter the picture – especially if petitions are filed by public interest lawyers, which is a common occurrence. And behind all of these potential intrusions into the village looms the Atrocities Act of 1989.[19]

The Act (which Dalit leaders often refer to simply as '1989') is a draconian law which characterises a broad array of actions – many of which stop short of violence – as 'atrocities' against Dalits. It empowers the authorities to jail alleged offenders immediately and without bail, on the strength of an accusation that an atrocity has taken place. It places the burden of proof on the accused rather than the accuser. State governments vary in the zeal with which they implement the Act, and many are less than assiduous in doing so.[20] Even when a state government seeks to make robust use of the Act, conviction rates for alleged offenders tend to be quite low. However, the low conviction rate should not blind us to the fact that even when a member of a 'higher' caste escapes conviction, s/he (usually 'he') must face a prolonged legal struggle – often lasting years – which is decidedly expensive and deeply inconvenient. It imposes huge opportunity costs, since it impedes the accused from getting on with other, highly important tasks such as cultivating land, marketing agricultural produce, developing other enterprises that may yield income, arranging loans, overseeing investments, and seeing that their children are properly educated and married off. For these reasons, even though it remains unlikely that the legal process will end in conviction, members of the 'higher' castes view the Atrocities Act with trepidation. In 1999, this writer saw palpable fear in the eyes of members of landowning castes when the Act was discussed even in the Gwalior region of Madhya Pradesh, where their social/political dominance and the old hierarchies had undergone little erosion.

All of these considerations weigh on the minds of the leaders of landed castes in most villages. They take them into account when deciding how to proceed when intercaste tensions arise, often as the result of a specific incident. These worries (and other considerations, discussed below) are usually sufficient to persuade them to seek to negotiate accommodations with Dalit leaders. Those accommodations are often uneasy and grudging, but they (and not violence) represent the predominant trend.

Regarding the types of 'incidents' that occur, there is space here only for inadequate comments on this complex, delicate topic – a full discussion of which will appear in a book-length study. But let us consider three types of incidents. Accommodations within villages are sometimes facilitated by a perception among most members of all castes that certain incidents – quarrels and modest ructions, however angry, between members of 'higher' castes and Dalits – are rather minor events that do not threaten the prestige of either group. This is often true of disputes that appear to all to involve unusually truculent individuals or households. They are perceived to be rather isolated, private squabbles that do little to disrupt the equanimity of social relations more broadly.

Another set of incidents, which are deeply serious, often trigger not violent conflict but frantic efforts to undo or otherwise resolve them – and to conceal them. This is frequently the response when amorous entanglements develop between individuals from Dalit and 'higher' castes, when individuals from those castes elope, or when rapes occur. All of these three occurrences have one thing in common: if they become known beyond the village, all of the young women of the village will be viewed by outsiders (unfairly of course) with suspicion – suspicion that loose morals prevail in the village, and/or that young women there may have been molested. These suspicions will make it difficult for all of those young women to find husbands. Such incidents may trigger violence, but that is not necessarily the most common outcome. Lest suspicions engulf all young women in the village, the first reaction by elders is not to resort to violence (which will only call attention to the embarrassment) but to hush things up. If an amorous relationship has developed between members of different castes, efforts are made to separate the two people, and perhaps to buy their silence. If an elopement has occurred, attempts are made to bring the pair back to the village, to annul a marriage if it has taken place, and again to separate the couple and use threats and/or enticements to break their links.

Rapes, which are obviously acts of violence in themselves, are even more inflammatory events and require more extensive discussion than is possible here. In some (but certainly not all or even most) parts of India, members of the landed castes have long routinely made free use of the bodies of Dalit women, and this vile practice persists in some areas. But now that Dalit and other organisations and the media have extended their reach into many rural areas, such outrages are more likely to become known – and under the Atrocities Act, action may follow. Given that possibility, and the importance of protecting the reputations of all the young women in a given village, efforts are again often made to hush things up, to intimidate those who might reveal that it has happened, and perhaps to compensate the victim.

Finally, let us consider a further set of events that are not trivial squabbles between individuals or households. They are not as salacious as amorous relationships, elopements, and rapes, but they pose genuine threats to peace in villages because they are perceived as serious insults to the dignity of 'higher' castes, and to what remains of the old hierarchical order. To illustrate this, consider two such incidents, both of which occurred in similar areas of South India but which produced contrasting outcomes. In the first, a few young Dalit men attended a village cinema. They had earned enough money to pay for the most expensive seats – for 'chairs' when the cheaper alternatives were 'benches' and 'floor'. During the screening, they placed their feet on the backs of the seats in the row in front of them – a row in which young women from the local landed caste were sitting off to one side. Such things are seen, in India, as a patently insulting act.

When word spread among members of the landed caste in the village, they were infuriated, and a few began violent attacks on Dalits which soon mushroomed into a killing spree that left many Dalits dead. Criminal investigations ensued, and several members of the landed castes were eventually convicted and jailed for long periods.

In the second case, three Dalit boys teased a lone boy from the landed caste which had formerly dominated social life in the village. When this was reported to elders of the landed caste, they gathered to consider what action to take. Some advocated violence, to teach the three Dalits a lesson, but the more influential elders argued that such action would produce too many lasting problems for the members of their caste, so they organised a meeting with Dalit elders. After some negotiation, it was agreed that the three Dalit boys would apologise to the boy whom they had teased – and after that happened, the incident was considered by all to have been closed. The kind of accommodation that was reached in the latter case is far more typical than the savage outbreak of violence in the first. There are, however, reasons to wonder whether such accommodations, which represent the predominant trend in recent years across most of rural India, will remain so. Doubts arise when we delve more deeply into the power dynamics that prevail within castes – and more specifically, into the influence of caste elders. Accommodations may not prove to be sustainable.

Accommodations are usually negotiated between senior figures from different castes, between elders. They share one common interest: no matter which caste they belong to, they see themselves as custodians of some sort of predictable 'order' in the village (or what is left of it after recent changes) – an 'order' within which they enjoy considerable influence and usually preeminence. Violence would threaten not just tranquillity but predictability, which is of great value to all of these senior figures.

Violence can threaten predictability in several ways. Quite apart from the injuries that it would (unpredictably) cause, violence could cause lasting disruption to daily village routines and make them less predictable. It might create longer-term resentments that would poison predictable intercaste relations, and thus the outwardly peaceable 'order' within the village, the maintenance of which is seen by many as the responsibility of senior leaders within different castes. Since that would impair their capacity to fulfil that responsibility, it would undermine their authority within their castes, and in general. Violence might also invite unpredictable interventions in village affairs by police or other government actors at higher levels, undermining the already limited autonomy of the village – autonomy which serves to make local affairs predictable. Even if no such interventions occurred, a spasm of violence would hand the initiative to those engaged in it – that is, to persons who were at least temporarily beyond the control of local leaders. It might thus have unpredictable consequences which could deprive those leaders of their much prized influence over village life. This in turn might open the way either to challenges by rivals or to a loss of discipline and coherence within their caste.

Accommodations negotiated by senior leaders of different castes are only enforceable if each leader has the authority within his[21] caste to persuade or compel his caste fellows to accept them. But in many localities, that authority faces the threat or the reality of erosion, by several different processes. Many of the changes, noted earlier, that have contributed to the declining acceptance of hierarchies by members of 'lower' castes also threaten the authority of elders *within* all castes. Education, occupational differentiation, and spatial mobility may make individuals within a caste less deferential to their own more senior fellow caste men. The emergence of local political entrepreneurs – 'fixers', *naya netas* – and of enterprising politicians on *panchayats* may also undermine the pre-eminence of caste elders. The problems that afflict agriculture and the sagging prestige attached to farming may weaken the influence of senior figures within landed castes.

The authority of caste elders is also sometimes undermined by actions which they themselves have taken. This is especially true of leaders of the landed castes. Three themes matter here: withdrawals, exits, and distractions. It was noted above that some senior figures within the once dominant landed castes have withdrawn from *panchayat* politics after becoming exasperated with the challenges and cross-questioning that they face there from opponents. Surinder Jodhka has shown that such senior leaders may invest funds in urban centres and establish second homes there for themselves or their children, where they spend part of their time. Even if they do not undertake part-time exits from the village, these things become distractions which prevent them from giving enough attention to affairs within their villages and their castes to maintain their influence there. These and other trends may damage the authority structures within castes, and even render castes leaderless. If that occurs, then it will become extremely difficult to arrange accommodations between castes and to enforce compliance once such accommodations are arranged.

This chapter is not intended to provide a final, definitive analysis. Rather, it seeks to open up discussion of several crucial issues which have, strangely, been largely ignored. But at least a start has been made here.

Notes

1 The author is grateful to the Harry Frank Guggenheim Foundation for the grant that made this research possible.
2 The plural is used here because not one but a great many different hierarchies exist within India. For example, crudely speaking, every linguistic region possesses its own caste system – which differs modestly or radically from those of other regions and contains subregional variations.
3 This chapter therefore omits discussion of conflicts and accommodation between Dalits and the 'Other Backward Castes' (OBCs) when the latter constitute the main group with which Dalits must interact. In villages where that is the case, the formerly dominant landed castes – for example, Marathas in Maharashtra, Kammas and Reddys in Andhra Pradesh, Lingayat and Vokkaligas in Karnataka, Jats in much of north India, etc. – are either absent or present in very small numbers. For complex reasons, it is usually more difficult for Dalits to forge accommodations with OBCs than with the landed castes.
4 It had largely confined members of various castes to traditional occupations – the least remunerative and respectable of which rendered poorer groups dependent on local elites.

As hierarchies wane 173

5 In some localities in various parts of India, Dalit efforts to obtain education have made them more qualified for employment in good jobs than OBCs and even formerly dominant landed groups in their localities. This is advantageous to Dalits, but it can also be a source of social tension.
6 They may obtain such employment partly as a result of connections with other Dalits, or with state institutions, or independently. In all of these cases, they become less dependent on other castes, and therefore disengage somewhat from them. Occasionally, however, they find such jobs as a result of contacts with members of other castes – and in such cases, they may not become less dependent upon and less engaged with members from other castes.
7 See the discussion of 'fixers' or *naya netas* (new leaders) elsewhere in this chapter.
8 For example, during an extensive exercise in field research in different parts of Maharashtra, Gopal Guru – who has a healthy scepticism about happy stories of change for the better – found abundant evidence of this trend. Interview with Gopal Guru, New Delhi, 7 April 2010.
9 A landless labourer in Bihar told Indrajit Roy that even though they could earn more money by migrating to Punjab for work, they preferred to stay at home because NREGA had made it possible for them to 'desist from working the *jamindar*'s (landlord's) land even if we stay in the village' – a choice that both reflected and hastened the erosion of status-based dependence. Another low-caste worker stated that before this programme, 'we were . . . subservient to the *jamindar*, and to the "high" caste. With the NREGA, we can live in the village without having to adhere to the village rules, of working the *jamindar*'s land. By seeing us in the village, without us begging him for work, he understands that we are human beings too, capable of a dignified life.' Emboldened by this display of assertiveness, another labourer added, 'His [the landlord's] economy be damned' (Roy, 2012: 26).
10 I am grateful to A. P. Kripa for an account of this incident.
11 Often, bonds of interdependence between 'higher' castes and Dalits no longer exist. If landed castes use machines for cultivation and harvesting or hire agricultural labourers from outside the locality to till their plots, the old bonds which tied local labourers into relationships of dependency are broken. A near total discontinuity separates 'higher' castes from Dalits, especially (as is common) when the latter inhabit separate hamlets or parts of a village which stand at a remove from the main settlement. Little or no social interaction occurs between the two groups. Paul Brass found numerous examples of this in rural Uttar Pradesh in 2013, and this writer saw this in several other regions (or districts within regions) in 2012 and 2013 – for example, in Mandya District (but far less often in neighbouring districts) of southern Karnataka.
12 I am grateful to Hugo Gorringe and A. R. Ventakatachalapthy for information on this trend. For evidence from Tamil Nadu of hitting back, see for example *The Hindu*, 9 November 2013.
13 The comments that follow are based in part on discussions with members of these groups in villages in nine Indian regions.
14 M. S. Swaminathan, 'The Crisis of Indian Agriculture', *The Hindu*, 15 August 2007.
15 Ibid.
16 Unusually in Karnataka, Brahmins own and cultivate land in Coorg and other pockets across the state.
17 Krishna (2002) calls these entrepreneurs '*naya netas*' (new leaders) and I call them 'fixers'.
18 I am grateful to K. C. Suri for stressing this point.
19 Its full title is the 'Scheduled Castes and Scheduled Tribes (Prevention of Atrocities) Act, 1989'.
20 See for example the cover story in *Frontline*, 21 November–4 December 2009.
21 The leaders are invariably men.

Bibliography

Charsley, S. R. & G. K. Karanth (eds.) (1998) *Challenging Untouchability: Dalit Initiative and Experience from Karnataka.* London: Altamira Press.

Deshpande, R. S. & S. Arora (eds.) (2011) *Agrarian Crisis and Farmer Suicides.* New Delhi: Sage Publications.

Dhas, A. C. (2009) 'Agricultural Crisis in India: The Root Causes and Consequence'. *Munich Personal RePEc Archive.* Working Paper 18930.

Gupta, D. (2004) *Caste in Question: Identity or Hierarchy?* New Delhi, London, & Thousand Oaks: Sage.

Gupta, D. (2009) *The Caged Phoenix: Can India Fly?* New Delhi: Penguin.

Jodhka, S. S. (2002) 'Caste and Untouchability in Rural Punjab'. *Economic and Political Weekly* 11 May: 1813–1823.

Jodhka, S. S. & P. Louis (2003) 'Caste Tensions in Punjab: Talhan and Beyond'. *Economic and Political Weekly* 12 July: 2923–2936.

Karanth, G. K. (1995) *Change and Continuity in Agrarian Relations.* New Delhi: Concept.

Karanth, G. K. (1996) 'Caste in Contemporary Rural India', in M. N. Srinivas (ed.) *Caste: Its Twentieth Century Avatar.* New Delhi: Penguin.

Karanth, G. K., V. Ramaswamy, & R. Hogger (2004) 'The Threshing Floor Disappears: Rural Livelihood Systems in Transition', in R. Baumgartner & R. Hogger (eds.) *In Search of Sustainable Livelihood Systems: Managing Resources and Change.* New Delhi, London, & Thousand Oaks: Sage.

Krishna, A. (2002) *Active Social Capital: Tracing the Roots of Development and Democracy.* New York: Columbia University Press.

Manor, J. (2000) 'Small-Time Political Fixers in Indian States: "Towel over Armpit"'. *Asian Survey* September–October: 816–835.

Manor, J. (2010, 2nd edn) 'Prologue', in R. Kothari (ed.) *Caste in Indian Politics.* New Delhi: Orient Black Swan.

Mayer, A. (1997) 'Caste in an Indian Village: Change and Continuity', in C. J. Fuller (ed.) *Caste Today.* Delhi: Oxford University Press.

Narayan, Badri (2011) *The Making of the Dalit Public in North India.* New Delhi: Oxford University Press.

Posani, B. (2009) *Farmer Suicides and the Political Economy of Agrarian Distress in India.* Development Studies Institute: London School of Economics.

Reddy, D. Narasimha & S. Mishra (2009) *Agrarian Crisis in India.* Delhi: Oxford University Press.

Roy, Indrajit (June 2012) 'Guaranteeing Employment, Forging Political Subjectivities: Insights from the NREGS'. Unpublished paper.

Srinivas, M. N. (1956) 'A Note on Sanskritization and Westernization'. *Far Eastern Quarterly* 15(4): 481–496.

Epilogue
Human and international security in an age of new risk and opportunities

Akio Tanabe and Minoru Mio

From 'nationally structured rule and development' to 'globally restructuring dynamics'

From the 1990s onwards, globalisation has interconnected the everyday lives of multiple and diverse peoples throughout the world. The flow of humans, commodities, money, and information has shaken the previously predominant ordering of social space within national boundaries, reshuffling borders and bringing about unexpected connections. This transformation on the international and domestic scene has brought about a 'paradigmatic shift' in our notion of 'security', as Crispin Bates points out in the Introduction to this volume. The notion of 'security' has shifted from the state-centric idea of national security based on military power to an understanding of security based on human concerns that transcend international boundaries, such as socio-economic development, human rights, gender equality, environmental degradation, terrorism, democracy, and governance. This shift is driven by systemic global changes, from the era of state rivalry, competition, and war in 'the short twentieth century' (Hobsbawm, 1994), to the post-Cold War era of global flow and mobility. The change coincided with the end of post-colonial nationalist regimes in developing countries, including India, which experienced a regime change from state-led development and centralised rule to economic liberalisation and devolution of power. In other words, there has been a shift from 'nationally structured rule and development' to 'globally restructuring dynamics' in which the notion of 'security' has also changed from national security to international human security.

The rise of mobility in the world has resulted in 'time-space compression' (Harvey, 1990) and 'liquid-modernity' (Bauman, 2000), causing traditional social structures to break apart. There has been a decoupling between the national order and capitalist economy, once united under the hitherto state-led economy, both of which have become fluid and mobile. Lash and Urry (1987) call this fragmentation of the socio-economic order, which is characterised by increasing economic and political disorganisation, 'the end of organized capitalism'. It is true that we are now witnessing a fluctuation of existing categories and groups, especially where new linkages across borders are taking place.

In the case of India, the prevailing post-colonial structures of elite dominance centred on the bureaucratic state apparatus and the traditionalised hierarchy of caste and class have been destabilised. This is not to say that elite rule is finished or that caste and class have lost their importance: the dominance of the urban high-caste elite persists, and the existence of inequality and discrimination is still prevalent. However, the nature of rule has undoubtedly changed and people are no longer silently embedded in structures of dominance and hierarchy. Today, diverse social groups participate in new ways in India's public life. Dalits; adivasis; Other Backward Classes (OBCs); minorities and women; individuals from rural areas, towns, and cities; the poor and the new middle classes – the 'vernacular publics' – are all raising their voices to demand, negotiate, and engage in dialogue with each other and the wider world (Neyazi, Tanabe, & Ishizaka, 2014).

The deepening of democracy in India, conversely, has undermined the liberal-democratic assumption of the gradual emergence of secular and rational citizen-individuals and has given birth to a multitude of vernacular publics that raise fragmented voices and form unexpected coalitions and alliances across diverse castes, classes, and religious groups according to the issues at stake (Kaviraj, 1991). In other words, in India, a new cross-border social dynamism is being realised through the restructuring and utilisation of existing social relationships and groupings. This can be seen in the formation of civil organisations, NGOs, and self-help groups based on various identities of caste, religion, and gender, as well as in the ways that kinship-caste-religious-personal networks are realigned and utilised to support mobility across the rural-urban nexus in search of better life chances through education and employment.[1] As a result, identity-based social relationships no longer imply a fixed structure that embeds individuals in a particular place and socio-economic position, but rather function as networks that support physical and social mobility. It also means that the apparent paradox between the continuity of identities and relationships based on kinship, caste, religion, and gender on the one hand and the vibrant dynamics of restructuring relationships, deepening democracy, and socio-economic mobility on the other is not an untenable contradiction but an expression of a 'long-standing dialectical and dialogical process' of engagement by various actors to creatively utilise new and old resources to secure and expand life chances (see Chapter 1). Human security in contemporary India must be understood with sensitivity to such socio-cultural, politico-economic, and historical dynamics.

Globalisation and South Asian development

The current transformation taking place in India as a result of modernisation and globalisation should not be understood as the total degeneration of age-old traditional structures, but as a process of reshuffling and realignment of the post-colonial national order. The post-colonial national order was Janus-faced: the modernising developmental state that emphasised democracy, secularism, and rationality belied the ingrained social structures of dominance and hierarchy based on caste, class, and gender. Since the 1990s, the forces of economic liberalisation, devolution and decentralisation, and globalisation have combined, causing mutual permeation among the global market, state governance, and vernacular society. In this hybrid space, where the global, the state, and the social meet, the pluralistic and diverse nature of Indian society is manifesting dynamic characteristics that go beyond the fixity of post-colonial structure that followed independence.

The globalisation process in India, seen from the perspective of the long durée, concurs with and progresses according to the South Asian path of development (Sugihara, 2010). While the Western path of development has been characterised by capital-intensive and production-centred economic growth along with politics of control in class society, and the East Asian path of development has been founded on labour-intensive and distribution-centred economies along with politics of cooperation in egalitarian society, the South Asian path of development is driven by diversity and a participation-centred economy along with politics of coordination within caste society (Sugihara, 2008). The South Asian path is thus remarkable in its ability to enable the reproduction of diverse social groups by ensuring entitlements to livelihood through what may be called the principle of 'segmentary participation and distribution' (Tanabe, 2015a).

In parallel with globalisation, the South Asian path of development has reacquired an open, diverse, and multicentred dynamism that goes beyond the post-colonial, nationalist socio-spatial rigidity. Here, the fixed structure of hierarchy and dominance that has characterised colonial and post-colonial India is relativised today by an ongoing process of redefinition of categories and relationships of caste, religion, class, and gender, as well as the development of social networks that support social and physical mobility. Kinship, caste, and religious affiliations that previously fixed a person within a hierarchical structure in post-colonial India today increasingly function as social assets that both enable and limit people's socio-economic mobility.

In order to understand the nature of economic development in contemporary India, we need to pay attention to the non-elite small-scale industries – the so-called informal sector. This sector indeed follows a 'diversity-driven path of development', in which different materials, technologies, and knowledge are combined to produce a large variety of goods and services on a small scale according to the wide range of needs and tastes arising from diverse social groups. Arguably, the competitiveness of the small-scale informal sector is due to its ability to respond to the diverse needs of various populations that large-scale production is unable to fulfil (Krishna, 2011; Datt & Ravallion, 2011). Regular employment in the formal sector, such as the much-celebrated information technology (IT) sector, remains a privilege of the few. On the contrary, the vigorous informal economy is currently experiencing a large increase in non-regular work, which is contributing to poverty reduction. However, the increase in self-employment and temporary employment in this sector means that it is necessarily unstable, even if the total income is growing for many people, and does not foster a sense of security (Nayak et al., 2010).

Regarding the question of inequality in contemporary India, caution is required as the simplistic image of caste and class hierarchy does not accurately reflect the current dynamism of restructuring. There is still a significant socio-economic divide; but the form of social differentiation that is manifested today is extremely complex. Categories such as 'low caste', 'religious minority', and 'women' contain much diversity as there are many axes of caste, class, religion, gender, and ethnicity that cut across these categories and interweave with each other.[2] Diverse populations attempt through political representation and social movements to enhance their life chances by utilising and expanding the various socio-political networks available to them, and by resisting and critiquing the socio-political oppressions that limit their socio-economic/political mobility.

When we look more closely at transformations in the market economy and democratic politics, contemporary India is not in the 'disorganized' condition by which Lash and Urry (1987) explain the European and American situation, but in a vigorously 'reorganising' phase where multiple social groups raise their voices and seek to improve life chances through multiple channels and networks. Diverse social groups and individuals utilise kin-caste-religious-personal ties, NGOs, and other and civil organisations to enhance livelihood security, life chances, and public participation and to redress historical disparity and inequality.

The rising influence of vernacular voices and the increasing political participation of diverse social groups reflect the principle of 'segmentary participation and distribution' embedded in the South Asian path of development. This means that the workings of the market economy in contemporary India do not lead to outright exclusion of the non-elite population, but rather that many individuals and social groups are able to find new opportunities, albeit opportunities that are often beset with instability and risks. The fact that the growth of inequality in India between 1980 and 2005 has been relatively small compared with China, where class disparities have rapidly increased despite its traditionally more egalitarian social structure, may suggest that the diversity-driven path of development has a significant role to play in allowing diverse population groups to participate in the growing market economy (see for comparison Swaminathan & Rawal, 2011).

Diversity-driven development also means, however, that access to opportunities and entitlements is related to the group and social ties in which a person is embedded. Therefore, although there is much dynamism today that goes beyond the old post-colonial structure of dominance and hierarchy based on state bureaucracy and landholdings, and a person can seek new opportunities and mobility in more open politico-economic spheres, social disparity has not been rapidly resolved but is being reproduced in other ways. The nature or the foundation of social disparity has changed from depending on the 'structure of positions and holdings' to being determined by an individual's 'life chances'. Thus the question of security and fairness must focus on how to prevent further growth of inequality and how to provide more equal life chances for all groups of people. The existence of the 'red belt' in eastern India, where Maoists are active, suggests that there are those who feel that the current democratic politics or market economy does not provide enough opportunity for them and that violence is the only means to change the current situation. This certainly reveals the limitations of the present state of democratic politics and market economy in India, and the need for immediate action.

Development as if all people mattered[3]: the importance of human capital

The new dynamism in contemporary India is concomitant with policy changes regarding the agency of development. The liberalisation of the economy from 1991 is often explained as a shift from the state-centred to a market-oriented economy. We should remember, however, that there are significant differences between the neoliberal economies in western Europe, North America, and Japan and the emerging economy in India, where human development, in terms of providing basic livelihood, health care, and education, must occupy one of the central concerns of the government. Moreover, India must manage to do this within the parameters of a democratic framework that includes freedom of speech and an electoral parliamentary system. This is in contrast to the 'developmental authoritarianism' in China and previously in Indonesia, South Korea, and Taiwan, where authoritarian regimes led development from above. In contrast to these regimes, India after 1991 may be called a 'developmental democracy' which aims to achieve not only economic development but also the deepening of democracy through human and social development, by promoting and ensuring opportunities for popular public participation (Tanabe, 2015b). We may argue that the main issue has shifted from the question of whether and to what extent India will succeed in national development to that of how India can provide better life chances for the multitudes of people in the global environment while minimising risks and securing inclusive development.

The policy shift in the 1990s did not, of course, bring immediate solutions to the problems of poverty and inequality. The situation needs much more improvement, and there is increasing demand and criticism from below through elections, social movements, and civil organisational activities. Widespread politicisation and subsequent criticism of poverty and inequality has also stimulated increasing public participation from hitherto marginalised populations, which has led to further dialogue, negotiation, and conflict among diverse voices in Indian politics. Thus the deepening of democracy also publicly accentuates the present predicament of poor and marginalised groups, and vice versa (Mehta, 2003). The symbiotic relationship between the deepening of democracy and the rising of voices from underprivileged people also supports the rise of 'developmental democracy' by augmenting the public participation of diverse social groups with contending viewpoints, interests, and values. This is a churning process that includes contention, frustration, and antagonism, but hopefully it will lead to wider socio-political participation and inclusiveness.

The widening popular participation under developmental democracy is relevant to our understanding of the current dynamism of Indian economics, especially since demand-led, small-scale industries that rely on popular participation hold growing importance to India's economic growth, alongside the country's export-oriented and elite-dominant large industries. The Indian economy started to change significantly in the 1980s (see Chapter 4) when government partial liberalisation and pro-business policies stimulated higher growth rates, alongside developmental policies that provided subsidies for the grassroots of society. This policy stimulated a demand-led economy from below, leading to India's New Economic Policy of 1991 which enabled much faster growth.

At the same time as it instituted growth-oriented economic policies, the government established various schemes to promote more equal opportunities, with the intention of providing human security and developing human resources. These have included Reservation for OBCs (1990), the Panchayat (local self-government) Reforms Act (1993), the Right to Information Act (2005), the Forest Right Act (2005), the Mahatma Gandhi National Rural Employment Guarantee Act (2005), the Right to Education Act (2009), and the National Food Security Bill (2013). These measures have not only provided a vital safety net for survival, but have also improved human capital from below (Becker, 1964). Building human capital in this manner is vital in economic development and vibrant democracy in general, but especially within a regime of 'developmental democracy', where the focal point lies in the model's human-centred, participatory, and inclusive nature.

Here, it should be noted that the dynamic vibrancy in contemporary India cannot be explained solely by the institutions of a free economy and representative democracy or the infiltration of ideas of liberty and equality. The more fundamental transformation lies in the expansion of entitlement and agency of diverse groups of people who gradually but increasingly have acquired better health, education, and public participation. This means that the particular social relations and cultural values that supported their participatory agency have influenced the way that India's political economy has developed in a path-dependent and yet open-ended way.

The following figures demonstrate the success of basic human development in India since liberalisation and popular participation took hold. Infant mortality has decreased from 11.5 per cent in 1961 to 4.7 per cent in 2010; state-wise, in 1961 there was a wide difference between the lowest infant mortality rate in Kerala, 5.2 per cent, and the highest in Madhya Pradesh, 15.0 per cent, but by 2010 the gap had shrunk dramatically to 1.3 per cent and 6.3 per cent respectively. The death rate has also dropped sharply and it is projected that it will drop to as low as 8 per cent in the 2010–2015 period. Over a similar period, the birth rate started to decline slowly and then more sharply from 60 per cent in 1966 to 1.7 per cent in 2008 (James, 2011). Literacy rates have risen sharply to 74 per cent in 2011; from 1991, there was a sharp rise in literacy particularly in the less developed states and among the less privileged social groups. While literacy rates for men have risen from 64 per cent in 1991 to 82 per cent in 2011, the increase for women was more dramatic, rising from 39 per cent to 65 per cent. The gap in literacy rate in terms of area, class, and gender has also shrunk in recent years.[4]

From the 1990s, the gap in economic performance between states, classes, and castes has been rising. However, we should also note that the gaps in terms of basic health and education are decreasing. This indicates that despite the widening economic gap, there is a rising potentiality for diverse and marginalised populations, in terms of area, class, caste, and gender, to participate in democratic politics and the market economy. It is arguably this expanding thick layer of human capital that sustains the vibrancy of the demand-led economy and participatory democracy in contemporary India. Having said that, there is still much room for improving human security in terms of health, education, and employment (see Chapter 5 for the importance of access to health care for human security), and it is vital to improve the quality of human security and human capital for sustainable and inclusive development in India.

International and human security in risk society

We have seen that the globalisation process in India ran parallel to a growth in the participation of vernacular society in democratic politics and the market economy. This has resulted in the 'glocalisation' of Indian society, where both the globalisation of everyday life and the localisation of identity ties and politics take place at the same time. Everyday life at the grassroots level in India today cannot be imagined without connection with the wider world, while the workings of governance and market are forced to respond and adapt to local situations. This contemporary paradox reflects the fusion of the (post)colonial dichotomies that hitherto characterised Indian society: state and society, urban and rural, market and community, democratic politics and lifeworld, elite and subaltern. These (post)colonial dichotomies, which were divided along the line of 'outer modernity versus inner tradition' (Chatterjee, 1986; 1993), have increasingly merged together, and diverse social groups are beginning to exert their agency in these mediating, in-between spaces, which we have called the 'vernacular public arena' (Neyazi, Tanabe, & Ishizaka, 2014). Here, both elitist dominance in the name of rationality in 'outer modernity' and the fixed hierarchical structure in the name of culture in 'inner tradition' have begun to dissolve, leading to connections of diversities in which multifaceted and multicentred dynamism takes place. Such transformation is concomitant with the infiltration of technologies of media, transportation, and communication which promote wider connectivity. Although this does not herald a sudden demise of the elite dominance or traditional structure of Indian politics, we note ample examples that suggest a gradual and significant restructuring of socio-politico-economic relationships.

The rise of wider connections in socio-politico-economic relationships combined with technological change, as well as the multifaceted and multicentred dynamism of society, means that a social, technological, or security risk that emerges out of friction, contradiction, or control-failure in a particular place becomes a potential threat for a much wider society. In other words, India has become a 'risk society' where the concern for risk and security has become one of the dominant socio-political themes (Beck, 1992). There are rising concerns about poverty, unemployment, Maoist uprisings, and terrorism in India, not just as issues of social welfare or national security, but as threats to the everyday social life of all sections of society. Furthermore, as the old elitist dominance or traditional structure can no longer be taken for granted, people have become more willing to take risks in challenging and going beyond existing structures of social relationships to seek better life chances. This risk-taking is a source of socio-economic vibrancy, but it also creates the conditions for further socio-political hazards through challenges from below and oppression from above. The 1980s and the 1990s saw a distinct upsurge in the outbreak of caste violence in India, but this was a period in which there was at the same time a rise in the voices coming from historically oppressed castes demanding more democratic and egalitarian relationships. There are also many cases where movements of assertion by regional, tribal, or other deprived groups have resorted to violent means to attract public attention, inciting oppression from the state (Chatterjee, 2004: 76). These movements raise questions and bring about fluctuations and reactionary shifts in the social order, which in turn present new opportunities for the hitherto marginalised while at the same time creating a sense of social insecurity as well as reactionary oppression from above.[5]

The glocalising transformation in India is related logically and factually to the changes in the wider world order. India has become increasingly important in the global political economy since the 1990s. Alongside this, there has been a shift in diplomatic policy, from a traditional non-alignment stance to a more pragmatic engagement with key countries (see Chapter 2). India is in the process of becoming a major power, and its global position is gradually gaining more weight (Chapter 3). The dynamics of contemporary India are leading to the emergence of a new international and glocal order in which socio-economic-political relationships at every level are being reshuffled and restructured. In this situation, the question of risk concerns both traditional international and national security and non-traditional human security. Within this, the agenda of how to secure agency, entitlement, and empowerment so that all humans may pursue self-actualisation in an inclusive, sustainable, and peaceful environment represents an important challenge for contemporary India and the world. The need to expand the concept of security is concomitant with the widening range of risks from which no country in the global community is exempt. There are social risks – such as social conflicts, social exclusion, and structural and physical violence; environmental risks – resource and energy problems and global warming; and technological risks – including genetic engineering and new reproductive technologies. There is a need to establish global, national, and local institutions in order to manage such a wide range of risks and to provide international and human security. Here, the questions of systemic risk-management and security-provision from above and of building human development, human capital, and human security from below overlap at the practical level. The new notion of security in the glocal risk society lies at this intersection between the expanding fields of international and human security.

Conclusion

This book has tried to answer the question 'To what extent has India achieved development since independence in multiple intersecting areas of international and human security?' We have looked at how India attempted to achieve disciplined disengagement from international power politics and concentrated on state-led national development in the first four decades after independence. There was a slow but constant growth in economic and human development, despite the underlying disparity in the distribution of wealth. From the 1990s, new opportunities and risks emerged as the post-colonial structure of elitist dominance and traditional hierarchy dissolved, and new networks of glocal connections began to be formed. Here, a new question appeared, namely, 'How are the new opportunities and risks, besides wealth, produced, controlled, and distributed within society?' The emergence of this new question is related to the expansion of the idea of security. The central problem here is which and whose security is to be achieved by whom. We contend that in order to deal with the new question of expanding risk and security, besides improving the governance of power and capital, it is vital to further promote capability, agency, and human capital among diverse sections of society through state-supported and human-centred forms of development. These measures, which promote the inclusion and participation of all citizens in public affairs, are critically important to the achievement of international and human security in India.

Notes

1 Chapter 8 explores this dynamic through the case study of women-focused microfinance in Tamil Nadu.
2 Chapter 6, for example, discusses the complex and multiple identities of India's Muslims.
3 The reference is to Schumacher (1974).
4 Data from IndiaStat.com, Economic Survey 2011–2012. www.indiastat.com/economy/8/economicsurvey/30416/stas.aspx [last accessed 4/215].
5 See Chapter 7 for a discussion of whether democracy can check violence; Chapter 9 for a sensitive, long-term observation of continuity and change in village life in India; and Chapter 10 for analysis of the cause and consequences of the declining caste hierarchy in rural India.

Bibliography

Bauman, Z. (2000) *Liquid Modernity*. Cambridge: Polity Press.
Beck, U. (1992) *Risk Society: Towards a New Modernity*. Trans. M. Ritter. London: Sage Publications.
Becker, G. S. (1964) *Human Capital: A Theoretical and Empirical Analysis, with Special Reference to Education*. New York: National Bureau of Economic Research.
Chatterjee, P. (1986) *Nationalist Thought and the Colonial World*. London: Zed Books.
Chatterjee, P. (1993) *The Nation and Its Fragments: Colonial and Postcolonial Histories*. Princeton, NJ: Princeton University Press.
Chatterjee, P. (2004) *The Politics of the Governed: Reflections on Popular Politics in Most of the World*. New York: Columbia University Press.
Datt, G. & M. Ravallion (2011) 'Has India's Economic Growth Become More Pro-Poor in the Wake of Economic Reforms?' *The World Bank Economic Review* 25(2): 157.
Harvey, D. (1990) *The Condition of Postmodernity: An Enquiry into the Origins of Cultural Change*. Oxford: Blackwell.
Hobsbawm, E. J. (1994) *Age of Extremes: The Short Twentieth Century, 1914–1991*. London: Michael Joseph.
James, K. S. (2011) 'India's Demographic Change: Opportunities and Challenges'. *Science* 333: 576–580.

Kaviraj, S. (1991) 'On State, Society and Discourse in India', in J. Manor (ed.) *Rethinking Third World Politics*. London & New York: Longman.

Krishna, A. (2011) 'Poverty Knowledge and Poverty Action in India', in A. Gupta & K. Sivaramakrishnan (eds.) *The State in India after Liberalization: Interdisciplinary Perspectives*. London: Routledge.

Lash, S. & J. Urry (1987) *The End of Organized Capitalism*. Cambridge: Polity Press.

Nayak, P. K., S. K. Chattopadhyay, A. V. Kumar, & V. Dhanya (2010) 'Inclusive Growth and Its Regional Dimension'. *Reserve Bank of India Occasional Papers* 31(3): 91–156.

Neyazi, T. A., A. Tanabe, & S. Ishizaka (eds.) (2014) *Democratic Transformation and the Vernacular Public Arena in India*. London: Routledge.

Schumacher, E. F. (1974) *Small Is Beautiful: A Study of Economics as if People Mattered*. London: Abacus.

Sugihara, K. (2008) 'Multiple Paths of Economic Development in Global History', in *Multiple Paths of Economic Development in Global History, Proceedings of the Symposium in commemoration of the Executive Committee Meeting of the IEHA*. Kyoto University Global COE Program on Sustainable Humanosphere & Osaka University Grants-in-Aid for Scientific Research Project on Global History: Center for Southeast Asian Studies, Kyoto University.

Sugihara, K. (2010) 'Miamiajiagata Hattenkeiro no Tokushitsu' [The Characteristics of the South Asian Path of Economic Development]. *Minamiajiakenkyu* [Journal of the Japanese Association for South Asian Studies] 2010(22): 170–184.

Swaminathan, M. & V. Rawal (2011) 'Is India Really a Country of Low Income-Inequality? Observations from Eight Villages'. *Review of Agrarian Studies* 1(1): 1–22.

Tanabe, A. (2015a) 'Kasuto Shakai kara Tayosei Shakai he: Gendai Indoron no Paradaimu Tenkan' [From Caste Society to Diversity Society: Paradigm Shift in India Studies], in A. Tanabe, K. Sugihara & K. Wakimura (eds.) *Tayosei Shakai no Chosen* [The Challenge of Diversity Society]. Tokyo: University of Tokyo Press.

Tanabe, A. (2015b) 'Conditions of "Developmental Democracy": New Logic of Inclusion and Exclusion in Globalizing India', in M. Mio & A. Dasgupta (eds.) *Looking beyond the State: Changing Forms of Inclusion and Exclusion in India*. London: Routledge.

Index

activism 12, 22, 108, 113, 154, 164
adivasis 176
Afghanistan 3, 41–6, 47n, 53
agriculture 5, 11, 13n, 23, 26–7, 45, 66–8, 70, 75, 77, 80, 85, 121, 146–7, 150–3, 158–9, 166, 169, 172, 173n
All-India Muslim League (Muslim League) 101, 106
autonomy 53, 75, 171
   material 164–5
   political 23
   strategic 51, 62
Ayodhya 6, 112–13, 115, 123
ayurveda 93

bankruptcy 9, 32, 34, 41, 45, 134–5
banks 67, 90, 129–31, 134, 136–7, 143n
   National Bank for Agriculture and Rural Development (NABARD) 130–1, 137
   Reserve Bank of India 5, 75, 85
   SEWA Bank 95
   Swiss Banking Association 46
   World Bank 26, 56, 66, 79–80
balance-of-payments crisis 5, 66–8, 75, 77, 79–80, 82, 85
Bharatiya Janata Party (BJP) 43, 52, 110–16, 122–3, 125n
Boundary Award 3, 33
Britain 36, 41, 45, 54, 101, 107
   British rule 15, 20, 30n, 33–4, 36, 65, 95, 102, 147
   relations with India 32, 53
   UK 42, 87
bureaucracy 23, 27, 32, 90, 102, 106, 134, 167, 175, 178

capitalism 23, 29, 143n, 175
caste 16, 18–24, 28, 102, 106, 111, 119–23, 126n, 134–5, 137, 142, 147, 150, 154, 162–72, 172n, 173n, 176–8, 180, 182
   accommodations 8, 162, 164, 166, 168, 171–72
   backward castes 119–22
   Dalits 8, 12, 103, 162–71, 172n, 173n, 176
   hierarchies 8, 137, 162–5, 167, 176–7
   intercaste relations 8, 162, 164–5, 167–72, 173n
   jati 19, 147, 149, 154, 163
   landed/landowning 8, 111, 119, 122, 162–4, 166–72, 172n, 173n
   OBCs 120, 172n, 173n, 176, 180
   riots *see* riots
   Scheduled Castes 120–1, 125n
   violence 110–11, 163, 166, 169, 182
Chanderi massacre 113, 124n
Chidambaram, P. 32, 46
China 4, 10–11, 34–6, 39–40, 42, 46, 50–1, 53–62, 63n, 65, 178–9
   India's relationship with 3–4, 9, 11, 32, 36–7, 40, 43–4, 46, 50–3, 57–62, 63n, 64n
civil society 99, 164, 169
class 2, 6, 8, 23–4, 27–8, 104, 110, 116–18, 120, 123, 128, 130, 135, 137, 142, 176–8, 180
   divisions 16, 20, 22–3, 28
   middle classes 128, 135, 176
   riots *see* riots
   violence 110–11
   working classes 17
climate change 57, 158
coastal communities 5, 96–8
Cold War 41, 50–2, 56–8, 62, 128, 175
communism 20–1, 34, 41
Communist Party of India 27
Communist Party of India (Marxist) 21, 24–5, 27

Index

Communist Party of India (Marxist-Leninist) Liberation (ML) 116–23, 125n
communitarianism 2, 101–2
Congress Party 17, 19, 21–3, 26, 38, 40–1, 62, 107, 112, 113–5, 117–9, 121–3, 125n
crops 142n, 146, 152–4, 156, 167
  cash 152, 167

debt 7, 24, 30, 46, 67–8, 79, 82, 130, 135, 138
defence 2, 4, 13n, 33, 40–2, 46, 54, 56, 59
deficit:
  fiscal 5, 67–8, 75, 77, 79–80, 85–6, 89, 95
  trade 4, 12n, 68
democracy 1, 6, 7, 16, 20, 22, 27–9, 40, 44, 59–60, 72, 75, 104, 110–1, 116–7, 119–21, 123–4, 162, 175–6, 179–81
  democratisation 12, 27, 119–23, 126n
  parliamentary 20, 72, 75, 116–7, 119–20, 123
development 2, 4, 7–9, 17–9, 24–7, 58–9, 65–8, 70, 77, 79, 82, 96, 128, 131–6, 140, 142n, 143n, 144n, 149, 154, 175–83
  discourse 18
  economic 17, 32, 37, 50, 54, 65–8, 70, 75, 179–80
  goals 24–6
  rural 96, 98, 146
  social 96, 131, 134, 179
  socio-economic 1, 175–9
disease 1, 91, 98
  non-communicable disease 92, 96

ecology 150–1, 158
economy 4–5, 8–11, 12n, 13n, 16–17, 23–8, 32, 40–1, 43, 45–6, 50, 52–5, 58–60, 62, 65–6, 70, 72, 75, 77, 79, 80, 82, 85–6, 132–4, 136, 140, 142n, 143n, 147, 150, 154, 163, 175, 177–8, 180–2
  crises 4–5, 65–6, 68, 70, 75, 79–80, 82, 85
  deficit *see* deficit
  development *see* development
  growth 5, 9, 11, 13n, 41, 50, 57, 66–8, 70, 72, 77, 79–80, 85, 177, 179
  'Hindu Rate of Growth' 70
  inflation *see* inflation
  liberalisation 4, 52–3, 66–7, 70, 72, 80, 82, 175–6, 179

macroeconomic:
  policy 4, 65, 72, 82
  performance 5, 65, 68, 82, 85
market 178, 180–1
policy 41, 46, 52, 180
political 23–6, 180, 182
reform 26, 67–8, 79
security 7, 128
education 2, 7, 10–11, 18, 89, 108n, 135, 143n, 146, 148–9, 154–6, 158–9, 163–4, 167, 172, 173n, 176, 179–81
  colleges 11, 89, 158, 167
  of girls 143n, 144n, 149, 155, 158
  schools 11, 135, 142n, 143n, 144n, 149, 150, 155–6, 160
elections 7, 15, 41, 68, 72, 75, 110, 112–23, 125n, 126n, 136–7, 179
electricity supply 97–9, 150, 154, 156
employment *see* work
environment 44, 58, 60, 146, 158
  degradation 1, 175
  global warming 56, 58, 182
  sustainability 146
exports 9, 11, 12n, 66–7, 77, 80, 93, 179

farming 27, 147, 149, 152–3, 172
  farmers 23, 25, 142n, 166–7
fishing 97
Five Year Plans 77, 79
  First 26, 65
  Second 66, 80
  Third 66
food 7, 26, 93, 98, 128–9, 142, 146, 150, 152
  imports 5, 67, 75, 77, 80, 85
  prices 9, 28, 72, 77, 88
  production 7, 26, 67, 77, 143n, 146
  security 92, 180
  shortages 41, 66
foreign direct investment 41, 82, 89
foreign policy 1–3, 9, 12n, 32–4, 36, 41–2, 44–6, 51–3, 56–7, 61–3, 99
  non-alignment 9, 34, 36, 39, 44–5, 51–2, 182
forests 158, 180
  forestry dept. 152, 158

Gandhi, Indira 3, 21, 23, 32–3, 38, 40–1, 66–7, 154
Gandhi, Mahatma 9, 30n, 112
Gandhi, Rajiv 25, 58–9, 67–8, 113, 115–16
Gandhi, Sonia 62
gross domestic product (GDP) 4–5, 11, 50, 53, 55–6, 68, 70, 75, 77, 79–80, 85–6, 95

Index

gender 8, 16, 128, 132–3, 137, 143n, 146, 149, 153–5, 176, 178, 180
  equity 1, 132, 146, 175
  roles 146, 154, 159
global warming *see* environment
globalisation 4, 29, 41, 62, 65–8, 70, 72, 79–80, 82, 132, 175–7, 181
glocalisation 8, 132, 181–3
governance 1–2, 8, 16–8, 25, 33, 175–6, 181, 183
government programmes 89, 92, 144n, 155, 163, 167
Green Revolution 5, 9, 67, 77, 85

health care 5, 86, 89–93, 96, 146, 148, 179, 181
  access 5, 86, 93, 99
  cost 90–1
  coverage 5, 90–1, 94, 99
  insurance 86, 89–91, 93–5, 143n
  private 86, 89–90
  provision 86–8, 91, 93
  rural 92–3, 148
  National Rural Health Mission 87–8
Hindus 20, 33, 38, 70, 101–2, 107, 113, 115, 125n, 147
  Hinduism 106, 165
  nationalism 105, 112
hospitals 86–92, 94–5, 129, 138, 148
housing 97, 134, 149
human capital 8, 132, 179–83

imports 12n, 41, 67–8, 75, 77, 80, 85
income 7, 72, 95, 128–33, 136, 139–40, 143n, 169, 177
  inequality 10
  per capita 10, 68, 70, 72, 77, 80
  tax 10
independence 1–2, 4, 6, 12n, 15–6, 20, 23, 29, 34, 50–1, 65, 67–8, 72, 80, 82, 99, 108, 110–12, 114, 123, 146, 157, 159, 162, 177, 182
  East Pakistan 39
industry 12n, 59, 91, 147
  heavy 66
  industrialistaion 16, 26, 65–6, 79
  industrial sector 23, 63, 66–7, 79
infant mortality 10, 13n, 88, 180
inflation 5, 10, 13n, 40–1, 67–8, 72, 75, 79–80, 85
information technology (IT) 5, 9, 90–2, 94, 96, 98–9, 177
International Monetary Fund (IMF) 50, 56, 67–8, 79–80

internet 98, 151
Islam 101–6, 108
  culture 6, 106
  Indian Islam 101, 104–5, 107
  religion 6, 104, 107
Islamist 6, 43, 104
  militants 46

Jammu-Kashmir 3, 33–4, 36, 38–9, 43–4
Janata Dal 27, 114–16, 120–3, 124n, 126n
Japan 4, 5, 10, 53, 57, 59–62, 63n, 87, 96, 98–9, 179
jati *see* caste
jihad 37–8, 43, 45–6
Jinnah, Mohammad Ali 6, 33, 101–2

Lakshmanpur Bathe massacre 122
landlords 101, 119, 121–2, 125n, 126n, 152, 165, 173n
  private armies 6, 111, 120–21, 123
  Ranvir Sena 6, 111, 120–3
lifeline infrastructure 96–7, 99
literacy 12n, 20, 108n, 146, 154–5, 180
  rates for men and women 180
loans 27, 129–31, 133–7, 139, 143n, 166
  national 41, 67, 80
Logain massacre 113
Lokpal and Lokayutas Act (2014) 12

Magalir Thittam 7, 126, 131, 136–7
  major powers 4, 45, 50–1, 53–6, 58, 61–3, 182
Mandal Commission report 6, 110–1
Maoism 6, 110, 116, 123, 178, 181
marriage 107, 155, 170
media 20, 35, 164, 169–70, 181
  social 97
Menon, Krishna 35, 37
microfinance 7, 129–30, 133–5, 137–40, 142, 143n, 144n
  microcredit programmes 131–2, 143n
migration 94, 147, 150, 165, 173n
  emigration 33
military 1, 33–7, 39–40, 46, 50, 54, 59–60, 99, 128, 142n
  army 37–8
  coup 111
  expenditure 4, 54–5
  navy 41, 50, 54, 59–60
  power 1, 4, 35, 50, 54, 56, 61, 142n, 175
mobile phones *see* technology
mobility 133, 175–7
  economic 8, 177–8
  political 178

social 8, 177–8
spatial 172
modernisation 16, 18, 20–1, 28, 54, 128, 146, 152, 176
Morley-Minto reforms 102
Muslims 102, 104–8, 108n, 111–6, 124n, 125n, 147
    communities 101, 103, 106–8
    culture 103–4, 106
    identity 6, 101–2, 104–6, 108
    India 5–6, 101, 103–5
    Islam *see* Islam
    nationalism 101–3
    Shia 46, 101
    Sufism 101–2
    Sunni 46, 101
    voters 113–6

National Rural Employment Guarantee Act (NREGA) 6, 87, 165, 173n, 180
nationalism 15, 23, 102, 104, 107, 175, 177
    Hindu *see* Hindus
    Muslim *see* Muslims
NATO 3, 46, 47n
natural disasters 5, 96–9
    earthquakes 5, 96–8
    management of 96, 98
    tsunamis 5, 96–8
        Indian Ocean Tsunami 5, 97
Naxalites 6, 110–11, 116, 120–3
Nehru, Jawaharlal 3, 15–6, 21–2, 26–7, 32–5, 37, 43, 53, 58, 66, 107, 111
Nehru-Mahalanobis model 66–7
non-alignment *see* foreign policy
nuclear:
    blackmail 43–4
    crisis (Japan) 5, 96–7
    deterrent 39, 42
    policy 3, 39–40, 42, 45, 51, 58, 61
    safety 44
    tests 2, 39–40, 42, 43
    war 33
    weapons 4, 39–40, 42, 45, 61

oil crises 4, 67, 70, 80, 82

Pakistan 6, 11, 13n, 33–4, 36–9, 42–6, 52, 59, 63n, 102, 106
    East Pakistan 39
    relations with India 32–3, 35, 37–40, 42–6, 52
    West Pakistan 39
panchayats 16–17, 172, 180
partition 5, 33, 65, 106–7, 110

phones *see* technology
police 113, 116–7, 121–2, 125n, 171
poverty 1, 13n, 16, 46, 99, 123, 128, 130–2, 139–40, 142n, 143n, 177, 179, 181
    absolute 5, 9, 13n, 72, 85
    alleviation 131–3, 137, 143n
    below the poverty line 13n, 131
    capability poverty 132
    income poverty 132
public health 5, 86–7, 93, 95–9
public transportation 20, 45, 148–9, 181

Ranvir Sena *see* landlords
Rao, Narasimha 3, 32, 41–3, 58, 68
rape 170
religion 6, 8, 16, 28, 104, 106–8, 134–5, 142, 159, 165, 176, 178
    Buddhism, conversion to 165
    deities 150, 159
    Hinduism *see* Hindus
    Islam *see* Islam
    riots *see* riots
reservations 12, 103, 108n, 163–4
Right to Information Act (2005) 12, 29n, 180
riots 17
    anti-Ahmadiya 106
    caste 6, 110–11
    class 6, 111
    religious 6, 110–12, 115–16, 123, 124n
        Bhagalpur 111–16, 123
        Bihar 6, 111, 114–15
        Gujarat 110–11
        Jamshedpur 112
        Sitamarhi 115–16, 125n
Rotating Savings and Credit Associations (ROSCAs) 130
Russia 34, 45, 53–4, 56–7, 65

sanskritisation 165
savings 91, 129–33, 136
Scheduled Castes and Scheduled Tribes (Prevention of Atrocities) Act (1989) 11, 164, 169–70, 173n
schools *see* education
Second World War 56–7, 80
secularism 2, 6, 103–4, 107, 113, 115–16, 176
Self-Employed Women's Association (SEWA) 94–5
Sharma Nagar 7, 134–5, 140
Shastri, Lal Bahadur 26, 38–40
security:
    definition of 2, 142n, 175

economic 7
global 1
human 1–3, 5, 7, 96–9, 128, 140, 142, 142n, 146, 162, 176, 180–3
insecurity 7, 122, 128, 142n, 147, 158, 159, 182
international 1–2, 175
national 1–3, 29, 46, 175, 182
regional 1, 8, 44
social 96, 128, 142, 142n
self-help groups (SHGs) 26, 130, 131, 134–9, 142, 143n 144n, 176
siddha 93
Singh, Manmohan 11, 32, 53, 58, 60–1
social capital 25, 132
social justice 26, 103, 119
socialism 24, 40–1, 102, 119–20
Soviet Union 35–6, 38–44, 50–3, 56–7, 62
subalterns 17, 19, 24, 29, 181
suburbs 7, 10, 128–9, 137, 139–40
Syed Ahmad Khan 101–2, 108

Taliban 44, 142n
taxation 9, 10, 27, 79–80, 94, 147, 159
technology 57, 90–1, 93, 96, 98–9, 156–7, 177, 181–2
  agricultural 5, 85, 147, 159
  computers 89, 92, 96
  information technology *see* information technology (IT)
  phones 97
    mobile 10, 96–8, 151
telemedicine 89, 91, 98
terrorism 1–2, 43–5, 57, 142n, 175, 181
  Al-Qaeda 44, 46
  Islamist 43, 45
  in Pakistan 43–5
  war on terrorism 44
trade 4, 11, 13n, 36, 58, 66, 68, 77
  deficit *see* deficit
  unions 18
tribes 11, 18–19, 89, 102, 182
tsunamis *see* natural disasters
two-nation theory 5, 101, 103–4

umma 101
United States 3–4, 16, 18, 26, 34–9, 41–6, 54, 56, 62, 65–6, 75, 151, 178–9
UN Security Council 1, 9, 11, 35–6, 39, 52, 57, 61

Untouchability Offenses Act (1956) 11
Urs, Devraj 24–5

Vajpayee, Atal Bihari 3, 43–4, 59, 63n, 112
vernacular publics 8, 176, 181
villages 19, 22, 95, 97–8, 113, 121–2, 124n, 126n, 130, 146–56, 158–9, 162–72, 172n, 173n
violence 2, 6–9, 108, 110–11, 116, 121–4, 142n, 162, 163, 167–8, 170–1, 178, 182
  caste-based *see* caste
  class-based *see* class
  domestic 130, 143n
  non-violence 110
vote-bank politics 41
vote banks 137

waste 150
water supply 10, 13n, 96–9, 154, 156–7, 159, 166
women 7, 12, 88–9, 92, 94–5, 128, 130–40, 142n, 143n, 144n, 153–8, 167, 170, 176
  education of *see* education
  empowerment of 130–4, 137–9, 143n, 144n
  pregnant 88, 92–3
  work *see* work
work 129, 150–1, 165, 173n, 177
  blue-collar 134
  children 149
  employment 9–12, 20, 89–90, 95, 102, 108n, 142n, 150, 155–6, 158–9, 164, 173n, 176–7, 181
    schemes 25
  government 158, 163, 167
  self-employment 131, 177
  unemployment 1, 10, 129, 156, 182
  urban 166–7
  white-collar 167
  women 12, 89, 95, 97, 128, 132–3, 138, 143n, 153–4, 158–9
  workers 11, 25, 28, 80, 91, 94, 134–5, 158, 173n
World Health Organization 96

Yadav, Laloo Prasad 115–16, 120–3, 125n